"If I were starting life over again, I am inclined to think that I would go into the advertising business in preference to almost any other. This is because advertising has come to cover the whole range of human needs and also because it combines real imagination with a deep study of human psychology. Because it brings to the greatest number of people actual knowledge concerning useful things, it is essentially a form of education. It has risen with ever-growing rapidity to the dignity of an art. It is constantly paving new paths. The general raising of the standards of modern civilization among all groups of people during the past half century would have been impossible without the spreading of the knowledge of higher standards by means of advertising."

Franklin D. Roosevelt, former U.S. President

"If you are ready to have it rain gold—in your business and life—absorb and use the eclectic, proven wisdom, experience, and profound insights of my great friend and trusted advisor, Joe Sugarman."

Mark Victor Hansen

"Joe Sugarman has managed to flush out the very subtle secrets to achieving success in a very entertaining way while leaving nuggets of wisdom in its wake. It's more than you'll expect from any book on success."

Jack Canfield

"What a trip you'll take reading The Seven Forces of Success *as Joe Sugarman, a true pioneer in direct marketing, reveals all his secrets for success in a way that will inspire you to take action. Get ready for a ride you won't forget."*

Joe Vitale

The Seven Forces of Success

12/8/15
To Marck
May the forces
be with you!

Joseph Sugarman

The Seven Forces of Success

Seven powerful ways to magnify your chances of winning in a competitive world.

Printed in the United States of America

Sugarman, Joseph "The Seven Forces of Success: Seven Powerful Ways to Magnify Your Chances of Winning in a Competitive World."

Attention: schools, ad agencies and corporations. DelStar books are available at quantity discounts with bulk purchases for education or business use. For more information, please contact DelStar Books at the address below.

ISBN 978-1-891686-12-2

DelStar Books
3350 Palms Center Drive
Las Vegas, NV 89103
Phone: (702) 798-9000
Fax: (702) (702) 597-2002
DelStarBooks.com

Book Design: Ron Hughes

This book is dedicated to Mary Stanke who has been my operations manager and company president for all my companies and has been with me more than 43 years. Her keen eye on the details of running my companies and her efficient handling of our operations gave me the freedom to use my creative skills without compromise.

Contents

Foreword

The first version of this book was published in 1980 by Contemporary Books. At the time, our company was recognized for selling the latest in space-age electronics. We had introduced the pocket calculator, the use of toll-free numbers for taking credit card orders, the digital watch, and other breakthrough products and marketing concepts.

Contemporary Books and its president kept after me to write a book. The public recognized our company from all our advertising, and it seemed natural to follow up this success in business with a book sharing the principles I had followed to achieve that success.

My premise would be simple—to provide valuable information and to inspire my readers on a personal level. I would help people and at the same time even acquire customers for my mail order company, JS&A Group, Inc. 100,000 copies of the book were sold.

Fast forward to February, 2009. I was at the SANG Conference (Speakers , Authors, Network Group) in Las Vegas where all of the top speakers, authors, and Internet marketers were assembled for speeches, information, and good old-fashioned networking. That evening I was tired after a long day and I opted to return to my home in Las Vegas rather than engage in the evening's networking.

As I crawled into bed, the phone rang. It was Gail Kingsbury, the event organizer. She asked me if I could return to the conference. I told Gail that I was already in bed but she insisted. "You've got to return. Dr. Pankash Naram from India came specifically just to meet you. He is one of the world's top healers and he's a big fan of yours." After a few moans, I said, "O.K. Gail, I'll be there in about a half hour," Upon arriving, I found Gail who took me into a private room where I met Dr. Naram.

Dr. Naram was a slight man dressed in all white and looking very much like an Indian guru. Gail briefed me that Dr. Naram's healing modalities were recognized throughout the world and he had offices in Europe, Asia, South America and the United States. He even had an Internet TV show that had a following of over 50 million viewers.

Using Ayvedic medicine, herbs and the ability to read a person's energy Naram was able to see and treat hundreds of patients a day. For example, when he was in the U.S. recently, people from all over the world flew in just to see him. And Dr. Naram indicated to me that he was booked three years in advance even though he was able to treat hundreds of people in the same day.

I was curious. Why would this world famous doctor be a fan of mine? Dr. Naram started to explain, "I studied medicine in India and learned my trade from some of the top healers in the world. I then started my practice and took on very few clients. One of them was David Ogilvy, a world-famous advertising man. Ogilvy had homes in England, a castle in France and an office in New York. His company, Ogilvy and Mather, was one of Madison Avenue's most successful agencies.

I knew of Ogilvy as I had read a few of his books on advertising. His philosophies were very much like mine.

Dr. Naram was a very modest man. He had learned a great deal from his masters in India—the people he studied under who lived well into their hundreds. He perfected his herbal formulations in India to help people rid themselves of disease and the difficulties associated with growing old.

His modesty was to some a weakness. Here, on the one hand, he had the power to heal but on the other not too many people knew about it. One of those who had heard about Dr Naram was David Ogilvy who soon became one of Naram's patients.

In appreciation for the work Dr. Naram was doing, Oglivy told him that upon Oglivy's death, he wanted to leave Dr. Naram his entire collection of books—a collection of books that ranged from spiritual to advertising to novels and non-fiction. Oglivy died in 1999, and true to his wishes, his entire book collection was delivered to Dr. Naram's offices in India. Examining the books, one stood out. "For some reason this book seemed to call out to me," said Dr. Naram. The book was *Success Forces*, the one I had written in 1980.

"I read the book," said Naram. "I can honestly say that it was one of the most significant books I have ever read and it inspired me to break through my shyness and timidity and to share with the world my gift with no fear of failure."

The copy of the book that he read contained hand-written comments from Ogilvy—comments indicating that Ogilvy had indeed read the book and used many of the principles I had espoused in *Success Forces*.

That night my head was spinning. It was one thing to learn that one of my mentors—an advertising superstar—had read my book and used the book's tools in his business life. And then to learn that someone, through a freak chance, had also read this book and it had changed his life as well was amazing. My book had served as an inspiration to Dr. Naram that put him on a mission to help millions of people throughout the world.

My purpose in life is to help the most number of people either through example or by inspiring them to greater heights. That is my number one goal and nothing else comes even close. To finally learn of the effect *Success Forces* had on just two people who shared just one of more than 100,000 books that were published and sold was humbling to me.

Everyone would like to believe he or she helps others and has a positive influence in life. But to have two shining examples right before my eyes, well, that was pretty exciting. If this were the case with Ogilvy and Dr. Naram, then certainly there are others out there who have been positively influenced by my book. And that's when I decided that if *Success Forces* helped people when it was first published, then maybe it was time to update it and get it into even more hands.

And now with *The Seven Forces of Success*, my wish to you is that you find, from what I offer, a set of tools and guidelines to add to your own business and personal success in life.

Acknowledgments

I would like to thank those who helped me produce this book. I would like to give a special thanks to my sister, Judy Sugarman, and Mary Stanke for their editing, coordination and talents. Special thanks also to Ron Hughes for his beautiful book design, and a special thanks to all of you who have contributed to my book and my life and who were willing to exchange their hard-earned money for my products and services. May you be as blessed in your life as I have been in mine.

Introduction

If you're thinking this is another one of those rags-to-riches success books, you're in for a surprise. What makes this book different is that I am not your average success story. I'm a college dropout with a whole bunch of failures to my credit. And even more incredible is that I have been able to make millions of dollars in spite of myself.

Now if you think that maybe I'm lucky, you're wrong. The truth is that I have probably failed more times than anybody reading this book.

But from all my failures, from all my dumb mistakes, I have discovered some interesting relationships.

Once you can recognize these relationships, which I call Success Forces, your chances of success will start to increase despite yourself. With a little bit of conscientious effort, Success Forces will propel you to heights of success you've never dreamed possible.

Once I started to experience success, I started to reveal my Success Forces at speeches throughout the country. I noticed people taking notes. It wasn't until a few years after those first speeches that I started getting letters from people telling me that my Success Forces worked. One letter told me how I had dramatically changed his life. Another told me how her business had profited as a direct result of my speech.

I published my Success Forces because people were asking for copies of my speeches. It was from this encouragement that I decided to write a book. That's how Success Forces evolved. And that was over 30 years ago.

Before I achieved my own success, I read all the popular books on success and interviewed successful people. I had great dreams of success. I knew that one day I, too, would be successful—despite my failures—and that success would not come because of the books I had read or the people I had met. I knew I had to study my failures to understand why I had failed and discover on my own the real forces that seemed to propel people to great success, while others seemed to fail no matter how hard they tried.

Some of my Success Forces may strike you as very elementary and others as complete surprises. That's fine. But don't underestimate any of the Seven Forces I present. Each one can be a powerful influence in your life if you'll accept my premise.

Do they work? What are these forces, and what can we do to make these forces work for us? What very simple basic things can we do in our lives that will force us to be more successful?

That's the entire premise of this book. Success Forces is a simple program that can be followed almost subconsciously. Any single

Success Force will work. Harness all of them and your chances of success will increase dramatically.

Remember, I'm not an author who writes about success and then makes a fortune from the sale of my book. I've already made my fortune and the techniques I've used have worked for me time and time again. Even if you've read other success books, this book will give you a totally different perspective.

I have developed these philosophies from my experiences and then observed them actually working. I have constantly questioned their validity and challenged them, only to discover a consistency that has proven to me that the philosophies I teach in this book do indeed work.

There is little that will be revolutionary and little that can be considered a breakthrough with the exception of the way I present this information. By presenting my concepts as "Forces" and showing you how to use them to be successful, I provide the basis for a new perspective on success, motivation, and self-improvement.

The Seven Forces of Success is really two books. The first book is autobiographical. I talk about my life, my experiences, and many conclusions I reached in the process of failure and success. The second section of the book is on the philosophy that I've developed through the years. You can actually skip the first part and go straight to the philosophies, but you'll miss some entertaining stories about my background so that you can truly appreciate the path I took and the lessons I've learned.

The Seven Forces of Success is my contribution to your success. I hope you enjoy reading it as much as I enjoyed writing it. Here's to your success.

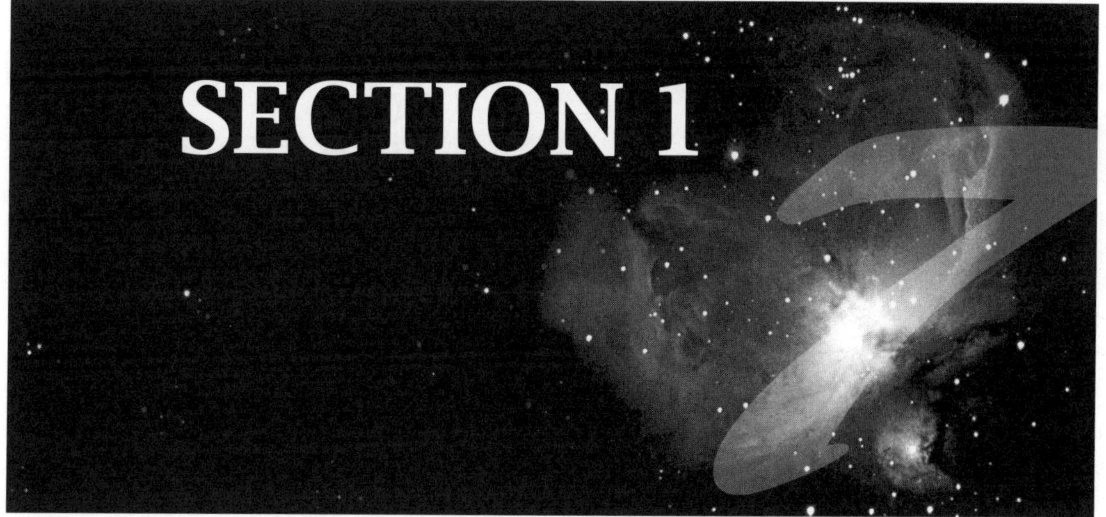
SECTION 1

1) The Start

"It is important to acknowledge a mistake instantly, correct it, and learn from it. That literally turns a failure into a success. Success is on the far side of failure."

T.J. Watson 1874—1956, founder of IBM

Before we discuss my philosophies, there are some things you should know about me, my failures, and the path that led me to this book. That's what Section I of my book is all about. After all, my advice won't be worth very much if you don't know how I developed my concepts and what I went through to develop them.

I was born on Chicago's west side on April 25, 1938, and I was eventually followed by three younger sisters: Barbara, Nancy, and Judy.

Our family had moved from Chicago to Oak Park and back a few times by the time I was 12 years old. Oak Park is a small suburb west of Chicago.

My father was in the printing equipment sales business. He was the president of his firm, Consolidated Photo Engraving and Equipment Company, which manufactured printing equipment and large process cameras for the printing and platemaking industry.

I can remember sitting at the kitchen table when I was three years old and watching my father read the newspaper. Suddenly he'd come to an advertisement and show it to me, saying, "Joey, look at this terrific ad." Later I would look at newspapers to see if I could find some "terrific ads." My interest in advertising never left me.

When I was eight years old, I lived in the Albany Park section of Chicago with my family in a three-story, six-flat apartment building.

An eight-year-old boy named Gene Rochlin lived in the apartment next door. Gene was a bookworm—one of those gifted children who sat down and read everything he could get his hands on. He was already into Shakespeare while I was still stumbling through comic books.

I can remember my mother always saying, "Why can't you be smart like Gene next door?" As a consequence, I grew up thinking I was not smart and had to try harder. Gene graduated first in his class in college and went on to write several books and papers. I am still in touch with him.

2) The Promoter

"Nothing can stop the man with the right mental attitude from achieving his goal; nothing on earth can help the man with the wrong mental attitude."

Thomas Jefferson

The first example that made me feel that maybe I did have a decent IQ came in first grade in the Hibbard Elementary School in Chicago. One day, each student had to read a few paragraphs in front of the class. Many of the students in my teacher's class stumbled through the reading, but when it came to my turn I breezed through it without a pause.

"That does it," proclaimed the teacher. "Pack your bags and come with me." At first I thought I had done something wrong. But I did a good job. What did she have in mind? I soon found out.

I was brought to the teacher of the advanced first grade class and told that I was being promoted. "Hey, I'm not that stupid," I thought.

The second inkling that maybe I wasn't as stupid as I thought came when I entered a citywide competition put on by the Chicago Association of Commerce and Industry. They were looking for a slogan for their Clean Up, Paint Up, Light Up, Plant Up Campaign. I entered, along with thousands of others, and won an honorable mention for my slogan. I don't remember what I submitted, but I was recognized by the school principal and given the award shown on this page.

THE CHICAGO ASSOCIATION OF COMMERCE AND INDUSTRY

Awards

This Certificate of Honorable Mention

to

Joseph Sugarman

Hibbard Elementary School

For an Excellent Slogan
for the
Clean Up, Paint Up, Light Up, Plant Up Campaign

December 6, 1949

John R. MacGregor
Chairman, Community Service Committee

My father was starting to do very well in his business and decided that living in an apartment building didn't make sense. It was time to move. He picked out a beautiful home in suburban Oak Park. And so, when I was in sixth grade, our family moved to Oak Park where I started grammar school.

In grammar school my favorite activity was writing. I'd write a story and if I was called on to read it, I would crack up the class. Back in sixth grade, I was the class humorist.

In sixth grade, I also had my first taste of the business world. My father helped me set up a small printing business. He bought me a printing press, type, and a small proof press. I paid for the equipment with time payments and money I earned.

That year I also invented a small game that I brought to my father's patent attorney to get a patent protecting it. The attorney also prepared a letter explaining the game so I could present it to the Parker Brothers Game Company.

The game was never accepted and the printing business soon became rather boring. But both were my first experiences in business.

At Oak Park and River Forest High School I joined the school newspaper photo staff and started writing my own stories, adding my own photos.

The school frowned on humor, so I didn't get much of a chance to use it, but I did write many stories and was the school's sports photographer. That got me to the sidelines of many of Oak Park's big sports events.

High school was probably one of the most exciting times of my life. Ernest Hemingway was a former student at Oak Park High, Frank Lloyd Wright had taught there, and the school was steeped with tradition going back well into the 1880s.

3) The Big Fight

"Great minds discuss ideas. Average minds discuss events. Small minds discuss people."

Eleanor Roosevelt

There comes a time when you have to stand up for what you believe and in some cases fight for your honor. Such a time came when I was in my senior year in high school and I was in chemistry class. We were all assigned lab stations to do our experiments. Unfortunately, I was assigned to a station next to Richard, a guy I did not get along with. He would make snide remarks to me. I'd counter with my comments and throughout the length of chemistry class, our banter escalated to the point where one day I turned to Richard and said, "OK, do you want to fight about it?"

Richard responded, "Oh yeah, you want a good fight?" I took another look at Richard. He was short and stocky and seemed like an easy pushover if I were to engage him in a fight. "Sure," I said. "You pick the spot."

"How about the baseball diamond at Greenfield Park? And how about 4 pm after school?"

"It's a deal," I said and proceeded to finish my experiment and head to my next class.

Greenfield Park was right across the street from where I lived. I had time to go home and change clothes. I was so confident of victory that I invited all my friends to witness the brawl, and I changed into all-white clothes. The white clothes were a subliminal message to the crowd. I was confident that I was going to punch this guy out with the first swing and walk away victorious without a single smudge to my pristine attire. OK, maybe a little blood, but it would be his blood, not mine.

We all showed up at the park—my friends and I. We were all anticipating Richard's defeat and I had my cheering section standing by to encourage me. The moment was tense. I first turned to my friends to acknowledge their presence. Then, as I turned around to face Richard and before I had a chance to strike a blow, Richard took a swing right at my nose. Wham.

The next thing I remember is blood gushing from my nose. The fight was over. I was doing everything I could do to stop the bleeding. My white slacks were full of blood. My clean white dress shirt was soaked, and I was heading back home for a ride to the hospital for a wound that surely needed stitches.

As I headed home, I realized that my mom was going to be in the kitchen preparing dinner for the family. And I also knew that she was very emotional. She would take one look at me, see the blood all over my clothes, and start screaming in a panic. I had to calm her down before she could actually see me.

As I entered the side entrance in my home, I called out to my mom, "Mom, I got into a little fight but please don't worry. I'm fine but I may need a few stitches. Promise you won't scream or get too excited."

"Don't worry about a thing, honey," she said. "I'll be fine. Let's take a look."

Now believe it or not, I was more fearful of my mom's panic reaction than I was about my wound. And my mom didn't disappoint me. She screamed at the top of her lungs, and once again I had to assure her that all was okay. She rushed me to the hospital, bloody clothes and all, where the bleeding finally stopped.

The story would typically end here. But wait, there's more (as I used to say in my mail order ads). Two years later, almost to the day, the jerk who punched me in the nose and beat the crap out of me, married my younger sister Barbara. Yes, it took two years, but I finally got even with him!

Richard Schultz turned out to be a nice and responsible guy. He completed law school and went on to achieve fame by being one of the government's prosecutors in the infamous Chicago Seven trial along with the chief prosecutor, Thomas Foran. And he's been married to my sister for 53 years and counting.

Today Richard and I have mutual respect for each other and both of us have accomplished a lot in our lives since those days in chemistry class. And from this experience I learned never to be overly confident. Anything can happen even if the odds seem like they're on your side. And of course, I learned that you should be careful with whom you pick a fight. He might marry your sister.

4) The Atom

"People of mediocre ability sometimes achieve outstanding success because they don't know when to quit. Most men succeed because they are determined to."

George E. Allen 1832—1907, publisher and author

In 1956, my senior year at Oak Park High School, I was getting frustrated with the limits placed on my writing by the very conservative school newspaper and decided to put out my own with my father's help and encouragement. The basketball players were scheduled to play in the finals. Having them on my staff was my insurance that I wouldn't get kicked out of school. If they kicked me out of school, they would have to do the same for the basketball players.

But I needed other talents on the paper as well. There was a guy whom everybody considered the school hoodlum. He flunked high school once and was therefore a lot older than his contemporaries. His name was Chuck Brightly and he was into fast cars and drag racing. I was into cars too so we became friends.

Our school had many children of Chicago's gangsters. Remember, this was shortly after the Al Capone era. At school this was just another profession. You could ask somebody what their father did and they'd tell you candidly that either they were a lawyer or a doctor or even a gangster.

But Chuck Brightly was no relative of an Al Capone gangster. Nevertheless, he had a lot of street smarts and I needed that for my magazine. I hired him. I needed the addresses of all the students at school in order to mail everybody a copy of my newspaper and figured Chuck was my man to do this. The mailing list was, of course, the property of the school and if they knew I was about to publish a student magazine and needed that list, they might get very cautious. But Chuck was up to the challenge.

Chuck Brightly dressed as a grandma to illustrate his recipe.

One day, with another student, he diverted the attention of the clerk in the principal's office, and he quickly went through the file cabinets until he found what he was looking for—the complete listing of all the students. He then snuck out of the office.

We quickly copied the names and returned to the office and once again diverted the attention of the clerk. Chuck replaced the listing as if nothing had happened. It took us a few days to copy all the names, but we did it and the school never found out.

The magazine was called *The Atom* and the subheading read: "Dynamic energy operating in a small orbit." I wrote it along with a few select writers from the school paper.

The ATOM was a big hit with the students although the school may not have felt the same way

I even had Chuck dress up to look like a grandma with a headdress and apron and featured him in a column entitled, "Grandma Brightly's Recipes" in which we had a humorous recipe for eggshell crunchies.

There were a lot of funny columns and material that were more interesting and relevant to students than what was in the school newspaper. And we went to various local businesses and sold them advertising to help pay for the magazine. *The Atom* was a big hit. It got written up in the local newspapers including the *Chicago Tribune* and the *Chicago Sun-Times*. The students loved it. And we didn't hear a word from the school.

The Atom only lasted one issue. To spend the time and effort to publish another edition would have been very time-consuming, and by then I was more interested in graduating than I was in becoming a publisher. I soon graduated from high school.

5) The University of Miami

"The person interested in success has to learn to view failure as a healthy, inevitable part of the process of getting to the top."

Dr. Joyce Brothers, psychologist and television personality

I enrolled at the University of Illinois in journalism, although my father had hoped I would choose engineering, as this was the area that would help him the most in his business. College was supposed to groom me to take over my father's company when he retired.

During that summer I convinced my father to buy me a beautiful 1956 racing Corvette with some of the money coming from cutting grass during the summer. It was the first of a new breed of Corvettes that was introduced at the Sebring race in Florida.

I was all prepared to go to the University of Illinois when I discovered that they didn't allow cars there the first year, and here I had this beautiful Corvette. So I worked for part of the summer and decided to take my last fling by driving down to Florida for a final summer vacation in my new car.

I had a few relatives who lived in Miami, and I was to stay with them. After spending a week in the beautiful Florida sunshine, I realized that attending the University of Miami made a lot more sense than attending the University of Illinois and besides, I could drive my car, so I compromised with my father and enrolled at the University of Miami's Electrical Engineering School. I had always liked electronic gadgets and radio communications (I was a general-class ham radio operator), even though writing was my first love.

One of the traditions of attending college is joining a fraternity. When I was at the University of Miami, the procedure was to attend several parties thrown by the fraternities. After attending these parties, you reduced your choice to three or four fraternity houses and then you attended a second round of parties, Finally by the third round of parties, you selected the few fraternities you want to join, let those fraternities know and they then either agree or disagree to have you join. But it doesn't end there.

Let's say you join a fraternity. You are what is called a "pledge." You are not a full brother but one who caters to the demands of the already initiated brothers. You go through a pledge period to prove to the other brothers that you are willing to take any kind of abuse just to join and become a full brother. The process they put you through is called "hazing" and it isn't easy. The idea is to put you through hell and if you can take it and want to join the fraternity badly enough, you endure it. Then after several weeks of hazing, you are accepted as a brother.

I attended some of the parties. I was sought after—partly because of the racing Corvette I drove and my friendly personality, not to mention my very attractive girlfriend. All the fraternities wanted me from the very prestigious to the worst. Finally, after the three rounds of parties, it was time to choose. Everybody was predicting the fraternity I would join—the most respected one on campus. But I was about to surprise everybody.

I joined the absolute worst fraternity on campus: Phi Sigma Delta. The guys were sloppy looking, their girlfriends were not attractive and it had so few brothers that it was easily one of the smallest on campus. Everybody was shocked by my choice, especially Phi Sigma Delta.

At my first fraternity meeting, they asked me straight out why I had chosen Phi Sigma Delta. Even the brothers couldn't figure it out. I then said, "When I become a brother, I will give you the key to expand Phi Sigma Delta into the most popular fraternity on campus bar none. I will give you two tips that, if you follow them, will build this fraternity like crazy.

Time passed and so did the hazing. Forced marches in the middle of the night, scavenger hunts, shining the shoes of the brothers—a whole series of petty harassments to the small group of us wanting to become brothers of the worst fraternity on campus. Finally, I was inducted into the fraternity as a full brother. And as part of the ceremony it was my turn to explain to the brothers my technique for a way to build the fraternity into the top frat on campus. It was midyear and the number of potential pledges was small compared to the beginning of the year at the start of school.

I got up in front of my brothers and explained that I was going to propose just two things. If my brothers were willing to do these two things, I would guarantee the biggest pledge class in their history—even

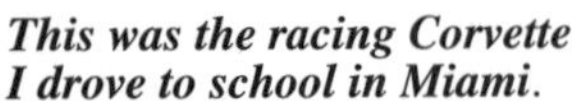
This was the racing Corvette I drove to school in Miami.

though it was midyear. They all listened intently as I proceeded.

"The first thing I am proposing is for each brother to take the potential pledge and introduce him to another brother saying something like, 'This is the nicest guy in the whole world. I would do anything for him' or something similar. The more brothers you introduce to the pledges in this way, the better. With each introduction you'll get in the swing of things and you'll be amazed at the results."

Many of the brothers disliked each other. Telling a brother how much you loved him when you actually hated him was going to be a challenge. "Now do you promise to do this? I guarantee it will do more to acquire a large pledge class than you could possibly imagine." The brothers nodded, chuckling at the idea that they would be doing this.

"Point Two. I would like to propose that I go to a Miami Beach strip club and recruit about three or four of the prettiest and hottest girls in the business—all to be hostesses at our parties. Keep your girlfriends at home. Do you understand?"

The brothers liked that idea. Their girlfriends were, at best, very average. "You follow just these two concepts and you will be

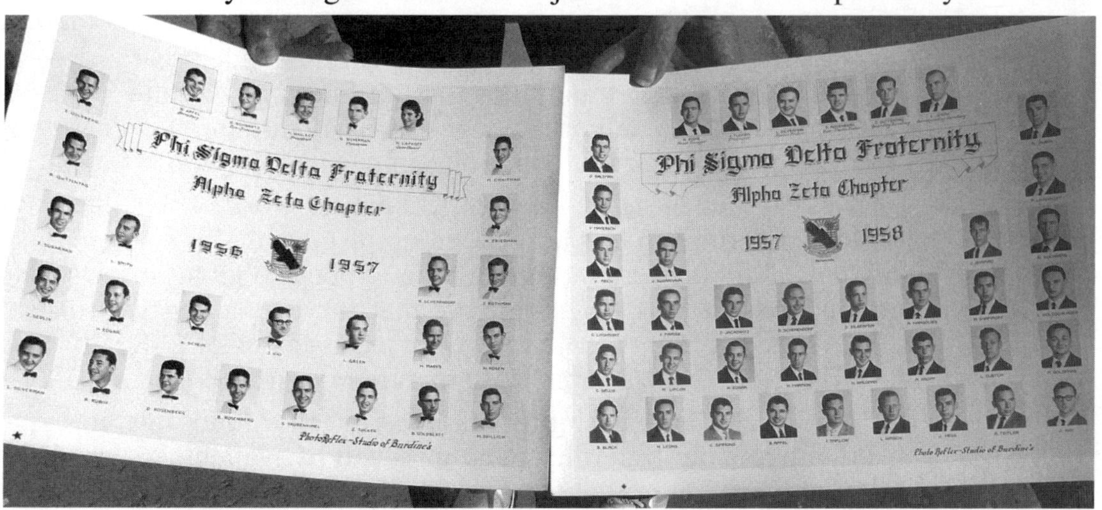

Before and after. Note the size of the fraternity before I got there and afterwards using the suggestions I made to my brothers. Not all the new brothers could fit onto the new photo spread.

amazed at the results. I chose this fraternity, not because I thought it was the best but because I thought it was the worst, and, if I joined, I felt I could turn this place around and build the best frat house at the University of Miami. Follow my advice and you will be blown away with what will happen."

To my delight, my brothers were all for my two ideas. And my visit to a few strip clubs produced four very sexy young ladies who loved the idea of being hostesses at a frat party. "Dress like college girls but very sexy," I suggested. And to my surprise they were willing to do it for free.

The first frat party was incredible. The brothers introduced themselves to the pledges, brought them to a brother and told the pledge how incredible the brother was. I mean they really got into this. Meanwhile the girls had dressed in short skirts and revealing tops and really looked hot.

Word got out. By the second party, the potential pledges increased dramatically. And the strippers had such a good time that they invited a few of their friends so that, without a doubt, we had the most attractive, sexiest girls of any of the parties—girls who were not shy about showing their physical assets.

By the third party, the crowd was so big that even I was surprised. The girls did a fantastic job of teasing the guys while the brothers did a great job of expressing their love and appreciation for their fellow brothers.

When invitations to join Phi Sigma Delta were passed out to the potential pledges, almost everybody who attended that last party wanted to join. Other fraternities did not fare too well and word got out that we had one hell of a pledge class. My mission was complete. I had turned the worst frat house on campus into the best.

Why did these two simple techniques work? I felt that guys joined a fraternity to be part of a group of guys that they would like and that would help each other in time of need. With all those strong introductions, it was not surprising that the perception was one of brotherhood—stronger than was expressed at any other fraternity. And the girls? Nobody else came close to our sexy girls.

Having the sexiest girls as hostesses left a subliminal message that if you join our fraternity, these girls will be available to date. Why do guys join a fraternity? On a hunch I had figured it out and turned the frat house from a bunch of losers into likeable guys who felt that the fraternity would also draw pretty girls. Our pledge class outnumbered the actual number of brothers, and it felt like a totally different fraternity. And those guys who had hated each other no longer did. I transformed the entire organization with two basic concepts and after that Phi Sigma Delta was never the same.

6) The French Hoax

"Many of life's failures are people who did not realize how close they were to success when they gave up."

Thomas Edison 1847—1931,inventor and businessman

While in college I always lived on the edge. I would do things that could get me in trouble, but I always managed to come out on top. One of the best examples is when I helped a friend of mine realize his talents.

My friend, Sanford (Sandy) Fink, was from Chicago and belonged to my fraternity. He had a very interesting talent. He could imitate several accents without actually knowing the language. For example, he could speak English with a French accent or English with a Russian accent.

He was so convincing that you could swear he was French or

The Miami  **Hurricane**

VOL. XXXIII | UNIVERSITY OF MIAMI, CORAL GABLES, FLA., AUGUST 22, 1958 | No. 32

Parisian Hoax Exposed By L' Hurricane

By PEG POWELL
Hurricane Staff Writer

A fantastic hoax by two University of Miami students that fooled thousands of people—and eventually would have taken in millions—was exposed last night by The Hurricane.

Sanford Fink, 21-year-old Miami Beach sophomore, who was passing himself off as a "visiting French disc jockey from Paris," and Joe Sugarman, 20-year-old junior from Chicago who posed as Fink's pen pal and sponsor were exposed by radio station WMET's disc jockey Sam Gyson on his 11 p.m. program in cooperation with Hurricane editor, John Garcia.

Fink, whose pseudonym was Marcel Voiture, and Sugarman had appeared on Gyson's program August 13 and fooled him as they had The Hurricane when interviewed by Larrie Schmidt for a feature story.

The two Phi Sigma Delta brothers planned the hoax in an attempt at nation-wide publicity to advance Fink's ambitions in the field of radio-TV.

They wanted to appear on as many local and national radio and television stations as possible with their goal being an appearance on Channel 4's "I've got a secret" program It all began last Monday when Sugarman telephoned Schmidt and asked him if he would be interested in interviewing his pen-pal, the French disc jockey.

An interview was held the next ... dance was Sanford Fink. Garcia then assigned Schmidt to investigate.

Telephone calls to the registrar's office and the office of the dean of men where student records and background information is kept, produced information that the "visiting Parisian" had never been to France.

Instead, he was born in Chicago, Ill., on July 11, 1937. At the time "Marcel" was supposed to have been

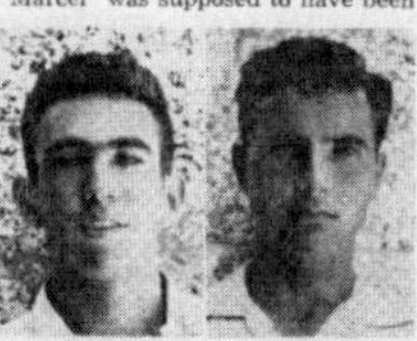

SUGARMAN FINK

attending Sorbonne University in Paris, he was attending Central YMCA High School in Chicago.

Fink had told The Hurricane and DJ Gyson that he worked for Radio France in Paris and that he came to America to visit this country and his pen pal and to study at the University of Miami this fall.

But Fink had already attended UM's first summer session and is presently attending the second summer session. Before coming here he was enrolled at the University of Illinois. He is a major in radio-TV, but prior to the hoax had never been on a radio or television program which made his role as a Parisian disc jockey extremely vul- ... farce, Fink and Sugarman said it was strictly a publicity stunt to help Fink in his Radio-TV career. Sugarman admitted to being the mastermind of the plot, but said he had nothing to gain from it personally.

"I am interested in engineering," he said, "but Sanford has such great talent that I hated to see it go to waste."

"He is a great actor and mimic and can do impersonations of French, German, Italian, Hungarian, and Irish accents that would fool even a native of those lands.

"This whole thing was my idea—and although we have fooled thousands of people—no harm was meant by the hoax.

"It turned out to be a tremendous adventure for both of us. An adventure that brought us romance and love, perpetual excitement, loads of fun and much publicity. We also learned a lot about the American people."

Fink, dropping his French accent and happy that the whole thing was over, said "Americans treated me wonderfully as a foreigner. Any body who says Americans aren't kind to their foreign visitors is nuts! Waitresses were especially patient and kind and helpful when they found that my English wasn't so good."

They said they first started fooling people when they broadcasted to many countries on Sugarman's ham radio set which he has installed in his auto.

"When we talked to a ham in Germany I used a German accent and when we talked with an Englishman I spoke with a British accent," Fink said. "And he fooled them too," chuckled Sugarman.

"Then Sanford and I decided to go into the masquerade seriously," Sugarman continued, "and that's when we called The Hurricane. After the interview with their reporter and news editor we contacted Sam Gyson at WMET.

"I had been on Mr. Gyson's program once before, several months earlier, in connection with a UM engineering function and considered him a highly literate and intelligent man—a man I did not think would ask Sanford a lot of personal questions that might have put him on a spot.

"Fortunately, Mr. Gyson, like so many other people, answered a lot of his own questions to save us embarrassment or exposure. Sanford had never been to Europe and I had only been to Paris once so we knew absolutely nothing about Parisians or the French way of life.

"Since we never had any idea what kind of questions people were going to ask Sanford about France, he had to make up answers right on the spot.

"He was in a couple of real tight jams when Schmidt and Mr. Gyson—both of whom have been to Paris—asked him questions concerning Paris, but Sanford resorted to evasiveness and pulled us out of a rut.

"That's another nice thing about Americans—they don't press you on answers. Whenever someone wanted to practice their French on Sanford, he told them he had promised me he wouldn't speak French while in the U. S. so that he could improve his English.

"Eventually, had we been successful with our hoax and appeared on the 'I've Got a Secret' show or the Jack Paar Show, we were going to write a book on the whole thing.

"Several times we were certain that the hoax had been discovered but we just kept on bluffing and bluffing. We knew that someone would catch on eventually, but we hoped we could carry the farce as far as possible before being discovered.

Improved Dial Phone Service Ready For Operation By Sunday

The hoax was exposed on the front page of the school newspaper. We didn't get in trouble but it stopped us from furthering Sandy's career.

Italian or even Russian whenever he would perform. His dream was to someday become a TV or radio talent, and his pronunciation skills were just one of many skills he had.

One day, sitting in a restaurant with him, I broached an idea I had. "What if we could call one of the big radio stations in Miami, get you an interview with the most famous of the radio personalities and have him ask questions to see how you view America, American women and the differences between France and the US."

Sandy asked, "Then what? How is that going to help my career?"

I responded, "Simple. We keep getting you radio gigs and eventually get you on one of the game shows like I've Got A Secret. With all that national exposure you're sure to get a job."

Sandy was a little reluctant at first but after awhile he agreed to go ahead with the hoax. I got him an interview with a top Miami radio personality and with the school newspaper, *The Hurricane*.

The interview on radio went very well. Sandy was humorous, expressed some controversial comments about American women and, after the interview, the disc jockey asked if he could return for another session. The audience loved Sandy. It went fantastically well.

He then was interviewed by a reporter from the University paper, *The Hurricane*, and it too went off smoothly. But then Sandy made a major mistake. He saw the Hurricane reporter on campus a few days after his interview and absentmindedly spoke to him without an accent, "How are you doing?"

It was enough to make the reporter realize that this was all a hoax, and without hesitation, Sandy confessed right on the spot. End of story and end of our big idea. But when the next issue of the paper was distributed to the students, the lead paragraph said it all:

"A fantastic hoax by two University of Miami students that fooled thousands of people—and eventually would have taken in millions—was exposed last night by *The Hurricane*."

We didn't get in trouble. But this is one of several out-of-the-box ideas I had while attending the university.

7) College and the Trade Show Promoter

"Create the highest, grandest vision possible for your life, because you become what you believe."

Oprah Winfrey, talk show host, actress, producer, and philanthropist

I spent two years in college getting average grades until my father asked me to help him run his New York office. He was having rough times during the 1958 recession and needed my help.

He owned a two-story office building in a poor section of town off 8th Avenue on 26th Street.

There used to be ten people in the office, but everybody quit or was fired during this period. I offered to work for him for nothing and acted as his salesman and serviceman even though I knew nothing about servicing printing equipment.

Despite my handicaps, I did manage to get by, and eventually I hired a few people and got the office functioning again.

During this time my father approached me with an idea. The Printing Industry of America was staging a printing exposition in New York, and they had reserved the New York Coliseum. Space at the show went so fast that almost all the foreign companies and many American companies were prevented from exhibiting and showing their products. My father suggested that I book the nearby New York Trade Show Building and stage my own show for the foreign companies that couldn't get space in the other show and for those American companies who also wanted to exhibit.

It sounded like a great idea so I reserved the New York Trade Show Building, called my exhibition Spectra '59, designed a full-color poster, a brochure and a space application form, and sent it to all foreign and American manufacturers.

Responses started to come in, but not as fast as I had hoped. The advertising materials looked very professional and were more exciting than those for the major show at the Coliseum. We actually looked like the major show in the eyes of the Europeans and Japanese.

But I was twenty years old at the time and looked so young that if a potential exhibitor would meet me, he would not have confidence that I could succeed. I couldn't use my father as the sponsor because he was competition for most of the exhibitors I wanted to attract.

The printing bills were starting to come due so I had to take some positive action. I hired a sixty-five-year old actor who looked as distinguished as the chairman of the board of any top U.S. corporation, and I told him what to say. He was to be my personal representative. Whenever I'd get a call from an interested party who wanted to discuss the show in more detail, I'd simply inform him in a slow yet deep voice that I was too busy and that I would send my personal representative to talk to them.

When things started to build and the sales started coming in, I called a college buddy of mine, Richard Pieper, and asked him if he'd like to help me out. He agreed and came up for the summer. He would handle the promotion and I would handle the sales.

Then I went to Europe to close a few deals that were pending. I know I must have shocked a few people. By this time I had turned twenty-one, but I probably looked more like eighteen, and my grey-haired actor was performing on Broadway and couldn't spare the time to travel to Europe for me.

Nevertheless, we managed to turn Spectra '59 into a very successful exhibition. The five floors of the New York Trade Show Building were sold out, we attracted a large crowd, and everybody was happy.

The exhibitors were pleased and the visitors were pleased. Dick Pieper and I ended up with nothing. We had spent our last pennies promoting the show and had nothing to show for our efforts other than plenty of experience.

But who cared? We had a lot of fun, learned what the real world was all about, and everybody benefited. Dick joined his father's small electrical contracting business back in Milwaukee and built it into a very successful company. I went back to school. Things sure seemed quieter.

Spectra '59 had the look and feel of a major trade show, as shown in this poster. We looked like the bigger of the two shows in New York.

8) The Cuban Adventure

"If you believe you can, you probably can. If you believe you won't, you most assuredly won't. Belief is the ignition switch that gets you off the launching pad."

Denis Waitley, author, speaker and trainer

Sometimes you go through life on a certain path and in a certain direction when suddenly something happens and you end up going in a direction you least expect. Such was the case with the Cuban Missile Crisis.

While in high school I earned my amateur radio license and became a general-class "ham" as we were called back then. It wasn't easy. I had to learn a great deal about radios as well as the Morse Code at 13 words a minute.

As a general-class ham and well before cell phones, I was allowed to broadcast from my car. While in college I bought myself twin Gonset radios and a large antenna. The radios themselves were large. One was the transmitting element and the other the receiver. Each of the two units was the size of a toaster and were located under the dash before there was a center console.

I enjoyed using these radios. I'd be driving along and broadcast, "CQ 20, CQ 20, this is K4TDL broadcasting from beautiful Miami, K please." Translated it meant that I was looking to talk to some other ham on the radio in some other location.

One minute I would be talking with somebody in California and the next with somebody in Germany and then a few minutes later I would be talking to some sergeant at a military base in Texas. I could also place phone calls by contacting a ham with a home station and an attachment to his phone. He would then patch me into his phone and would dial up the person I wanted to talk to for a few brief moments. For example, if I was heading home and got a ham with a base station and asked him to connect me with a buddy of mine to tell him I was heading back to my fraternity house, he would, as a courtesy, make the connection.

So one day I was driving down Coral Way in Coral Gables, Florida, when somebody pulled along next to me, started honking their horn and signaled me to pull over to the side of the road. I pulled over and a man in his thirties said, with a Spanish accent, "You are a ham radio operator, no?"

From the size of my antenna and the letters on my licence plates K4TDL, it wasn't too hard to figure that out. "Yes, I am. Why?"

The man started to explain that he was with a group that was planning on invading Cuba to take it back from Castro. They needed communications equipment and he thought that maybe I could help them source it. I then followed him to a home where I met the former head of the Air Force, Pedro Dias Lance, and several high-ranking military personnel along with a few Americans. I was welcomed to join them anytime.

I went back to my apartment, called the FBI, and they visited me. I explained the entire plan that the Cubans had briefed me on and the FBI agents simply said, "We know all of that and we are monitoring it closely. Just be careful."

I did help the Cubans but did not want to go on any invasion of Cuba. Some of the Americans I was introduced to at the Cuban home were eventually caught as spies and hung. I heard about it on the radio. And of course the Bay of Pigs invasion of Cuba failed miserably.

9) The Rise and Fall of Joe Subway

"Continuous effort - not strength or intelligence - is the key to unlocking our potential."

Sir Winston Churchill 1874—1965, Former British Prime Minister

After my Spectra '59 and Bay of Pigs experience, college took on real meaning for me. I was now a more serious student. My grades improved dramatically and I spent less time on social activities.

I dropped out of the fraternity house and rented an apartment off campus. During my stay at the apartment, I studied at the kitchen table every evening. Keeping the radio playing softly in the background, I listened to Bob Greene on Miami radio station WINZ. I learned how to concentrate on my studies despite the radio which would play the novelty and hit rock and roll songs of the late fifties.

One evening at a party I met Neil Sedaka, a rock singer who had cut a couple of records and then rose to the top of the charts. He was a regular sort of guy who told me how he really hated the music he sang, but because of its commercial success, it made it possible for him to occasionally play and sing the music he really enjoyed.

After meeting him and knowing every rock and novelty tune on the music charts, the idea of writing my own song and singing it really appealed to me. Sedaka was an average guy from Brooklyn, not especially good looking, who was the hit of the party. Girls were chasing him because he had plenty of money and he was living a very exciting and interesting life. Why couldn't I do the same?

The key, of course, was a hit record. I had to write one first. I had already written lyrics for a song during my stay in New York around the time of several successful space flights by American astronauts. The song was called "Santa's Got a Problem," and the theme was quite topical. What if Americans soon lived on the moon? How would Santa deliver toys? "Santa's got a problem, for very very soon, good girls and boys would want their toys delivered to the moon." So the song went. A great idea, I thought—until I tried to sell it. Despite many weeks of knocking on doors in New York. I couldn't interest anybody.

I met Archie Bleyer, the band leader who also managed the Everly Brothers. We were on a plane to Europe where I was trying to sell exhibition space for Spectra '59. He told me how impossible it was to sell a record, let alone a seasonal song like mine. Despite my setbacks, I was determined not to give up.

During a break from school in 1960, I met an old high school friend, Dick Bjork. Dick was an excellent piano player who was always the hit of any high school party. I convinced him to write some music for my Santa song and a few other novelty songs I had written while at school.

I wrote a song, "Is It Chilly in Chile during Christmas?" The weather, was warm during the cold Christmas season in the U.S. I needed a flip hit for my Santa space song and it fit the bill perfectly.

Then I wrote a novelty tune that played to a calypso beat called "Mudder Goose." It was simply an up-to-date rendition of the Mother Goose nursery rhymes had they been written in 1960. Some examples:

Hickory Dickory Dock. The mouse ran up the clock. The clock struck one and blew up. It was a time bomb.

Little Miss Muffet sat on her tuffet eating some curds and whey. Along came a spider who sat down beside her and said, "Like what's happening?"

[Chorus] Mother Goose was a very hip poet. She was hip but we didn't know it. It wasn't until later years that her modern version made our ears.

Dick collaborated with me in writing the music and I contacted a local recording studio in Miami and told them that I wanted to record my songs. I didn't need musical accompaniment as I had the recording with Dick playing the piano.

When I arrived at the recording studio they gave me Studio A and I pulled out my music. I had never sung before in my life. They rolled my music tape and I started to sing "Santa's Got a Problem." From the expressions in the control booth, I was convinced I was not doing a very good job. There was agony written on the face of the engineer who stepped out of the control booth and spent two hours trying to get me to sing the song correctly. Finally we resorted to singing it several times and he would very carefully splice sentences, words, phrases—anything that would sound right—into a single tape.

It was a rather humiliating experience that convinced me that I definitely was not naturally endowed with much of a voice. Frank Sinatra certainly had nothing to worry about. Finally, after another two hours, the engineer realized that the song wasn't going to sound like much unless I had a professional singer. He politely suggested that he could get me a singer to cut the record if I wanted. As I was really only cutting a demo record anyway, I agreed, and after lunch a local nightclub performer showed up and sang my two Christmas songs. He was able to do them in a matter of minutes.

I still insisted on doing my "Mudder Goose" song because the nursery rhymes were not sung but rather recited in a rather stupid-sounding way. I was perfect for that.

Early the next summer, in 1961, after school let out, I took my records, or dubs as they were called, to a few record companies. Mercury Records rejected them. Several other local companies rejected them.

I went to New York, using some of the money I had earned working for my father, and after several days of rejections left New York for Chicago where I decided to investigate the black record companies.

I called one of them, Apex Records, and spoke to a Dempsey Nelson, the president of the company. Nelson invited me to stop by and I played my music for his producer. Apex Records was located on the south side of Chicago. After entering a small storefront entrance, I was greeted by a receptionist who brought me to a small waiting room outfitted with rather old beat-up furniture.

I waited for about an hour. The producer for the company greeted me and took me into a rather barren room with just a record player and speakers and played my Santa song. After a few seconds, he flipped it over and listened to "Is it Chilly in Chile during Christmas?" A few seconds later he said, "I'm afraid ya ain't going to make it with that stuff. What else ya got?"

Mad Records and my first "hit" song, Mudder Goose.

I then gave him my "Mudder Goose" dub and he played it. After each rhyme, he laughed loudly and listened to the whole tune. He then said, "Wow, good friend, you've got a smash."

He quickly ushered me into the president's office. Dempsey Nelson was a large man with a mustache who chomped a cigar and smiled simultaneously. The producer told him, "We've got a stone smash single, Dempsey. Don't let this guy leave until we sign him up."

Dempsey heard my dub, laughed louder than the producer and convinced me to sign up with him. "I'll call RCA records, rent their largest recording studio," he said, "and you'll be on the air in a few weeks."

Here I was on the way to stardom. So of course I signed the contract. "Could you write a few more songs," Dempsey urged. The session would require four songs.

"Yes, I will," I assured him and off I went. I contacted Dick and we worked out a few more songs for the session, such immortal songs as "Flip-flop Fanny," for example. I can't remember the other two, but they definitely weren't classics.

Dick would accompany me on the piano and would attend the session and get paid musician's scale for his effort. Meanwhile, Nelson hired four backup singers and an entire band and we were all set for the big evening session at RCA Studio A. What a thrill. Look what I had created. All these people there because of me.

At the session, the group played the songs, the backup singers accompanied me and there I was, hearing my songs for the first time—and, boy, did they sound great. Everybody was patting me on the back. "Joe, you've got a stone smash hit."

To say that I was thrilled was putting it mildly. Dreams of fame, of beautiful women begging me for my autograph, of national publicity as my novelty tune hit the top of charts—all this raced through my mind during those few days after the session.

As a recording artist, I also changed my name to something better fitting the image of the song. I called myself Joe Subway.

With fame assured, I gave serious thought to quitting school for a semester so I could tour the country and make personal appearances. I found it difficult to go back to work for my father to be a delivery boy and do other odd jobs. The excitement and expectations kept me on a high for over two weeks.

But for some strange reason I hadn't heard from Dempsey. So I called him. "How's it going?" I asked.

"Not too good, Joe. Could I see you?" he said in a rather concerned and serious way.

What's wrong?" I asked.

"Just come down and I'll explain," he said.

I arrived at his office and was told to take a seat in his reception room. All sorts of horrible things passed through my mind. Dempsey kept me waiting for two hours before I was escorted into his office.

"We've got a few financial problems," said Dempsey. "That last record we had didn't take off as we had expected. We're very short on funds, and to be frank, Joe, we don't have the money to pay for the sound mixing and the records to get this thing kicked off."

"How much will it take?" I asked.

"About $1,500 to get to the record pressing stage," he replied as he shrugged his shoulders.

"If I raise the money to get the records pressed, could I put the record on my own label and work out a joint venture with you?"

"Sure," said Dempsey. "What label have you got?"

"I don't have any yet, but give me a few days and I'll get one," I answered.

I saw this whole turn of events as a great opportunity to start my own record company. Not only would I have my own song, but I would own half the company as well. Dempsey had agreed to pay me back half of everything I spent to get that record pressed, and I felt I couldn't lose.

I managed to convince my father to loan me $1,500 and I proceeded to get the MAD record label for my very own. In about three weeks I had pressed over a thousand records and was now well on my way to stardom. I dropped off a few hundred records with Dempsey and told him that he could "do his thing"—get that record on the radio.

Dempsey, however, called me a week later and told me that before anybody would play it, there had to be some publicity and advertisements in Billboard and Cashbox magazines. No problem, I thought. With such a smash hit, I wasn't going to let a few advertisements get in the way, so I contacted some advertising people and created a series of three advertisements which I gave Dempsey to run in the various magazines.

Meanwhile, I called Richard—a local disc jockey who owned a record store on the south side—and offered to give him some free records if he would play the tune. I sent out mailings to radio stations all over the country. I sent letters to disc jockeys and I tried to get Dempsey to run those advertisements in the magazines. But I couldn't seem to reach him.

Nothing worked. We did sell a few records in Richard's record store, but the mailing didn't work, the disc jockey mailing produced nothing, and Dempsey Nelson literally disappeared. His storefront business closed and his creditors were now after me to pay all his other bills—none of which were ever mine in the first place.

My dreams of becoming a great songwriter, a star performer—even a record company owner—slowly crumbled around me. I was in debt to my father for about $3,000 and figured that I'd just be able to pay him back if I could work the rest of the summer and the next Christmas break. Which I did.

I still had about five hundred records left but, unfortunately, nobody was interested in Joe Subway's latest smash single. Not even my father.

SELECTIVE SERVICE SYSTEM

LOCAL BOARD NO. 104
SELECTIVE SERVICE SYSTEM
7520 MADISON ST.
FOREST PARK, ILLINOIS
(LOCAL BOARD STAMP)

IN REPLY, REFER TO:

15 August 1961

Mr. Joseph Sugarman
1201 Woodbine Avenue
Oak Park, Illinois

11-104-38-126

Dear Sir:

This is to advise you that the local board members would not recommend a cancellation of your Order To Report For Induction. They were of the opinion that you had waited too long to request any kind of a deferment. Each man that is pulled out of induction must be replaced by another man. Your order was mailed 4 August 1961, and nothing heard from you until 14 August 1961.

The members also felt you had been negligent in never having your school send in anything certifying to your attendance therein nor had any request ever been received from you for a student deferment. You had plenty of time to do this when the Current Information Questionnaire was returned to the local board on 12 December 1960, at which time you stated you were a student at the University of Miami. Your file lacks information or certification of what you have been studying and whether or not you ever received a degree or even how many years you have attended any school as a student.

The local board members wanted this information furnished to you so that you would appreciate their position in the matter.

Very truly yours,

FOR THE LOCAL BOARD

Margaretta S. Pierson

(Mrs.) Margaretta S. Pierson
Chief Clerk

Overlooked was my 3-1/2 years in ROTC and my years studying electrical engineering. But this wasn't the first time I experienced our bureaucracy.

10) Defending Our Nation

"What you can do or think you can do, begin it. For boldness has magic, power, and genius in it."

Johann Wolfgang von Goethe 1749—1832, Poet, Novelist and Scientist

It was now my last year of college. My grades were excellent, I was active in extracurricular activities and I was even enjoying ROTC (Reserve Officer Training Corps). For some reason I liked the military and ROTC gave me the opportunity to go into the army as an officer. It didn't work out that way, however. After spending three and a half years in school, I received my draft notice.

I took the notice and returned it to my local draft board, advising them that I was a student in the university's engineering school and that I was in ROTC and needed just one more semester to graduate and also become an army officer.

The draft board had different ideas. It would not grant me a deferment. I had violated one of its regulations by not reporting my school status, and despite my good grades, my ROTC status, and my appeals, they refused to defer me for one more semester. The Berlin Wall had gone up and the draft quotas were taking quantum leaps. They needed me to fill their quotas and there was nothing I could do to change their minds. The army ironically lost an officer and the world lost another electrical engineer.

So off I went to Fort Carson, Colorado for basic training. When I arrived at the camp, I took a series of tests along with the rest of the troops. Coming right out of college, I scored almost 100 percent on everything. After about six weeks of basic training, I was called to attend a special meeting conducted by some men wearing civilian clothes. The meeting started out like a scene from a stereotyped war movie.

"We called you out of the company because of those high scores you got on your tests. We've got a special mission for you if you'll accept it. If not, no problem; you can go back to your squad."

They explained that if I would enroll for an extra year—three years instead of the mandatory two years—I would be eligible for Army Intelligence. They would send me to a spy school at Fort Holabird, Maryland, and there they would teach me the tricks of being a spy and a secret agent. Then they would send me to some exotic foreign country, teach me the language and I would never have to wear a uniform for the rest of my tour.

That extra year bothered me but it made sense for me to extend.

Look at the adventure and education that was awaiting me. So I enrolled for another year, finished basic training and went off to Fort Holabird.

The school had a typical Army feel to it. We slept on bunk beds, and in the washroom where we showered and shaved was a large room with showers on one side and sinks and mirrors on the other side. Unfortunately there was a big fan in the middle of one of the windows to draw out the air so the mirrors wouldn't fog up.

It was the middle of winter and very cold outside and with that large fan blowing, it was cold taking a shower. So one day, out of not wanting to take another cold shower with cold air blowing through the shower area, I went over to the fan, flipped off the on/off switch and went to take my shower.

No sooner had I stepped in the shower then somebody flipped the switch and turned the fan back on again because the mirrors were getting fogged. "This isn't good, I thought." I tried the next day to turn the fan off, but somebody just as quickly turned it back on.

After a few days of taking these showers with cold air blowing through the shower stalls, I finally came up with a plan. I would go to the local office supply store in town and get materials to make up an official looking Army sign and place it by the fan. The sign would say, "Anybody turning the switch to this fan either on or off will be subject to dismissal from this school and prosecuted under part 407 of the military justice act." There was no such part 407 but it made the sign that much more official looking.

In the middle of the night while everybody was sleeping, I made the sign and placed it next to the fan. I went back to sleep and woke up the next morning anxious to see if my plan worked. I can remember walking into the washroom, walking up to the fan, turning it off and then stepping into the shower while everybody was looking at what I had done. Obviously they thought, I had not seen the sign. I took a long shower. Guys were wiping the fog from the mirrors, but nobody would dare turn the fan switch on for fear of being prosecuted under part 407 of the military justice act. I then walked up to the fan, turned it back on and took my shave with a clear mirror.

I also noted that a lot of the guys would wait for me to walk into the washroom and take a shower while I was taking mine. I'm sure everybody thought, "This guy Sugarman is in deep trouble if he is ever caught."

I did this for almost a month and then one day I got called down to the Commanding General's office. "Sugarman, sit down. I understand that you have been consistently violating part 407 of the military justice act. What do you have to say for yourself?"

At first, I was stunned. What do I tell him? How can I explain what I did? All sorts of images flashed through my mind. Was I going to be thrown out of the program? Was I going to be severely disciplined or even thrown in jail? Despite my worst scenarios I did what felt best. I told the truth.

Halfway through my explanation, the general started to chuckle and by the time I finished he was laughing out loud. "Sugarman, we need men like you. That was very clever on your part and that's what we need in Army Intelligence. I'm going to deploy you to Germany. I'm going to suggest you enroll in the German language school over there and then I want you assigned to a special unit in Frankfurt, Germany. You're a clever guy and you'll do well in this tough business.

And that is what happened. I was sent off to Germany, and I enrolled in a German class where there were two teachers and only six students. The study was intense and I attended two of these schools—one in Wiesbaden and the other in Oberammergau, Germany. After six months of intense language training I spoke German so convincingly that you couldn't tell I was an American. I was then assigned to a special top-secret unit of the Army based in Frankfurt and traveled throughout Germany. On occasions I would be assigned to the CIA to watch over Russian defectors during their interrogation by the CIA. They were usually low-level army defectors who were in the process of being debriefed by the CIA, and it was my job to keep them out of trouble.

The defectors would get an allowance and freedom to move about Frankfurt as long as I accompanied them. And where did they go every night? Down to Kaiserstrasse, Frankfurt's red-light district, to watch all the strip shows and blow their allowances. I soon got to know every stripper on Kaiserstrasse.

After my three and one half years with the army, I was discharged in Europe. I went to visit some of my father's European business associates who were interested in having me help them open up a ski-lift sales organization in the United States.

I was given a two-week tour of the Austrian Alps and its ski resorts with my own personal ski teacher. I also invited an engineering friend from Miami, Sam Bonasso, to take the tour with me. After my tour I returned to Frankfurt to get my things packed and think over the ski deal. I arrived at a small Frankfurt hotel near the American Consulate. While waiting at the reception desk to be assisted, I overheard the man in front of me talking to the receptionist in German. I knew German so well that I was able to also detect if the person speaking was from a foreign country. I detected a Russian accent from the man in front of me. While he was waiting and the clerk was answering the phone, I asked him a few questions and discovered he was the Russian ambassador to Germany. I then knew from my intelligence training, what to say to convince him that I had valuable information he might possibly be interested in.

I dropped into the hotel unexpectedly, so the chance meeting could not have been preplanned. Realizing the valuable intelligence contact I had just accidentally made and with three solid years of intelligence experience and training, I knew exactly what to do to make the Russian think that I was willing to get him all sorts of valuable information for a price. Yes, I became a double agent.

He thought he really had a hot source. Little did he know that I had contacted my friends at the CIA and worked under strict cover until things got too hot for me and I left Germany after a few months of top-secret activity. I learned later that my chance contact turned into a very valuable operation for the CIA and my replacement managed to carry on nicely after I left.

Back in the States, I held three jobs. One was with my father, helping him with advertising, the second was organizing the newly formed ski-lift company with the help of my friend, and the third was still in the Army being part of the Army Reserve—3 ½ years active duty and 1 ½ years in the reserve. I was twenty-seven in 1965 when I returned from the Army and set up Ski-Lift International.

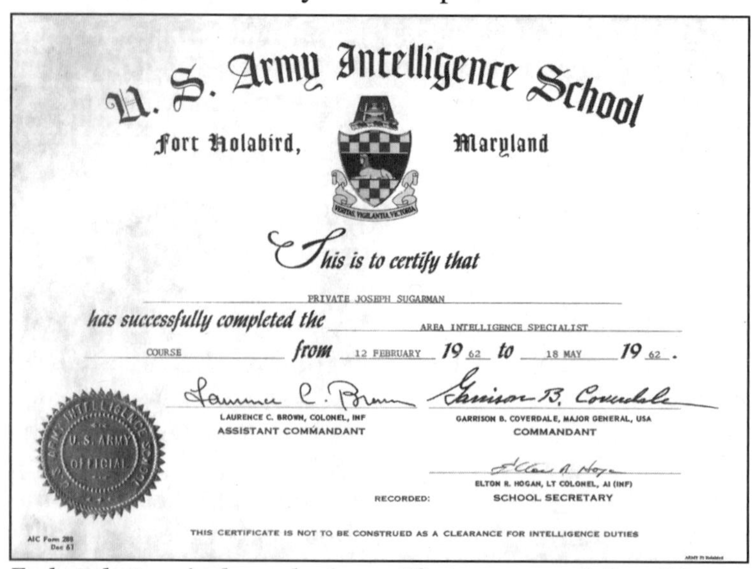

U. S. Army Intelligence School

Fort Holabird, Maryland

This is to certify that

PRIVATE JOSEPH SUGARMAN

has successfully completed the AREA INTELLIGENCE SPECIALIST

COURSE from 12 FEBRUARY 1962 to 18 MAY 1962.

LAURENCE C. BROWN, COLONEL, INF
ASSISTANT COMMANDANT

GARRISON B. COVERDALE, MAJOR GENERAL, USA
COMMANDANT

RECORDED: ELTON R. HOGAN, LT COLONEL, AI (INF)
SCHOOL SECRETARY

THIS CERTIFICATE IS NOT TO BE CONSTRUED AS A CLEARANCE FOR INTELLIGENCE DUTIES

AIC Form 289
Dec 61

Each student received a graduation certificate upon completion of the rigorous training at the Ft. Holabird Intelligence school.

11) Batman and Robin

"There's plenty of intelligence in the world, but the courage to do things differently is in short supply."

Marilyn vos Savant Columnist, Author and Lecturer

During my first year with SLI (Ski-Lift International), with the help of artists and designers, I created sales literature, brochures, magazine advertisements, and direct mail promotions. The material was so professional that we looked like a real contender in the ski-lift industry in which we had nine competitors.

Sam Bonasso, my engineering school classmate and new partner, was one of those hail-fellow-well-met types who always had a smile on his cherubic face and knew how to charm people. He was in charge of sales and engineering and once I developed a hot lead, he'd follow it up for the final sale.

But I was too blunt to satisfy our Swiss and Austrian owners. While I was in charge, they would try to overload us with inventory or tell us how to run things and I was very quick to point out my dissatisfaction.

They could convince Sam of their ideas, but they couldn't convince me. I only had a 10 percent interest in the company—the same as Sam—and although I did not have control of the company, I did call the shots in the United States.

On a few occasions when we sold a ski-lift, the resort that purchased one was so impressed with our promotion and advertising that they asked me to help them with their advertising. Before long I had two ski resorts for clients, and between SLI, my ski resort clients, and my father's business, I decided to form my own advertising agency to capitalize on the 15 percent advertising commission normally given agencies by the media.

Within one year SLI was profitable and held a very visible position in the industry. I was quite proud of the job I had done, and so was Sam, But the Europeans were not. I was a thorn in their side, a pain in the neck who didn't give them the freedom they wanted to control our company from abroad. In addition, they tried to get us to hire the Austrian inventor's brother-in-law. I disapproved. Finally, after one and a half years, they met with Sam and me and asked me to resign.

They appointed Sam the new president and asked if I would continue handling some of the advertising. Sam took over and I helped him a little with the advertising but decided later to drop the account entirely and sell my stock back to the group.

Sam did well for a short period of time but floundered and control was then passed to the Austrian inventor's brother-in-law. He practically drove the company into the ground. SLI went bankrupt a few years after that, with a loss of several million dollars. I took no great pleasure in the news. I'm sorry to see anybody lose like they did, but it was their company and their folly, and it gave me the confidence that maybe I really did know what I was doing.

Out of this experience I formed my own advertising agency. At the time I had four accounts, a secretary, and an office at my father's factory on the south side of Chicago. His company was then called Consolidated International.

The Batman Credit Card had the potential to earn my first million. Then tragedy hit.

My accounts included Bryces Mountain Resort in Bayse, Virginia, Schuss Mountain in Mancelona, Michigan, and an assortment of small restaurants. I used outside typesetting and I wrote the copy.

In early 1966 the Batman fad swept the nation. Whatever product had the Batman name on it sold like hot cakes. There were Batman t-shirts, Batman toys, Batman combs, even a Batman peanut butter—you name a product and there was a similar product with the name Batman on it. Around the same time, credit cards were also becoming a big fad. Bank Americard and Master Charge had just announced their programs. American Express and Diners Club were growing rapidly.

I had a wild idea right at the very start of the Batman craze. Why not produce a Batman credit card—a plastic card embossed with a person's name and a special personal number? The cards would resemble a real credit card in size, shape, and thickness. A Batman credit card, however, would have no value. It was really just a satire on the new credit card explosion.

My idea involved advertising the card on radio stations throughout the country and selling them for one dollar with the owners' names embossed on the cards. For every card we'd sell, we would also capture that person's name on a mailing list. With the mailing list we could send out a Batman catalog, conduct contests, and really tie the whole fad nicely together.

I called up the Licensing Corporation of America, the group that was licensing the rights to Batman, and finally, after several calls, I got through to Murray Altschuler, one of their representatives.

I told Murray that I had an idea for a new Batman product that could be the hottest-selling item in their entire line. Murray replied, "Joe, we've already got Batman t-shirts, Batman toys, Batman shoes-what could you have that's different? Everything possible is now licensed and on my list."

I said, "Well, I've got a Batman credit card." There was silence. It was as if Murray was looking up and down his list, unable to find a Batman credit card.

"That's certainly different," he said. "Tell me about it." I proceeded to tell him about my idea, the catalog, the mailing list, and my marketing approach. Murray thought it sounded so good that he asked me to come quickly to New York with my plan. He wanted to present it to the principals of LCA (Licensing Corporation of America).

I flew to New York with my presentation. I had drawings of the card, mock-ups of the mailing packages and radio scripts for the spot commercials. Despite the few days it took me to put it together, it looked good, and I was totally prepared.

I arrived in New York, walked into LCA's office and waited to see Murray. I noticed how busy the phone lines were and how quickly people were moving. It was really a madhouse—something you could imagine from the way the Batman fad was taking off.

Murray brought me into his office and I made my presentation. When I was half finished Murray picked up a phone and called in Allan Stone and Jay Emmett, the two principals of LCA. "I've got something you've got to see," he said calmly. "It's very important. Hold all your calls."

After my presentation to the group, all they could do was shake their heads and smile. "Fantastic idea," said Stone. "Would you entertain a partnership or joint venture to really launch your concept?"

The idea appealed to me. Rather than be selfish and hog the whole deal for myself, by sharing it with them I'd have an advantage no other licensee would have. I'd have their full cooperation on making my program a success. And then if any future deals came up, I'd have first shot.

It took me about four seconds to accept. "It's a deal," I said. shaking their hands.

"Go back to Chicago and get those cards printed," said Emmett. "This fad hasn't peaked yet and we don't want to be too late."

They suggested I print a quarter of a million of them for the first run and get my lawyers to draw up the corporate papers. We were to split everything on a fifty-fifty basis, and they agreed to put up half the money so there was less risk on my part.

I flew back to Chicago dreaming of the millions I was going to make, of my new Playboy mansion, and of that chauffeur-driven Cadillac limousine I was going to drive in.

The first thing I did was contact my attorney, George Cohon to get him started on the contract. Then I went to the credit card printer.

I picked the best credit card printer in Chicago—the one that all the banks were using to print their credit cards.

When I arrived, I was met by the chief credit card salesman for the company. I introduced myself as being from my advertising agency and he took me for a tour of the facility where I saw huge presses churning out all sorts of plastic cards. There was plenty of security, and at every entrance armed guards stood by, making sure nobody walked off with the plastic money they were printing. In a way, it was like touring a mint.

We then sat together in the salesman's office to discuss my big project. "I'll need a quarter of a million credit cards," I said.

"For what bank?" he asked.

"Not a bank," I replied, "but for a major national account—Batman."

"Batman?" he asked, rather puzzled.

"Yes, we need a quarter of a million Batman credit cards by next week," I said. I then explained my idea, how I had called Murray and then flown to New York. I described how LCA had fallen in love with the idea and become my new partner. I told him how vital it was that I get the cards as quickly as possible because we did not know the duration of the fad and we wanted to capture Batman's momentum before it peaked. "How soon can we get a quarter million Batman credit cards?"

The salesman looked at me and shook his head. "The best I can do is eight weeks."

"Eight weeks? That's no good. It's got to be this week or we may miss the fad. Why eight weeks?" I asked.

"You have to wait two weeks for plates," he replied. "And then we have a dozen customers waiting to get on press. That alone will take six weeks."

I couldn't believe that my big dream was about to crumble because I couldn't get on press. "Could I have the name of your platemakers? Maybe I can get a plate faster if I explain my problem."

"Sure," said the salesman. All the power to you." Even if you can get the plates sooner, I still can't help you because I've got so many customers waiting in line."

There had to be a way. I couldn't let this opportunity pass. "What if I took the names of your customers and convinced them all to let me get in front of them? I'm sure they'll appreciate and understand the urgency of what I'm doing."

"Joe, if you can do it, be my guest." And with that he pulled out eight files from his drawer and proceeded to read off the names and phone numbers of his customers.

Without wasting any time, I drove straight to the platemaker in downtown Chicago and spent an hour trying to convince him of the importance of the job. I finally got a commitment from him that he'd have the plates for me in two days.

Returning to my office, I called all the names the salesman gave me and got enough of his customers to let me step ahead of them so that I was assured of getting on press within the week.

One of my calls was to the First National Bank of Chicago. They not only let me step ahead of them, they offered to put their data processing department at my disposal.

We worked out a deal whereby the First National Bank would receive the orders, deposit the checks or cash, and then produce a magnetic tape that could be used by the embossing company to emboss the credit cards and would also be used by the company that would later mail out the cards.

I also got Addressograph Multigraph Corporation to commit to embossing the cards and a large Chicago mailer to mail them out.

Meanwhile I had sent out the corporate contracts to LCA and was waiting for their licensing contract.

Within one week after I returned from New York, the credit cards started coming off the presses and I started storing them in my office. I conducted a few tests with adults who were unaware of my involvement with the program and was offered $5 for an unembossed card—a card we were going to sell for $1. If you remember the fad, the demand for Batman products was so great that companies couldn't produce them fast enough. And I had the first really unusual Batman product—one that appealed to adults as well as to teens and children.

I produced my radio spots at WCFL, a local Chicago radio station. Dick Orkin, one of the station's creative talents, had just started a radio series called Chickenman which was a spoof of Batman, and his series was being aired daily on WCFL. I had him do the spots for me and placed a schedule on the radio station to start at about the time the credit cards were supposed to be completed. The six spots were humorous satires on the whole credit card scene and cost me over $1,000.

I called an old friend from my Army Intelligence days, Greg O'Bierne. He was in between jobs but agreed to join me in my venture and move from Philadelphia to Chicago with his wife and child. He moved almost as quickly as I did, and he had an apartment and his belongings in Chicago within a week.

I had everything covered. I had the printing, promotion, fulfillment, and help and was even working on some future projects when I realized that I still had not received the contracts and the license to sell my Batman credit cards. The radio schedule was all set to run and everybody was primed and ready to roll, but I didn't want to give the station the approval to run the spots without a contract.

So I called Murray. He was busy, so I left a message. Still no word from Murray so I called again. He was still busy so I started getting concerned. The radio station was calling me and my room was filling up with Batman credit cards. A quarter of a million Batman credit cards, incidentally, would take up an entire ten-foot-by-twelve-foot room. That's a lot of credit cards.

It was obvious after two days of calling Murray and his two associates and not getting a call back that something was wrong. I quickly flew to New York, went to their office and waited in the reception room for two hours—just to see Murray.

Murray finally walked into the reception room looking very sheepish. "Joe," he said as he cleared his throat, "I don't know how to tell you this, but we couldn't get your license approved. All licenses must be approved by Mr. Liebowitz, the chairman of the board of National Periodical Publications, owner of the Batman rights. And Mr. Liebowitz didn't like your idea and refused to sign the contract."

I wasn't daunted. I had been told it took eight weeks to get on press, and we had our cards in a week. Now my challenge was to convince the only person left who could stop me. So I had Murray call Mr. Liebowitz so I could meet with him personally.

Mr. Liebowitz was a short pudgy man who sat behind a large, clean, polished desk. As I walked into his office he pressed an intercom button to page his secretary. "Marie, get me a cigar," he said.

I expected to see Marie walk in with a cigar but instead she walked up to the edge of his desk, opened a small wooden box on his desk, pulled out a cigar, unwrapped it and put it in his mouth and lit it. When I saw that, I knew I was in trouble.

"Go ahead kid. What's on your mind?" he said.

I proceeded to explain the history of the program. I explained how I had a quarter of a million Batman credit cards sitting in my office. I told him how I had my entire savings in the project and that I owed thousands of dollars to my suppliers. I asked for his understanding and mercy. Then he finally spoke: "I don't like it. I've made $60 million already with this Batman thing and I've made enough. Besides I don't like your idea. Period."

I pleaded with him to let me sell just enough to pay my bills. He refused to budge an inch and stuck to his decision. "And if you dare do this without authorization, I'll sue your ass. Now get out of here."

And my partners at LCA were no help either. "Sorry, Joe. You did it without a license. It's your tough luck. We can't help you," said Murray.

There was nothing I could do or say. It's one thing to realize that you have lost an opportunity to make a million, but it's another thing to realize that you are now broke and owe people money.

I had the opportunity of a lifetime snatched from my grasp and suddenly it all collapsed. It was almost too hard to believe.

I returned to Chicago and promptly canceled the radio spots. Then I totaled all my expenses. Aside from what I owed, I had two other problems. First, I had no idea what Greg, who moved to Chicago, could do at this point. Secondly I had no idea what to do with a quarter of a million Batman credit cards.

The Batman experience was a very traumatic one for me. If I ever had to list my biggest disappointments, my Batman experience had to be near the top.

I didn't give up, however. I moved the Batman credit cards to a warehouse and stored them there. If I had owned Batman T-shirts, I probably could have sold them in some other country or offered them to some ravage-torn disaster area. But I had Batman credit cards—useless pieces of plastic with no intrinsic value. There was nothing I could do with them short of burying them or holding on to them.

I tried to keep Greg busy in my advertising agency, but we both realized that the handwriting was on the wall. I was thousands of dollars in debt and there was little that Greg could do to help me at that time so he packed his belongings and he, his wife and child returned to Philadelphia.

I called each of my suppliers and told them what had happened. I also shared with them that I couldn't pay them but I promised them one thing. I said that I would send them a check each month until their bill was paid off. Some months I told them the check would be for a small amount and some months more, but every month they would receive a

CHICAGO TRIBUNE, THURSDAY, DECEMBER 8, 1966

ADVERTISING/MARKETING

Holy Credit Card! He's Swamped

BY JAMES SMITH

Someone out there may be able to help Joseph Sugarman who has 240,000 Batman credit cards.

Sugarman, 28, and Gregory O'Beirne, are principals of a small advertising agency at 4501 S. Western blvd. Last June they hit upon a variation on the Batman theme. It went like this:

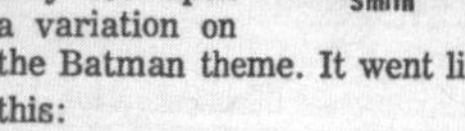

Smith

With Licensing Corporation of America, which controls the Batman franchise, they proposed to distribute Batman cerdit cards to teen-age listeners of rock and roll radio stations.

The credit cards weren't good for much credit [except a spanking for deliquencies], and they were to be accompanied by a Batman credit card insurance policy which wasn't worth much either.

Too Bad, Dad

"This policy does not cover the loss of any other credit card. If you lose any other credit card, you are out of luck, Charley," the policy read.

It also promised a free surprise to be sent in a few months. This was a catalog of Batman gifts offered thru Licensing Corporation.

Commercials prepared by Sugarman thru WCFL radio spoofed the daylights out of the credit card and its rivals "American Surpress, Diner's Grub, Carte Bunk, Air Gravel, Charge America, Charge Europe, and Charge the British Are Coming."

After considering the possibility of misuse among honest-to-goodness credit cards, Licensing Corporation nixed the idea.

Well, What Now?

By this time Sugarman & Associates had a massive case of 250,000 Batman credit cards sitting in the front office.

In an effort to lessen the floor load somewhat, Sugarman took his idea to the Diner's club as a possible promotion. It was rejected.

He then suggested it to a Chicago department store as a means of disposing of all Batman goods before Christmas. It again was vetoed.

On Way Out

"At this point, people began to tell us Batman promotions were on the way out," Sugarman said.

As a last resort he managed to sell about 10,000 of the credit cards as premiums thru ads in Advertising Age.

As to the remainder: "I think we'll just dig a hole someplace and bury them," Sugarman said.

Meanwhile, the agency is moving ahead with a new promotional idea which it hopes to launch thru American Symbolic corporation, which it just established.

Better Than No Breath

It's a garlic and onion flavored candy mint called Bad Breath, "for very popular people who wish to reduce their popularity somewhat."

"My dilemma made the Chicago Tribune and attracted my next losing opportunity."

check from me until it was all paid off.

Sure enough, after two years I found myself signing the last check. Everybody was paid back and I had kept my word. And it reminded me to give Murray Altschuler a call. Batman was now into re-runs and the fad was clearly dead. Maybe now I could get a license and revive the fad.

"Murray, this is Joe Sugarman," I said.

"Joe Sugarman, Joe Sugarman . . ." said Murray.

"Remember," I said, "the Batman credit card?"

"Joe Sugarman, sure, the Batman credit card. How are you?"

"Fine, Murray," I said. "You know I still have a quarter of a million Batman credit cards and the thought occurred to me that maybe I could get my license now. The Batman fad is dead and I thought maybe my efforts could get things rolling again."

"Joe, it's funny you called," replied Murray. "LCA was just acquired by National Periodical Publications and now that we're all one team, you may have a chance. Let me check out the idea and call you back."

It wasn't long before Murray called me back. "Sorry, Joe, but the answer is still no. Mr. Liebowitz still doesn't like your idea. Maybe some other time."

A few more years went by and I called Murray again. I had just moved the credit cards to a new location and I was curious to see if Murray was still around. The switchboard operator connected me to a young lady who said, "Mr. Altschuler's office." Evidently Murray now had a personal secretary.

When Murray finally answered, it didn't take him too long to recognize me. "Murray," I said, "this is Joe Sugarman."

"Joe," was the reply. "How are you?"

"Fine," I said. "I was wondering if you would consider resubmitting my Batman credit card for a license? I still have a quarter of a million of them."

"Joe, it's funny you called," he said. "National Periodical Publications has a new president. He's Jay Emmett. Do you remember him?"

What a break, I thought. Here was the same guy who loved my idea back when I first presented it and now he was in charge of the company that owned the Batman rights.

"Of course," I replied. "I remember him well. See if he'll go for me trying at least a test to see if I can sell the card. The fad has been dead for years. I can really accomplish something if I can get it going."

It didn't take Murray longer than a few days to call me back. "Sorry, Joe, I checked with Jay and he told me to take a pass on the deal. He's new as president and doesn't want to make a move for awhile that would upset Mr. Liebowitz. Call me in a few years."

About three years later I called Murray again. It was now 1976,1 had my own mail order business, and I had achieved some visibility and success.

"Murray," I said, "I thought I'd give you a call again to see if there was a possibility of having you license my Batman credit cards. I still have a quarter of a million of them."

"Joe, it's funny you called," Murray said. "National Periodical Publications was just bought out by Warner Communications and I'm sure they'll be interested. Warner is really promotion-minded and I think we'll have a chance."

Murray called back a few days later. "Joe, they rejected the idea. They're too early in the merger for a deal like this. I would suggest calling back once they get their feet on the ground."

It was in early 1978 that I called Murray back. Warner Communications was working on its $40 million Superman movie that was scheduled for release at the end of the year.

Batman was still running on TV, both as a cartoon show and in reruns from the 1966 show. It was now twelve years later and it appeared that Batman was actually going through a slight revival.

I now felt better about my chances than ever before. So did Murray when I called him in February.

"Joe, it's funny you called," said Murray quite optimistically. "Warner Communications is really promotion-minded now — especially with their Superman movie coming out this year. Maybe there's a chance. Let me call you back."

And so I waited, and a few days later I received a call from Murray. "Joe, I don't know how to tell you this, but they've accepted your request for a license and I want you to come to New York so we can sign the papers and celebrate."

What a thrill! After waiting twelve years to get the license, I finally got it. What a tremendous feeling of accomplishment I had. And then I thought that maybe it was fate. Here I was with twelve years of experience in mail order—better qualified to handle the promotion than ever before. Finally I had the opportunity I had worked twelve years to get. "Murray," I shouted, "I'm so thrilled. I can't begin to tell you how I feel."

And Murray, who sounded as thrilled as I was, said "Joe. I have never felt as good about issuing a license in my life as I feel about the license I'm about to issue you. Congratulations!"

"Murray," I said, "I'm not going to disappoint you. I'm going to write the best damn mail order ad of my life. You'll be proud as hell, Murray. I promise you."

So I flew to New York, had a celebration luncheon with Murray and some of the principals of Warner Communications, and received a contract which I promptly sent to a different lawyer from the one who had the original corporate papers I signed twelve years earlier. My original lawyer was now the head of McDonald's in Canada and was no longer practicing law.

Maurice Raizes, my new lawyer, looked over the contract and approved it. The contract gave me the rights to conduct a test campaign for which I was under no obligation. If the test proved successful, I would pay them $25,000 as a guarantee against a certain percentage of the sales of the cards.

Here, after being in my own mail order business for almost seven years and with all my experience, I now had the opportunity to run an ad that meant more to me than any other advertisement I had ever written.

I worked on my Batman mail order ad for two solid weeks. I was determined to make it the finest ad I had ever written. And indeed it was. After I finished it, I was proud. It was the type of ad that I knew would work.

So I ran the advertisement in the southwestern edition of the Wall Street Journal where we test all our advertising. From this test I have always been able to determine exactly how many items I could sell through hundreds of other national magazines and newspapers.

Instead of selling the card for $1, my price was now $5. Inflation had taken its toll. And instead of using radio commercials, I was using magazine and newspaper advertisements.

The ad needed only two hundred responses to break even, and I was so confident I geared up for over one thousand responses. When the ad finally ran, my response was only a total of twelve orders.

The ad failed miserably. I had tried and failed for twelve straight years only to fail once and for all.

I wrote Murray and thanked him for his help and advice and for sharing the joy of issuing the contract. I told him of the dismal results and gave him my best wishes for his new Superman movie.

But, I wasn't finished with my Batman saga. I waited a number of years and found out that they were coming out with a Batman movie and that the movie might revive the fad. I contacted Murray only to find out that the licensing arm for the picture was now located in Los Angeles and that I had to contact the new head of licensing there.

When I appeared at their offices in Los Angeles and told them the whole Batman story and how I felt that now was a good time to come out with the card, they advised me that they actually just licensed a real affinity Visa credit card with the Batman logo and that there would be too much confusion if they licensed me.

Once again I packed my things and returned home to Northbrook, Illinois. I can't tell you the number of times after that I contacted them with fresh new ideas on how to do a promotion that wouldn't cause confusion. The story would end here had it not been for something that happened in the year 2000.

I was giving a seminar on Maui and I had invited Dan Kennedy, a successful direct marketing consultant, as one of my guest speakers. During one of the breaks, Dan approached me and said, "Joe remember that Batman credit card you used to have quite a few of?"

I nodded. "Yes, I remember them well."

Dan continued. "Well, you gave one to a friend of mine and he gave it to his son. His son put it on eBay and it sold for $400.

I was in a state of shock. I excused myself and went to my office in my home, took out a calculator and entered $400 times 250,000 but the calculator was only an 8-digit one and I needed one with ten digits. Still visibly shaken, I found one and figured out that I owned 100 million dollars worth of Batman credit cards.

I still own pretty close to the 250,000 Batman credit cards. I learned that if you keep something long enough, it might even have some value.

12) The Great Teeny Bopper Society

"Most great people have achieved their greatest success just one step beyond their greatest failure."

Napoleon Hill, Author of Think and Grow Rich

In 1966, when I first discovered I had a quarter of a million Batman credit cards and no license to sell them, I was really crushed. My dreams shattered, I realized I had to pick myself up and start over.

One of the first things I did when I realized my plight was to get some publicity with the hope that somebody might be able to help. I called up the Chicago Tribune advertising editor and told him about my problem. He laughed and decided to do a story.

A model demonstrates the Teeny Bopper at the New York Toy Show.

The story started out, "Can anyone help Joe Sugarman?" and told the tale of my Batman adventure.

The article drew a number of letters and even dollar bills for the credit cards and a strange call from a Mr. Frank Camp.

"Mr. Sugarman, I read about your story in the Chicago Tribune and I think maybe you can help me," he said in a slow, raspy, deep voice. "I've got a quarter of a million Twist'n Pops sitting in my warehouse and I thought you might be just the guy to help me get rid of them."

So I went to Camp's warehouse and saw what a Twist'n Pop was. It was a plastic paddle ball game about two feet long with two big paddles separated by a plastic rod. A ball on a string was tied to the middle. The object of the game was to bounce the ball from paddle to paddle. It was easy to master, and once you got the ball moving it looked as if you were doing the twist—a dance rage of the early sixties.

But here we were in 1966. The twist as a dance was dead and along with it the Twist'n Pop. Like Joe Sugarman, Frank Camp was the victim of some major miscalculation and ironically, by the same quarter of a million.

Seeing Camp's predicament didn't make me feel too bad. A quarter of a million Twist'n Pops took up an entire 50,000-square-foot warehouse. The cartons were stacked ceiling high and everywhere you looked there were Twist'n Pops—in his office, in the locker room, and on top of the loading dock. Only in the narrow aisles and around a few machines were there open spaces where Camp stacked small wire garden fences he manufactured for Sears.

"You sound like you might be good at promotion," commented Camp. "Why don't you work out a program? I'll supply the Twist'n Pops, you supply the promotion, and we'll share the profits."

I certainly understood Frank's predicament. He seemed like an honest guy who had obviously made a big mistake.

So I accepted the challenge. The deal was simple. I would put up $10,000 worth of my time and promotion money and Frank would give me 10,000 Twist'n Pops in return. After I sold my 10,000 pieces, I would then start to sell his product and share the profits.

The first thing I did was change the name. The dance called the twist had been dead for several years, but a new term was now part of the nation's vocabulary—teeny bopper, the new name for the music-loving teens of the late sixties. Lyndon Johnson was president and his "Great Society" program was also the nation's new buzz word.

So I renamed the product the Teeny Bopper and I decided to form a club—the Great Teeny Bopper Society. I got a popular WCFL disc jockey, Ron Britain, to work with me on a radio promotion for his show.

The idea was exciting. Members would join the club by sending a self-addressed stamped envelope to the station. In return they would get a membership card, button, and bumper sticker. Hopefully, this would create the first wave of a fad that would eventually help sell our warehouse full of Teeny Boppers. All we would have to do is announce the Teeny Boppers' availability on spot radio commercials and everybody would rush to the store and pick one up.

I had 20,000 membership kits printed up. I still owed money

from my Batman fiasco, but I was convinced that this promotion would be a huge success and worth the gamble.

Then I had my next-door neighbor, Sam Bird, read the Great Teeny Bopper Society pledge. Sam was ninety years old and sounded every year of it. He loved the idea and recorded the pledge on my small tape recorder. We played the pledge every day on the air, and hearing the Great Teeny Bopper pledge being read by a ninety-year old man was the talk of the station.

Then I would take the tape recorder and record other people. The

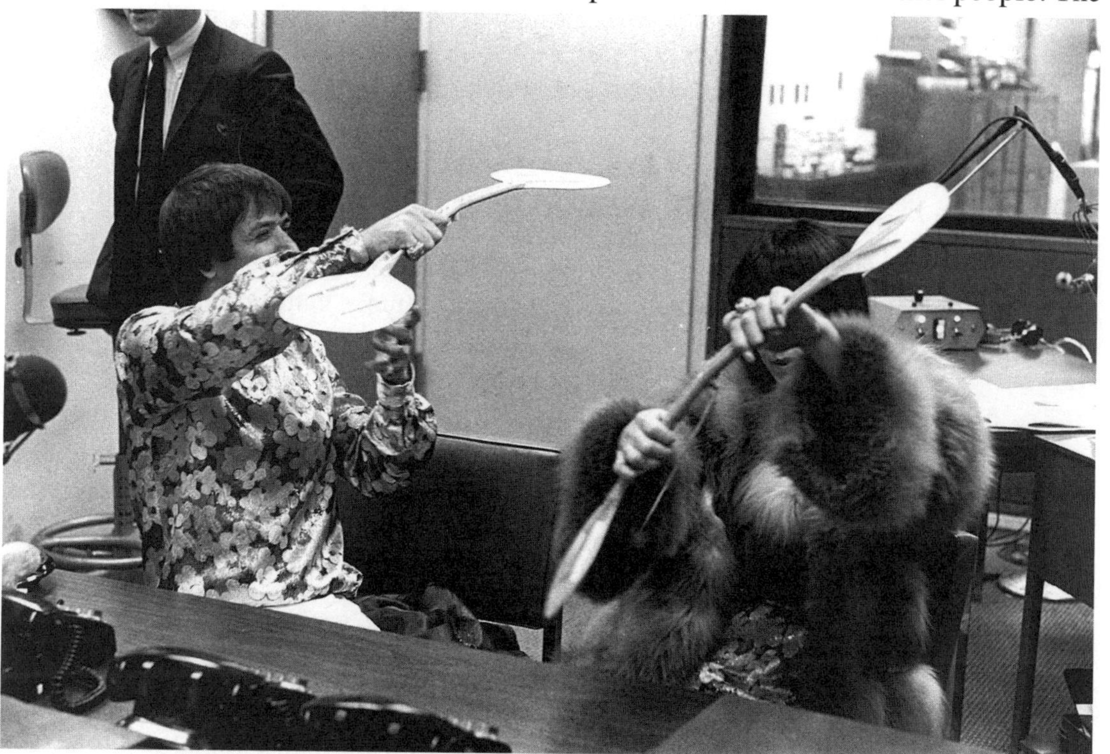

Here's a shot of Sonny and Cher at the WCFL studios in Chicago trying out the Teeny Bopper.

mailman would come to my door and I'd give him a script to read: "My name is Sam Konitz and I'm a mailman, I'm also a proud member of Ron Britain's Great Teeny Bopper Society."

I got over fifty people to read something similar. I got our butcher, my lawyer, several people at a nursing home—anyone over fifty years old qualified perfectly for my recording sessions.

When the responses came in, they poured in. Ron Britain would play the tapes on the air and then urge his audience to send for the kits and join the Great Teeny Bopper Society. I had my whole family helping me stuff envelopes. Letters came in from all over the Midwest—from doctors and lawyers as well as teenagers.

I then selected a chain of discount stores throughout Chicago to stock the Teeny Boppers and contracted for a series of radio commercials announcing the Teeny Boppers' availability at those local stores. With 20,000 members of the Great Teeny Bopper Society I would be able to launch the product, and if Chicago proved a good test market, I could launch the campaign nationally.

Meanwhile, I had received a call from Bruce Gilbert of the Coca-Cola Company in Atlanta. I had sent them information on the Great Teeny Bopper Society on the hunch that if I could tie in with them and have them sponsor the program nationally, we'd have a huge success. They were interested and asked that I fly to Atlanta and present the concept to them.

Before I left I stuffed two big suitcases with the responses we had been getting from our promotion. The envelopes were already filled with the membership materials, so I figured I'd mail them from the Atlanta airport before I returned. I wanted them with me in case Coca-Cola wanted to see the responses we were actually getting.

I arrived in Atlanta, went straight to Coca-Cola's main office on Peachtree Street, and made my presentation to Gilbert and his staff. It went well and then they popped the question, "What kind of response did you get?"

I told them to see for themselves, and on their big conference room table I poured out the contents of the two large suitcases. A heap of mail stared them in the eyes. They started sorting through the letters—nuns from Indianapolis, employees from Xerox Corporation and General Motors. The return envelopes looked so impressive that they were going through them like kids in a candy factory.

I packed my suitcases and left with the feeling that they were genuinely impressed. I even left with a few recordings of their voices saying things like "I'm Ralph Pinzer. I'm a brain surgeon and I'm a proud member of the Great Teeny Bopper Society." They, too, were joining in on the craziness.

They were to call me with a decision shortly after my big Teeny Bopper promotion which was coming up the following week. The radio commercials were being aired as I returned to Chicago. I had already filled the stores with Teeny Boppers, and I was gambling a thousand dollars of my own money to pay for the radio spots.

I had selected one of Community Discount's larger stores as the key introductory store, and I had hired models to demonstrate my Teeny Boppers. Who were the models? The members of the Grandmothers

- ✶ 3 BANDS
- ✶ WCFL's RON BRITAIN
- ✶ TEENY BOPPER GIVE-AWAY
- ✶ FREE BATMAN CREDIT CARDS
- ✶ NEW GIRL ROCK BAND
- ✶ FREE BUTTONS, STICKERS, CARDS
- ✶ BIGGEST DANCE OF THE YEAR

The New TEENY BOPPER

COME TO FRANK BOND'S BIG

TEENY BOPPER DANCE

MAY 14th—7 to 10:30 PM

Dance to 3 bands at Frank Bond's dance of the year. Ron Britain of WCFL will give away 50 Teeny Boppers (the newest most exciting fad to hit the nation) in a sweepstakes drawing. The Maybees, The Presidentials, and Stuarts Private Blend (4 gals and a guy) will entertain and official Ron Britain Great Teeny Bopper Society membership cards, stickers, and buttons will be given to all attending. Those coming before 7:30 p.m. will receive a free Batman Credit Card. Admission is $2.50 at Frank Bond's Teen Club, 3243 South Harlem, in Berwyn, Ill.

FEATURING:

RON BRITAIN
America's First Psychedelic Disc Jockey

THE MAYBEES
Popular Rock and Roll Recording Group

The Teeny Bopper was my next promotion and then tragedy struck again.

Club of Chicago. I couldn't think of a more appropriate group.

I also hired Ron Britain to make a personal appearance, hired a rock band, and planned for a real gala event.

I was really taking a chance. I had lost a fortune with my Batman promotion and I was still paying it off. I had to do well with the Teeny Bopper program or I was going to have one awful time surviving.

But I wasn't worried at all. The promotion was going so well that I couldn't help but succeed. I had a big potential program with Coca-Cola and it looked like clear sailing in Chicago. I had no product to manufacture, and if the thing took off, I had a great chance to make that million dollars I missed making with the Batman promotion.

I just knew the promotion was going to be a huge success. It was April, the weather had been warm, and the Teeny Bopper would make

We even had gift certificates for people to give TeenyBoppers as gifts.

a great spring product. The radio station was being inundated with calls from people reconfirming the time and place of the big unveiling. The discount stores had received so many calls that they moved the planned location of the Teeny Boppers to the entrance. I couldn't ask for better cooperation.

Everything was in place that Friday. I had scheduled the introduction for two o'clock in the afternoon, and each hour of the day leading up to that time I checked off what had to be done. I absolutely was not going to let one detail slip through my fingers. This time I wasn't going to be stopped by the lack of someone's approval as I had been with the Batman credit card. I was confident that nothing short of an act of God was going to stop me from making it this time.

A few hours before my scheduled grand opening, a tornado struck the Chicago area, killing several people and wiping out my promotion. It was the blow that I didn't expect—the act of God that proved fatal for the entire program. I couldn't reschedule the campaign because I was broke. I had lost all the money on the radio spots, the band I had hired, and myriad other expenses. And once I lost the momentum, that was it.

In addition, Coca-Cola called me the following week to advise me that they were no longer interested in the program. Time magazine had mentioned in an article that Teeny Bopper was the name associated with dope-swallowing teenagers, and Coca-Cola didn't want to hurt their image.

Within just a few years I had been struck by more disappointments than most people could take in a lifetime. Two major promotions had success written all over them and yet they collapsed.

But I did not give up. As long as I could feed myself and pay back my debts, I would continue. I simply took most of my 10,000 Teeny Boppers and put them next to my quarter of a million Batman credit cards and carried on.

THE MAYBEES
WILSON PICKETT
ARTHUR CONLEY
JAMES BROWN
SAM & DAVE
MAYOR DALEY
EV DIRKSEN

all play good soul music - but only one will appear April 21st at Richard's Teen Club!

"The promotional flyers for the dances were zany, full of humor and drew big crowds. This was one of the first flyers I made promoting the dance featuring the Maybees."

13) Teen Club Promoter

"When you get into a tight place and everything goes against you, never give up then, for that is just the time that the tide will turn."

Harriet Beecher Stowe 1811-1896, Writer and Abolitionist

During my Teeny Bopper promotion, I needed a band to entertain at my grand opening. I heard a group called the Maybees playing in a nearby suburban bar. My girlfriend Wendy and I had stopped in to go dancing one evening and really enjoyed their music. When I needed a group to perform for me, I thought of the Maybees and went back to the bar where I had first seen them. But they were gone. The manager told me that they were now playing as a regular group at Frank Bond's Teen Club on Harlem Avenue in Berwyn, a western suburb.

I went over there one evening and met Frank Bond—a Damon Runyon-type character who owned a restaurant and bar and a large banquet room. Bond would rent out the banquet room on Friday nights to a local promoter who would stage live rock bands for the kids in the area. The promoter would book the rock groups, charge for admission, and pay all the expenses. What was left was split between Bond and the promoter.

When I stepped into his bar, I found him sitting at a table eating dinner with his girlfriend. Bond was about fifty years old and reminded me of a stereotypical Chicago gangster from the early twenties.

"Sit down," he grunted. "What can I do for ya?"

I introduced myself and told him that I was staging a big promotion and needed a rock group. I told him about the Teeny Bopper, how we had had a big campaign on WCFL, and how I had heard the Maybees at another bar and tracked them down to his place. I explained that I wanted to hire them for my big promotion.

Bond just listened as I explained, and after I finished he paused for a minute, chewed his food, and then said, "How would you like to promote this place? The guy who's doing it now isn't worth a damn. I end up running the dances myself."

"All you do is book the group, hire a disc jockey, and sell tickets at the door. Then at ten o'clock ya kick the kids out, pay the group, pay $100 for the rental of the room, and we split the profits. Ya can't beat that. It's a smooth deal."

I accepted the challenge, but on the condition that it wait until my Teeny Bopper promotion finished the following week. And as you know, it indeed was finished the following week.

Frank Bond couldn't have come at a better time. Broke with just barely enough to pay rent and eat, I needed the extra work. It was at night too which meant it left my days free to do my advertising.

Frank Bond's Club was fun. It was there I really learned the art of promotion. Whenever I would try to hype a big dance, it would flop. Whenever I presented the dance honestly, the kids responded. And I never really knew for sure which dance would be big and which dance would be a bomb. There was always the element of surprise.

Wendy took tickets at the entrance and I was the MC on stage. I tried different promotions. During one dance I called for a battle of the bands. Normally, groups battle each other by playing their music with the audience voting for the best group.

My battle was different. I had both groups put down their instruments, put on boxing gloves, and battle it out on stage. It usually drew a big crowd and occasionally a little blood-but the kids loved it.

I'd hold dance contests with no music, and if you ever wanted to see a strange sight, that was it—squirming, gyrating teens moving to no sound.

On special occasions I'd offer unusual prizes like Joe Subway records, Teeny Boppers, Batman credit cards, and even a round trip for two to the Brookfield Zoo in a Brinks armored car.

The money from Bond's wasn't that great, but it kept me fed and helped me repay many of my debts. It also gave me an opportunity to produce full-page flyers announcing the next dance, which we passed out at the end of each dance.

Prior to this, I got my art and typesetting done by outside artists. One artist was very reasonable, but he was too busy most of the time. The other artist was quite expensive, but he was generous enough to wait for his money, so I would occasionally use him.

But for the Teen Club I didn't need any great artwork, so I started doing it myself. I would use pieces of art supplied by an art service I subscribed to and typesetting that I would buy in sheet form and then press together letter by letter. I had watched my artists doing paste-ups before, so I got myself a T square, some rubber cement, and a drawing board and became an artist. The Teen Club flyers gave me the experience, and I got better with every flyer I designed.

Around this time I was still doing work for Schuss Mountain, one of the ski resort advertising accounts. My other ski resort, Bryce's Mountain, refused to pay me $2,000 they owed me, claiming they never authorized certain ads. I had to file suit, and two years later I won by

My car wash account never paid me and went bankrupt. I learned a big lesson here.

showing several letters of authorization they had issued me.

I also landed a new account. My former next-door neighbor in Oak Park called me and asked me if would mind working on a new car wash brochure his company was preparing.

I agreed and spent two solid months preparing the brochure for his company and having it printed for them. Although I had learned my lessons from Bryce's Mountain Resort and had contracts with his company and made sure everything was in writing, as a stalling technique the company refused to pay the $10,000 they owed me. I sued them, only to have them go bankrupt on me. They were dishonest and I fell for their ploy.

I was still paying back the money I lost on the Teeny Bopper and the Batman credit card when this latest disaster hit. Now I was so broke and so much in debt that I was seriously thinking of getting a job. Wendy and I got married at this time and she got a job while I prepared myself to look for one, too.

Things were probably at their lowest.

14) Pulling Ourselves Out

"A hero is an ordinary individual who finds the strength to persevere and endure in spite of overwhelming obstacles."

Christopher Reeve 1952—2004, Actor and Speaker

Wendy was now working and I was looking in the papers for a job at an advertising agency. It was the summer of 1968, around the time of the Chicago Democratic Convention.

A group I had hired at the Teen Club asked me if I wouldn't mind managing them and helping them cut a record. The idea appealed to me. I had observed dozens of bands and felt that the group that came to me was probably among the best. I had also had my experience with Mad Records and felt that maybe this time I would be luckier.

Cutting a hit record was one way to make it rich quick. With my experience as a promoter and my need to be able to pay off my debts, it was very tempting.

Through my contacts at the local radio station I got the name of Royal Disc Distributors, an honest record distributor and one that could give me good advice. So I prepared to go to downtown Chicago for an interview with an ad agency and then, later, get some advice from the record distributor.

When I arrived at the Albert J. Rosenthal ad agency I was ushered into the office by one of the agency executives. He asked for a resume. I had none. I just had samples of my work. I had never had to get a job before so I never even thought about preparing a resume.

I showed him my work and he looked it over carefully. "What do you do?" he asked.

"I do copy, paste-up, typesetting—anything you need help in."

"But we're looking for someone who is very good at one skill. In an agency like ours, we would place you in one position and that would be the position you would grow in."

"Well, I could be a copywriter," I replied.

"Yes, but we're really looking for experience—agency experience, and I don't think you'll quite fit in."

So I left their offices. I was disappointed, but I quickly learned what I needed for an interview—a resume and some experience.

I have often thought to myself how my life and that of the Rosenthal agency would have changed if I had been hired. But I wasn't, and I left for my second appointment—at Royal Disc Distributing.

Royal Disc was owned by Kent Beauchamp and Edward Yalowitz—two young men in their thirties who were willing to give me advice on cutting and promoting records. They weren't very encouraging, though. Apparently the record business wasn't that simple—something I had already discovered.

During our discussions I explained what I did for a living and they asked me if I wouldn't mind spending the time reviewing their advertising and future promotion plans. I agreed.

Their office was located on Michigan Avenue, and I can remember driving on that street during the days of the 1968 Democratic Convention with the National Guard on one side of the street and the protesters on the other side. But I didn't have time to stop or observe. I was too busy trying to survive.

I still had a quarter of a million Batman credit cards stored in the basement of my apartment building along with assorted Teeny Boppers, Joe Subway records and car wash brochures. Life had definitely not been very kind to me. My job interview flopped, but I ended up with the opportunity to land another account.

The relationship with Royal Disc progressed well. Pretty soon they asked me to develop a corporate logo for a new company they had formed called Alltapes—a company organized to sell stereo tapes, a new, rapidly-growing segment of the music industry.

Schuss Mountain was my other account. In my lawsuit against the car wash manufacturer I had met Joseph W. Smith, chief of the States' Attorney's Fraud and Complaint Division. Joe was impressed with my work and asked that I help him on his campaign as a representative for the Illinois Constitutional Convention. Now, suddenly, with a few new accounts I was back in business, I soon started doing other political work for the Democratic Party while my involvement at Alltapes grew. Pretty soon I was doing a tremendous amount of work for Alltapes—so much so that they gave me my own office and asked me to troubleshoot a direct mail tape club they had started.

The orders were taking up to six weeks to fill and they didn't even know if they were making any money from the club. They had three people working on it with procedures that didn't make sense. It was a real mess.

Within three weeks I had worked out systems that permitted every order that came in the morning to get out that day. I had reduced the paperwork to the bare essentials, and I had reduced the staff to just two people.

Then I observed a very poor system they were using to pull tapes to fill their regular store orders. I called a special meeting of their entire organization and convinced them that they should change their entire warehouse and showed them how to do it. Within two weeks they had changed their system to mine.

Meanwhile, I produced a great deal of advertising for the group, really putting their image in front of the financial community.

I involved myself in practically every aspect of their business. They used me as a consultant, as an advertising man, and I even organized many of their warehouse procedures. They put me on a retainer of $400 per week and they really got their money's worth.

They went public about this time and I bought $10,000 of their stock. By 1969 I had paid all my debts and had earned about $10,000 from my active work at Alltapes, so I felt that putting that money back into the company was a worthwhile investment. How could I lose? The stock market was making everybody wealthy. Now it was my turn.

Within a few months of my investment, the stock dropped from $12 a share to $4 a share. It was my first experience with stocks and another failure I found very disappointing.

During my activities at Alltapes I did very well with all my other accounts, and if it hadn't been for the stock loss, I would have done well. I actually was earning about $80,000 a year—mostly tax-free as a result of my previous losses. And now Wendy and I were starting to save.

In 1970 Wendy and I decided to take a trip to England to visit Wendy's parents. We had also just bought a 1970 Oldsmobile station wagon—a big purchase for us at the time.

Things looked very good. We had some good accounts, I still had the Teen Clubs, and Wendy and I finally had a few dollars saved in the bank.

While we were in England, Wendy and I spent about $8,000 on clothes and gifts—something we had denied ourselves during our years of struggling.

Upon our return we started looking for a home. Wendy was pregnant and we thought we'd find one before we had our first baby.

We did. But it was a lot more than we could afford. The house cost us $70,000 and at the time was a dream come true for us and a real steal. At that time houses weren't selling because we were in the midst of a recession. It had a huge basement, a garage, and, in fact, the whole house was awfully big for the little furniture we had in our small one-bedroom apartment.

With some financial help from my mom and a banking connection from my brother-in-law Richard, I was able to squeak out a mortgage. But we were flat broke. Everything was gone—between the money for the car, the trip to England and the down payment. The mortgage took everything we had.

Then it really hit. The 1970 recession grew deeper and All-tapes needed to cut expenses. I convinced them that they should cut out their stereo tape club. I showed them where they weren't making any decent profits and that the club wasn't worth the salary they were paying me. They responded not only by dropping the club but by asking for my resignation. The recession was hitting them hard, and without the tape club, with few advertising requirements, and with the poor economy, it seemed a good move to them.

Since they represented over half my business, I had to carefully watch every penny. Not only did we have a new house to pay for, but we had a baby on the way.

Again, we were confronting financial problems, but thanks to a few of my accounts and my teen clubs, I was staying afloat.

15) Rock Group Promoter

"A great attitude does much more than turn on the lights in our worlds; it seems to magically connect us to all sorts of serendipitous opportunities that were somehow absent before we changed."

Earl Nightingale 1921—1989, Philosopher and Syndicated Radio Personality

In 1967 a rock group called the Dontays approached me to manage them. The group consisted of five guys who played the usual guitars, bass and drums, but who could also play brass, piano, and flute. Each member had more than one function—whether it was playing two or three instruments or taking the lead singing assignment.

I was really impressed with the Dontays, and based on the groups I had seen, they seemed like one of the better groups in Chicago.

Come to the Grand Opening of the most exciting new teen club in America! It's Jim Stagg's GRAFFITI—the new talent showcase of the Midwest. And don't miss opening night. It's Tommy James and the Shondells singing everything from *Hanky Panky* to *I Think We're Alone Now* to *Say I Am* to *Mony, Mony*. It's the Shadows of Knight introducing their new smash hit: *Shake*. And then for dancing —it's the big brass sounds of the Dontays. It's a night you won't want to miss—7pm, Saturday, October 12th at 950 East New York Street right in Aurora. Grand Opening admission—$3.00. Don't you miss it!

The grand opening of the Graffiti featured two very popular groups and the Dontays who I managed.

I agreed to handle them as their manager and I would get 10 percent of their earnings. They were getting $100 a performance and my first project was to get them a good booking agent and more money for their performances.

I took photos of them, created flyers and posters, and helped them get new equipment and a van to carry all their amplifiers and instruments.

The next thing I did was to get the names of all the other teen clubs that hired live groups. Then I created a newsletter called The Chicagoland Teen Club Report. Ten clubs got the report, along with a dozen booking agents and press people, but my motivation was not circulation.

I had a want ad section in my newsletter and put into it a series of free ads for other groups that needed bookings. The ads listed their fees—usually around

$100. For the Dontays I listed a fee of $350.

About three issues of the newsletter had been published before I raised the price of the Dontays to $450. I would call each teen club owner to gather the news from the club for my newsletter, and they would see their names in print and cooperate the next time I called.

Finally, after about six issues, I raised the Dontay's salary to $650 and had my booking agent call the club owners to get them to book the group.

The booking agent would then cut a deal for a special "teen club owner's price" of $300. The deal seemed so good that nobody refused. After all, the Teen Club Report had their fee at $650. From then on I was just building on their success, and by the end of the summer they were getting paid $1,000 a performance and were doing concerts with the Beach Boys and other famous groups. There was no secret that I was their manager, but I tried to get most of the deals through the booking agents so they would give the group some really good exposure. For the teen club owners, we kept the price at about $350.

About this time I took over a teen club in suburban Glen Ellyn. The club owner had been getting my newsletter and thought I could do a better job of promoting his club than he had been doing.

"GIVE US YOUR TIRED, YOUR POOR, YOUR HUDDLED MASSES, AND WE SHALL BLOW THEIR MINDS!"

the DONTAYS

EXCLUSIVE MANAGEMENT
Joseph Sugarman & Assoc.
Call (312) 262-5300

Here's a poster I made of the Dontays, the group I managed.

As a result of the newsletter, I was also asked by a disc jockey to form a teen club with him in Aurora, Illinois, a small town about forty miles west of Chicago.

The disc jockey, Jim Stagg, had located an abandoned supermarket in a poor section of town and felt that with his connections the club would be a great success. He also felt his influence at getting top name groups at low prices would be very helpful.

So we met with the building owner, Zander Bowman, and agreed to test the facility for a few months. Stagg did very little other than show up for the dances and name the club the Graffiti, and I doubt if his influence helped book any groups or got them for anything less than I could have gotten them for.

For some reason the club wasn't successful. The room was so big that even an average crowd seemed small. If there is one thing the teens never liked, it was the feeling of a poor turnout, and no matter how successful a turnout we had, the room still looked empty. Since we named the place the Graffiti, we let the kids loose with marking pens and markers to decorate the walls, but that didn't help much.

The grand opening was a huge success. Over a thousand teens showed up for the three groups we booked. But then it was all downhill.

The neighborhood was bad, and a number of neighborhood problems such as vandalism, rapes, and muggings didn't help things.

Meanwhile, we were losing money. The groups we were hiring were a lot more expensive than the club could support, and before we knew it, we were committed to groups a month in advance, with no hope of making any money on the program at all.

I had three teen clubs at the time: Frank Bond's in Berwyn, the Spectrum in Glen Ellyn, and the Graffiti in Aurora. I was taking all the money I was making at the Spectrum and Frank Bond's and covering my losses at the Graffiti.

Finally, Jim Stagg and I parted company and agreed to dissolve our partnership. The owner of the facility urged me to stay on and split the profits but not the risk. He would promote the club himself and all I had to do was book reasonably priced groups to keep our costs low. That didn't work either, and before a month went by I dropped the club completely and concentrated on the other two.

Shortly after I dropped the Graffiti, I was approached by Emerson Whitney, the new owner of the huge Aragon Ballroom on Chicago's north side. The Aragon used to be a plush Chicago landmark during the twenties, thirties, and forties, but the changing neighborhood, the deterioration of the facility, plus the general fading of interest in the big-time dance halls had all caused the Aragon to lose its popularity. It staged boxing matches instead of dances.

Whitney wanted me to do the promotion for the Aragon which was going to start promoting rock shows. He had been one of my Teen Club Report subscribers and thought that I was the perfect guy to help promote his big shows. He changed the name of the Aragon to the Cheetah to give it more of a contemporary feel and wanted me to book some really big name groups.

He had a great sense of humor and was very shrewd when it came to knowing how to get publicity. One day, after spending two solid months getting all sorts of good publicity for the Cheetah, I shot a picture of him lighting a cigarette for a performer in one of his acts. She wore a very, very low-cut dress, and I snapped the shot just as she was bending over Emerson's desk and he was lighting her cigarette.

The picture was really quite funny. It was a very suggestive picture of this girl leaning over his desk with her breasts close to falling out of her dress and a big smile on Emerson's face as he lit her cigarette.

Knowing that Emerson had a great sense of humor, I had the shots developed and put a caption at the bottom of the photo as if I were preparing it for a publicity re-

I designed and made the flyers announcing the next dance by myself using a service from which I bought the illustrations. The more bizarre or off the wall the flyer, the better the response.

lease. The caption read, "Light my fire. Emerson Whitney, Aragon owner, seems absolutely elated as he lights the cigarette of the lead singer of Johnny and the Greenmen now playing at the Chetah."

Emerson wasn't in when I brought it to his office, so I left it with his secretary with a note saying, "Here is that photo we released to all the newspapers today. They loved it and promised to use it."

I never sent it to the papers, nor would I without Emerson's approval. I knew he would realize this and would take the whole thing as a joke. But his wife happened to stop by the office after I left and saw this urgent-looking envelope lying on his desk. Mrs. Whitney was very conservative; she also did not have a very good sense of humor. She opened the envelope and the next day I was fired. Emerson had no choice.

The owner of the Spectrum in Glen Ellyn decided to close down his club rather than renew his lease, so I was left with just Frank Bond's Club. I then tried an unsuccessful concert in Traverse City with the American Breed, that had played for me at Bond's and had already played quite successfully in Traverse City a few months before. I lost over $2,000 on that concert.

Finally, Frank Bond sold the banquet hall to another restaurant owner and the club was renamed Richard's, but soon attendance dropped because summer came. We agreed to close the club for the summer. I never reopened it, and the facility was turned exclusively into a banquet hall.

That left me managing just the Dontays, and although they were doing well, it was obvious that they weren't going places unless we got them on records. About the time I had closed my clubs, I decided to get the Dontays a recording session and put them under contract, so I contacted a prominent Chicago attorney who specialized in working with artists.

The attorney, Dick Shelton, was very helpful in setting up all the contracts I needed, but he also put me in touch with Buck Ram, the producer of the Platters, the million-selling record group. Buck was trying to revive the Platters and was looking for a good Chicago publicist

When I met Buck and his partner, Jean Bennet, we hit it off very nicely. They asked me to do some publicity for them and we agreed on a fee. I then told Buck about the Dontays and he agreed to hear them in concert and give me his opinion. He liked them and agreed to record them if we could raise the money for the session.

We raised the money, but the session never resulted in a hit. I pressed records and tried to have them played, but it was rough getting air time and the record never sold. On top of that, Buck never paid me for all the publicity I did for him, and he disappeared once the record flopped.

The Dontays played a debutante coming-out party, and the daughter's father owned a radio station and a Cadillac dealership. He was so impressed with the group that he agreed to put up the funds for a record session and to use his station to promote the group. He was a tall man who had inherited most of his money from his father, but he appeared to be a shrewd businessman.

He had the Dontays spend two weeks recording his radio station jingles, and then we signed a contract in which he was to take half ownership of the Dontays for $1,500. He agreed to record and promote them within a period of six months. After the jingle sessions, he wanted to back out of the deal and we refused. After all, the Dontays had done the equivalent of $8,000 worth of jingles and hadn't been paid a penny. So I sued him, and four years later I was awarded $1,500, which I gave to the Dontays. By the time I collected, it was 1974 and I was delighted to surprise the group with the bonus they had worked so hard for many years before.

The Apocryphals was another group that often played at my clubs. They were very popular with the kids and were a well-disciplined, hard-working group. They approached me to be their manager and I suggested we do a few records together. My plan was to get them recorded so that I had something that could be played on some of the stations that were perfect ven-

CHICAGO'S AMERICAN, THURSDAY, APRIL 18, 1968

ps, Road to Success Is Ro

Joe Mantegna of the Apocryphals, whom I also managed, plays the guitar before a group of admiring fans. Mantegna went on to appear in 87 movies and dozens of TV shows.

Joe Mantegna stands closest to the camera with his fellow musicians.

ues for their soul-based music. So I signed a contract on February 19, 1968, went into a studio and recorded four songs.

I started plugging the songs in Traverse City, Michigan where we were going to hold a big concert with the American Breed and as a result of our upcoming event, the radio stations were playing the Apocryphals' songs.

The Apocryphals didn't last very long. They broke up and their lead singer, Joe Mantegna, decided he liked acting better than being a rock musician. He quit the band and joined the production company of "Hair" in Chicago, performing in that play for almost two years. He was then discovered by David Mamet, a famous screen writer and director, who got Joe some great exposure in such plays as Glengarry Glen Ross for which Joe won a Tony Award. His most famous role, however, was in the movie The Godfather III playing Joey Zasa.

He has appeared in hundreds of movies and TV productions with the latest being the CBS series, "Criminal Minds" in which he starred for over seven years. He has a star on the Hollywood Walk of Fame, has been a great supporter of the military and his daughter is in show business as well. He also has appeared on the Simpsons as "Fat Tony" over the last 23 years.

Joe Mantegna starred in the TV series "Criminal Minds" for over seven years.

I have worked with dozens of artists and one never knows who will break out of the pack, become very successful, and make a big name for themselves. Joe certainly turned out to be the guy. He is very kind, modest and has lived a very ethical life—earning and deserving all of his success.

I had a lunch meeting with him recently after seeing not seen him for almost 20 years and I asked him what he remembered about me during those days of the teen club and the interaction we had with his band. He said "in the business we were in, there were a lot of dishonest and unethical people. You were probably the most honest person we dealt with."

The music business was very hard to break into. There were things going on with disc jockeys being paid off in what they called "Payola" back then. And since I wasn't that experienced in the promotion of records to radio stations that took bribes, success eluded me in the music industry. It was a costly experience but one that taught me a lot.

16) Publicity

"If you do build a great experience, customers tell each other about that. Word of mouth is very powerful."

Jeff Bezos, CEO of Amazon.com

After my experiences in the record industry and with my teen clubs, I was in my new home and we had managed to make it through the winter without too much difficulty. Our first child was born in January, 1971. She was supposed to be born in February, so we named her April. You figure that one out.

My office was in one of our four bedrooms. This was where I wrote my advertising and did my paste-ups. April kept me company in her crib while Wendy was typing my letters and retyping my copy.

I was really getting good at doing artwork and I was doing my own full-color brochures. Much of my work was now being done for various political candidates and for Schuss Mountain, which was still one of my major accounts.

I got along quite well with the resort's president, Daniel R. Iannotti, who put me in charge of advertising and publicity. I took a great deal of interest in the resort, often driving up there with Wendy during the ski season. I would write copy, conduct business, take pictures, and Wendy and I would do a little skiing.

After April was born our trips stopped and we had most of our contact with Dan over the phone. One day Dan called me and said, "Joe, our snowmobile program is not doing well. What can we do to encourage people to go snowmobiling here?"

I thought for a while and told him that I would call him back. This was 1971 and the women's lib movement was getting tremendous publicity.

It took me about an hour and I called Dan back. "Dan, let me read the release I just wrote. The headline is 'Resort Bans Women Snowmobilers,' and the story reads like this: Daniel R. Iannotti, president of the Schuss Mountain Ski Resort in Mancelona, Michigan, announced that he will no longer allow women to drive snowmobiles at his resort. Said Iannotti, 'If there's one thing worse than a woman driver, it's a woman snowmobiler.'"

Dan was a little taken aback. "But what about the protests we are going to get?" he said.

"So what? The worst that can happen is that you'll get more publicity," I replied.

Dan agreed. And I released the news item on the City News Bureau wires. The item immediately hit the national news wires and the news item was read on national TV news and radio and appeared in newspapers all over the country. Overnight Schuss Mountain's snowmobiling became the focus of national attention. Articles appeared in newspapers nationwide, and news commentators on network programs such as the Huntley/Brinkly Report ended their news coverage with the item.

Now we braced ourselves for the onslaught of women protestors. But nothing happened. Only a few nasty notes. That's all. One week after the big publicity hit, I called Dan. "We can't let these women's lib groups do that to us."

"But Joe, they haven't done anything," Dan replied.

That's just it," I said. "At least if they would have protested, we could have had more publicity. But that shouldn't stop us. You did get a few nasty notes, didn't you? Let's issue the following release:

WOMEN'S PROTESTS CAUSE BAN TO LIFT

'Because of the pressure from Women's Lib groups upset over the recent ban against women snowmobilers, Daniel R. Iannotti, president of the Schuss Mountain Ski Resort in Mancelona, Michigan, has lifted his ban.'

The second release made about half as much news as the first release did. But interestingly, it was the women reporters who were doing the interviewing and covering the story.

The publicity event gave the nation a lot of laughs, poked fun at the excesses of the women's lib movement, and drew so many snowmobilers to Schuss Mountain that their revenues were four times those of the previous month and stayed at that level for quite a few years.

Publicity has always been a fun game for me. I look at it as a creative challenge—a challenge to view and report the news in a different way or make the news fit the assignment.

During my years with Schuss, I was a member of the City News Bureau, which let me, for a fee, put my news releases on their news wire that fed Chicago's media. Often the other wire services pick up the stories, and TV and radio stations soon followed.

Probably the biggest press conference I've ever conducted took place in a most unusual setting. I received a call one day from a young man, Earl Kitover, who had heard from my recording contract attorney that I was a good publicist. He wanted to talk to me about promoting his wife. Who was his wife? Miss Nude America, a popular exotic striptease dancer.

I invited him and his wife to our home to discuss their objectives. Apparently there was a big contest in Indiana at a nudist camp and the winner was Valorie Kitover. Earl Kitover had quit an engineering job to act as her manager.

Valerie was only getting a few hundred dollars a performance at the local clubs and Earl thought she deserved a lot more. He told me that with the right kind of publicity Valerie could command a thousand dollars a performance, but it took some major publicity to command that kind of fee.

Valerie definitely did not look like a stripper. She looked and acted like the neighbor next door—an innocent-looking, well-built, clean-cut girl whom you'd never expect to strip on stage at a striptease show.

But she did strip and Earl assured me that she'd do anything to get publicity—even dance in the nude if she had to.

Meanwhile, my wife was sitting there listening to the entire conversation in our den, thinking that the Kitovers had to rank as the weirdest account I'd ever had. I agreed to give their problem some thought and get back to them.

The next day I called Earl. "Earl, can Valerie perform at the Rialto?" I asked.

"Sure, they'd love to have her," he replied.

"Great. Get her a booking there and I'll do the rest. Are you sure she'll do anything?" I asked.

"Anything! You get her the publicity," he replied.

To get publicity for any politician in Chicago, all you had to do was attack Mayor Daley. But if you praised the mayor, not a word would appear in the papers. I realized this from handling many politicians during the past few years and knew what Chicago reporters would respond to.

I also knew that reporters would respond to the story I was about to release to the City News Bureau. Imagine yourself a reporter for a Chicago paper seeing something like this come across the wires:

MISS NUDE AMERICA CHALLENGES MAYOR DALEY

Miss Nude America will conduct the city's first nude press conference in the basement of the Rialto Theatre in which she will announce her intentions to remove all her clothes on stage at the Rialto Theatre to challenge Mayor Daley's nudity ordinance."

I have conducted several news conferences in my life for everything from politicians to products, but never have I had such a large turnout as I did for this one. Everybody was there.

I even had reporters from the Wall Street Journal with cameras, even though the Journal at that time had never printed a photograph in their history. The TV news people were there from every Chicago TV station—including an educational channel and two I never knew existed.

But Mayor Daley was not to be undone by Miss Nude America. Although he had succeeded in successfully challenging more formidable opponents, Miss Nude America presented a totally different threat. He responded by sending the fire department to inspect the Rialto for fire violations, and the fire inspectors found several.

However, when the fire inspectors saw the big press turnout, they realized that to disappoint the press would cause more headlines. After a few calls to key city officials, the situation was reassessed and the Rialto got just a warning.

Meanwhile, the press gathered outside Valerie's dressing room (or, should we say, undressing room) and had their cameras ready and their notebooks out.

Finally, Valerie emerged, just as promised, wearing only her high-heel shoes. Her figure left no doubt about how she had won the Miss Nude America contest. I can remember a pause when she stepped up to the microphone as the reporters prepared for probably their most unusual press conference. The only sounds you could hear were the whirring of seven TV cameras and strobe lights flashing.

Valerie stepped up to the microphone to read a prepared statement I had written for her the day before. She read it as if she were a high school student standing before her class reciting a composition. She seemed as innocent and as naive as the little girl next door, and I'm sure that also took the reporters by surprise. Her statement was really a rehash of our press release, so there was nothing new, but it was important that a formal announcement break the ice. From then on, it was downhill all the way.

She then announced she would take questions from the reporters. With every question I started to look for a hole to crawl in. For example, when asked why she was doing it, she answered honestly, "I want to get enough publicity so I can charge more for my exotic dancing." After this disarming answer, the questions continued.

There was no doubt that the reporters were enjoying the answers and, quite frankly, they probably couldn't have cared less. Cameras were shooting photos that would never see the pages of any newspaper. TV news cameras were taking footage that viewers would not be permitted by law to view.

After her press conference she went back into the dressing room, put her clothes on, and proceeded on stage to undress before the thinnest crowd ever to attend the Rialto. Apparently nobody wanted to be in the audience with all that publicity except the handful of reporters-all in the line of duty.

The next day Valerie was front page news in all four Chicago newspapers and on all the TV shows. All the papers and TV newscasts showed was her portrait and not much more.

Later her price went up to $1,500 a performance and she was Chicago's top stripper, an honor directly related to her Chicago publicity campaign. The Rialto closed down shortly after that.

I handled other publicity during this time, as it proved to be the least expensive way to advertise my clients' products or services. I did publicity for the Spot Restaurant in Evanston, north of Chicago. I was

Jerry Herman of the Spot restaurant shows his bra-shaped pizza which created a lot of publicity for his restaurant.

doing their advertising and the restaurant owner, Jerry Herman, told me that his dream was to get some publicity on the Johnny Carson show.

One day on the air Johnny Carson started kidding Ed McMahon, who claimed that mayonnaise originated as a result of his distant relatives.

I saw an opportunity to capitalize on the statements. I immediately prepared a label for a large jar of mayonnaise and called it Ed McMahon Mayonnaise. In the ingredients we listed 5 percent alcohol to add to the ribbing that Carson always gave McMahon. I also listed a whole series of humorous instructions that tied into the show and sent Carson a letter from the Spot about the product's popularity. I did mention a problem, however. The stuff couldn't be served in Evanston because alcohol was not allowed in the North Shore community. Evanston was dry.

Carson gave three minutes to the bit and the Spot was deluged with calls and customers for some time afterwards.

Another time, Herman wanted me to come up with a different promotion. His specialty was pizza. A new fad was taking hold at this time. Women were not only going all out for women's lib, but they were removing their bras as a sign of their independence. So I suggested the world's first bra-shaped pizza which consisted of two small round pizzas connected by a strap. It, too, made the Chicago papers.

Around this time Spiro Agnew was becoming a household name. In fact, Agnew's name was unknown before the 1968 political conventions and Nixon's statement "Agnew is no household name" was often bantered around.

So I created a series of products, some of which included Spiro Agnew facial tissue, toilet paper, drain cleaner—an entire line of Spiro Agnew household products. Then I sent out the release. I really had no client to promote and quite frankly didn't intend to promote the product anyway. But I thought it would give the public a good laugh and be perfect for those humorous bits at the end of the news shows. Hopefully, the publicity would land me a new client.

Sure enough, it got good national coverage, but I quickly discovered something about making fun of politicians. I got bomb threats with people calling me on the phone and yelling at me. It wasn't much fun after all, and I didn't get any new clients.

I've also had some promotions destroyed because of poor timing. The Teeny Bopper promotion was a good example, but I've had others that were just as bad.

I've released a promotion the same day that four major news

stories broke, each one of which would have rated a huge front page headline by itself. The paper that day had four large headlines and my big story was totally ignored.

Then I had a front page picture in the Chicago Sun-Times yanked the hour Eisenhower died in 1969. The picture did run, but only in the earliest editions of the paper.

Publicity was always lots of fun and I never lost my shirt, as I did with my other paid promotions.

Another restaurant wanted to meet with me as I was starting to develop a reputation for the creative PR approaches I used. Court of the Lions was an upscale North Shore restaurant that appeared at first to be an expensive place to eat. My idea was simple. Create a menu with

WEATHER
Cloudy, warmer, chance of showers. High in the lower 50s. See Page 92.

CHICAGO SUN-TIMES

©1969 by Field Enterprises Inc.

★ ★ ★ ★ FINAL

Vol. 22, No. 47 | Phone 321-3000 | FRIDAY, MARCH 28, 1969 | 136 Pages, Two Sections—10 Cents

New Rock All-Stars, Kids: It's The Fuzz!

By William Granger

Five youths wearing beards, satin shirts and wildly printed trousers sat calmly in a pleasant Southwest Side home Wednesday night waiting for the cops to come.

At 7 p.m., five policemen, complete with pistols and nightsticks, entered the home at 4835 S. Leamington.

"It's the fuzz," said one youth, going to the door.

"No," corrected Joe Sugarman. "It's the South Side Fuzz."

The policemen and kids shook hands all around and then got down to the serious business of singing songs.

What's going on here?

Patrolman Robert Altobello, one of the five policemen from Worth, explained:

"We wanted to put on a dance for the youths in the southwest communities. They're always complaining they don't have a place to go. So we contacted this rock group, the Dontays, and asked if they'd donate their services for a dance."

Sugarman, the Dontays' manager, said, "I suggested that not only we play but some Worth policemen form a quartet and appear with us."

Sugarman talked about the generation gap and said "you can imagine what the police gap with the kids is."

Altobello, head of the Worth Police Assn., agreed to the idea, so he found four volunteers. They decided to call their group the South Side Fuzz.

The Fuzz will make its debut Saturday night in Richards High School, Oak Lawn, and kids from throughout the Southwest Side have been invited.

Sgt. Charles Walsh laughed. "Don't expect much. We aren't even amateurs."

The South Side Fuzz give out with "The Sound" under the direction of rock musician John Canning (right), during rehearsal for Saturday night's big bash. The singing Worth policemen are (l. to r.) Sgt. Charles Walsh; Sgt. Art Ziehlke; Greg Walsh, the sergeant's brother, and Bill Demblon. Frank Rondero of the Dontays holds the music for the bluecoat quartet. (Sun-Times Photo by Jack Lenahan)

Cong Call Thieu Bid Trick

Stories On Page 2

We had the Worth, Illinois police department perform for the teens. Shown above is John Canning of the Dontays helping the police blend their voices. The publicity stunt made the front page of many newspapers but was promptly replaced with news of Dwight Eisenhower's death which took all of the headlines.

their regular reasonable pricing and then create one with the prices three times their regular price.

You take your girl to the restaurant. She gets the high-priced menu, you get the regular menu. Your girl is impressed that you're taking her to a fancy and expensive place. We had a few other pranks that the waiters and waitresses were trained to do to impress dates.

The program was called "The Snow Job" and we created flyers, passed them out at Northwestern University and at the local high-rise buildings, and waited for the response. It was very slow until the story broke in the Chicago Daily News on a cool November day. The response was fast and heavy, and both the new customers and the waitresses were having a ball watching the expressions of the ladies the men were trying to impress.

CHICAGO DAILY NEWS, Monday, November 16, 1970 Section Three 23

Charm chick with meal check

Restaurant's 'Snow Job' does trick

By Robert J. Herguth

Poverty-level boy friends can now pretend they're rich sugardaddies, thanks to Chicago's Joe Sugarman.

Joe has developed something called "The Snow Job — A Guaranteed Way to Impress Your Next Date" for a North Side restaurant:

(1) Boy friend phones Court of the Lions restaurant before dinner date, gives his name, and makes reservations for "The Snow Job Special."

(2) Boy friend and date arrive at restaurant. Hostess greets boy friend effusively by name and says, "How nice to see you again" even if hostess never laid eyes on him before.

(3) At the table, hostess hands boy friend menu containing our regular low prices. But your girl gets our menu containing prices that are three times the real ones. One look at the menu and your girl has got to say, "Man, is he blowin' the bread!"

(4) "You'll get only one wine list but it will be four times the regular prices — so simply divide by four." Let your girl see the wine list.

(5) "Now comes the good part. The waiter brings over the wine. You taste it. You pause. You grimace. You say: 'Take it back — it's lousy.' Our waiter will apologize and pretend to get you a new bottle." The girl friend is thinking "Malcolm Timlich, you groovy cat!" If your name is Malcolm Timlich.

(6) After the wine and a fine meal, boy friend pays the reasonable check with no extra charges, and checks out with marveling chick.

"WE STARTED the 'Snow Job' service last weekend but haven't had any takers yet," said Bill Nopar, co-owner of the restaurant at 6935 N. Sheridan.

"We distributed fliers among Northwestern and Loyola students, and in Sheridan Rd. high-rises.

"Several parents wanted to know if their teens can substitute sparkling grape juice for the wine on dates." (Yes).

Handpicked waiters and waitresses handle "The Snow Job" because they must be good at acting.

WHO IS Joe Sugarman, creator of "The Snow Job?" He is 32, a Chicago adman, an Oak Park-River Forest High grad who majored in electrical engineering at the U. of Miami in Florida.

Basically, Sugarman is an idea man. He recently developed the popular Spiro Agnew Effete Powder for those with athlete's effete.

But he bombed with his Batman Credit Card — the "only credit card you had to use cash with.

"We made 250,000 of the cards and we were eventually stuck with them."

The Snow Job not only brought a lot of business to the Court of Lions restaurant but the waiters and waitresses were having the time of their life.

17) Politics, the Tooth Fairy, and the Calculator

"Don't be distracted by criticism. Remember the only taste of success some people have is when they take a bite out of you."

Zig Ziglar Author and Speaker

After losing Alltapes, my biggest account, I started to look for additional clients.

It was 1971 and the recession was in full swing when I got a call from Dick Orkin, the talent who had created Chickenman and who originally had produced my Batman radio spots.

Dick had created another radio series called "The Tooth Fairy" for his own newly-formed company. He wondered if I'd be interested in creating all the promotional materials for the series. Each radio station that bought the program would want to promote the show and give away bumper stickers, buttons—the same stuff we used for our Great Teeny Bopper Society.

The deal was simple. I would own part of a company called The Tooth Fairy Company and we would split the costs of producing the materials as well as the profits.

I accepted and started to design and produce the materials. I then sent mailings to all the radio stations carrying the program. I sent samples of the t-shirts, the bumper stickers and the buttons.

In a very short time we realized that the world was not going crazy for the "I Believe in the Tooth Fairy" goodies we were trying to peddle, and we abandoned the project. Although the show was popular, the promotional items didn't sell. Dick and I parted on the best of terms.

There wasn't any money lost on the project—just a lot of valuable time. But I had enough work with my political candidates, the Schuss Mountain Ski Resort and a few restaurant accounts to pay my mortgage and generate enough money to buy a photo typositor—a new typesetting machine for my small advertising agency.

It was now spring of 1971 and I was heavily involved with the gubernatorial campaign of Thomas A. Foran, the former chief government prosecutor of the Chicago Seven trial in Chicago. His assistant in the trial was Richard Schultz—my brother-in-law. Dick recommended me to Tom Foran and I became the campaign's advertising man.

In the process of the campaign I noticed that a few of his assistants were using an electronic calculator they had rented to total up the campaign statistics.

I asked to borrow the large Sharp brand desktop unit that I took home to try. I used it to figure out my mark-ups, add up my charges, and compute discounts, and I found it to be a tremendous time-saving tool for my agency. I was going to buy one until I discovered that the unit sold for $600—little more than I could afford at the time.

The Foran campaign continued. I was producing beautiful campaign literature and doing excellent photography, but Foran's efforts weren't paying off and I was replaced by a few other advertising people who didn't save him either. Foran's campaign was designed to convince Mayor Daley to select him to run for governor, yet Foran couldn't muster enough support to get Daley's backing and he eventually dropped out.

My political advertising activity was quite successful, even with the Foran loss. They said that if more than 60 percent of your candidates won, you were a good advertising man. My record was 87.5 percent winners—an incredible record. But there was a catch. Fifty percent of my winners were eventually either indicted or sent to prison—but then that was Chicago politics.

One day while glancing through Business Week magazine, I came across an article about a pocket calculator that would sell for $240 and would add, subtract, multiply, and divide.

I thought about my desire to own one of those units and called the manufacturer. After numerous phone calls, I finally reached

THOMAS A.
FORAN
CAN BE
A GREAT
GOVERNOR
WITH YOUR
HELP!

Thomas A. Foran is well known for his effective prosecution of the "Chicago 7." But he's done a lot more than that...

Here is a brochure I prepared for the Foran for Governor campaign. Although he didn't win, the ads were recognized for their copy and graphics.

Craig Corporation in Compton, California. I expressed my interest in their new pocket calculator and asked if our agency could introduce the product through a direct mail campaign. I talked to a Loren Davies who was their national sales manager.

I explained to Loren that I could tell him very quickly, through my testing, whether or not the pocket calculator would sell. The idea intrigued Craig's marketing people. They weren't sure whether the product would sell and we gave them a good test vehicle. They had a representative who happened to have one of the first prototype samples with him, and he would be instructed to stop by and pay me a visit.

Alex Molnar, a soft-spoken, slim man in his forties stopped by my home. It was October of 1971, and Alex presented me with my first pocket calculator. I looked it over and asked him if I could buy it, giving Alex a check for $141, the wholesale price at the time.

I told Alex that first I wanted to show it to a client of mine for a possible direct mail advertising campaign and that I would get back to him within a few days.

I brought the calculator to my former client at Alltapes. I showed them the unit, demonstrated it, and asked Kent Beauchamp if he thought a mailing to his stereo tape club list was a good idea.

"Who would pay $240 for a pocket calculator through the mail that nobody heard of?" said Kent. "I don't wanna take a chance."

So I drove home thinking what a great opportunity it would be for me to try. But I was still struggling to make a living, and with a baby I had other responsibilities to consider. I couldn't take a chance.

All my life I've always had people telling me, "Joe, if you ever need investors, let me know. One of these days you'll strike it rich." But I never had the guts to ask anybody for money, and thank goodness—I would have caused many people to lose their money.

When I arrived home I received a call from Ed Bauman. Ed was a forty-year-old real estate salesman who also managed a rock group called the Family. Ed's group played at my clubs and I used to sympathize with his problems of managing rock groups who never appreciated their managers.

He was trying to interest me in a possible real estate deal. I told him that I couldn't afford it, but I asked him if he'd like to double his money within a few short months.

"Great," he said. "What's the deal?"

I described the pocket calculator and the economics of direct mail. I told Ed that most direct mailings have a 2% response rate. With the pocket calculator deal, a 2% response would double our money the first week. I asked him if he would like to be an investor.

Ed got all excited and drove out to my home where I showed him the unit. "With just a simple mailing piece and renting just the right lists, we could easily double our money," I assured him.

The deal I worked out was simple. I told Ed that I needed

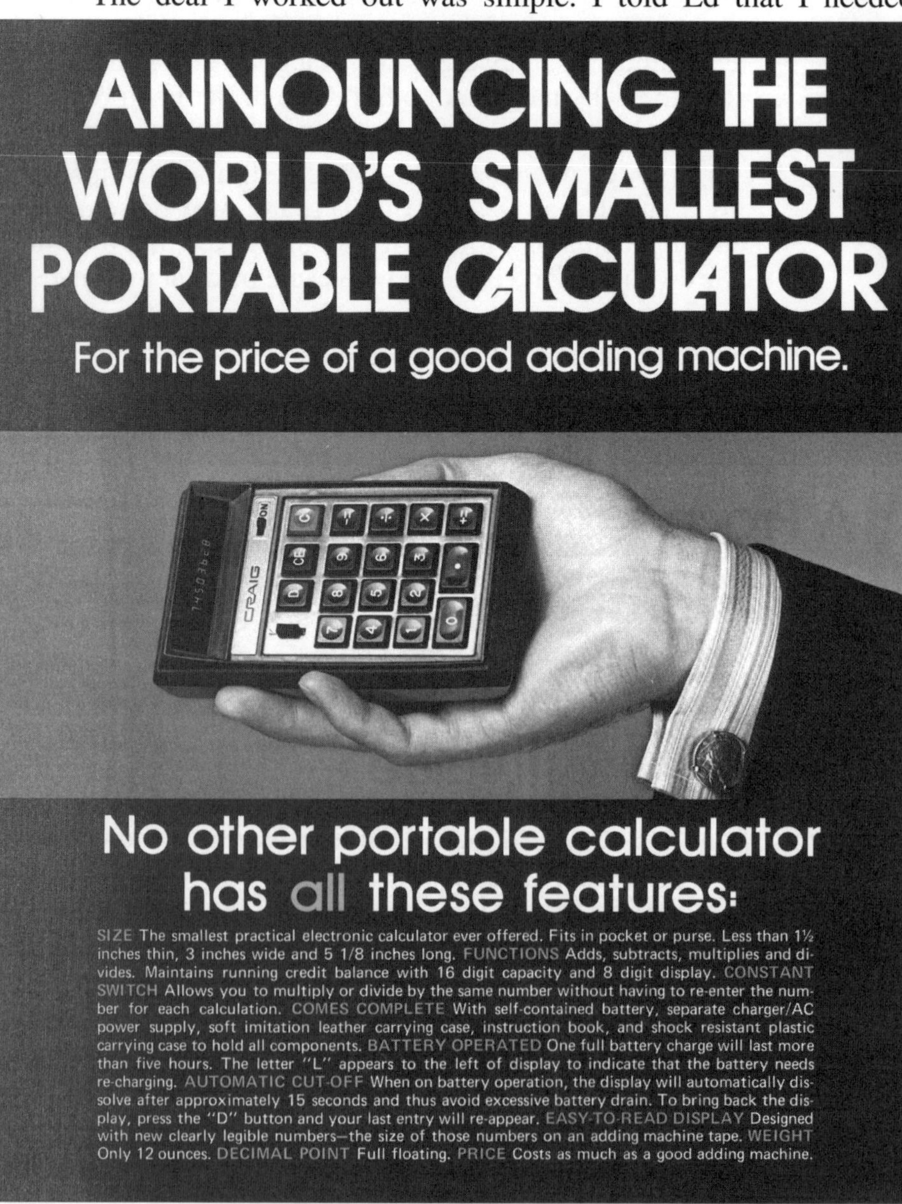

This was the brochure I prepared to sell the first pocket calculator. It was accompanied by a letter and return order card which I coded and which proved to be the key to my eventual success.

$12,000 for the campaign. If he would raise the money, I would agree that the first profits to come in would go to him and his investors until he doubled his money and his investors got a 50-percent return on their investment. Then I would make the rest. I would also own the business and have no further responsibility to the group after our goals were met.

Ed agreed and I presented my concept to a group of his friends. We raised $12,000 and I proceeded to rent 50,000 names using ten different mailing lists. I rented a list of 5,000 accountants, 5,000 engineers —all the people who I thought could use a calculator.

I quickly arranged for a photo session and hired a hand model. When the hand model arrived, he had a brief case with him into which he had just the sleeves of suits and shirts plus an array of cuff links. I asked him, "Where did you get all those sleeves."

He confided in me, "I just go to a department store and when nobody is looking, I cut off a sleeve or two and then leave."

After hearing that and paying him an expensive hand-modeling fee, I decided from then on to become a hand model myself. And for the rest of my career, each time you saw one of our products being held by a hand, it was my hand. In fact, my hand has appeared on billions of pages in print and it all started that eventful day.

I raced to print the full-color flyer and letter and got Craig Corporation to start shipping me calculators in November.

I had all my forms ready to go. I bought a tape machine to seal the packages and Wendy bought plenty of stamps. Wendy and I were going to work together to open the mail, and although I felt that we could handle everything ourselves, I knew that there would come a day when we'd have to get help if my little mail order company succeeded.

I had named my new company the JS&A National Sales Group. I already called my advertising agency "JS&A Advertising," an abbreviation for Joseph Sugarman and Associates, so I was able to answer the phone with "JS&A."

The mailing went out and I waited for the response. All I needed was a two-tenths-of-one- percent return to break even. Later we discovered that our company was the first to introduce this untested, unproven product—a product that launched the micro-electronic revolution.

I'll never forget the first response I received. My feeling at the time was, "You mean somebody would buy a $240 calculator through the mail?" It just seemed so incredible that the concept had worked—but did it? I needed a lot greater response than one order.

The final response was poor. After a dozen or so orders, I

realized, based on projections, that we were going to lose half of our money.

The first time I had attempted to get investors for a venture ended in failure. I would have to confront them with the sad results.

To prepare for the meeting I decided to run an analysis of the response. In testing the ten lists, I gave each reply card a special code that corresponded to the mailing list I used. To my surprise, I discovered that two of the lists were actually successful and that the others were so bad that they brought down the total overall response. The two lists were the last two I had selected.

I remember Jim Pheta, my list salesman, telling me to try the presidents of million-dollar corporations which I thought was a rather stupid choice. Certainly engineers and accountants would respond in droves, but presidents of big corporations didn't have time to read advertising literature sent through the mail from unknown companies.

But I accepted Jim's suggestion, and to my amazement, he was right. The only successful lists were the last two I selected and the two I would have never expected to succeed.

After my analysis I saw that had I used just those two lists, I could have doubled my investors' money and made a profit myself. The calculator was selling for $240 and costing me around $140, so I made a little less than $100 per unit after the credit card charges were deducted. We were using Master Charge, Bank Americard, and American Express, although most of the orders came in with a check. (Note: Master Charge changed their name eventually to MasterCard and Bank Americard changed their name to VISA.)

"If only I could convince my investors to stay in," I thought, "I know we could make it."

But Ed Bauman needed some of his money back and his investors were pestering him, trying to find out the results. I had to move quickly.

On a hunch I called Craig Corporation and talked again to Lauren Davies, the national sales manager. He was anxious to find out the results of our campaign, so I leveled with him. "Loren, it didn't go very well, but we did discover the types of people who would buy the calculator." I then proceeded to describe my findings.

Loren advised me that I could sell the calculator for $180 because the costs were starting to drop. My new wholesale price of $103 would be effective February 1.

When I got my group of investors together, I told them of my results, of the new price, and of the excellent chance we had of succeeding. "If you guys decide to back out, I'll definitely continue on my own," I said.

They all agreed to stay in after a brief series of questions. It was now December and most of the responses were in. Indeed we had lost half the money. Even if my investors wanted back what was left of their money, I probably would have eventually paid all their money back anyway.

The mailing I wanted to conduct included a million names. The 10,000 names that worked were taken from a list of a million names that I had great confidence would work. The $6,000 that was left would just cover about 25,000 mailing pieces, and yet if I was going to score big, I had to roll my campaign out quickly and in great numbers to beat the competition.

I was thirty-three years old, just barely able to pay my mortgage, and had a wife and child to support. I knew that each time in my life that I had felt I had a sure winner, something came up at the last minute and grasped success from me just as I felt it was within reach. I knew that if I invested the huge sums of money I needed to make this program a success and lost, it might be a blow I wouldn't recover from for years.

I realized that I'd risk my home, my car, and everything I owned if my mailing failed. And I was concerned that something was sure to happen that I least suspected but would certainly end up in disaster.

I remember the confusion that I felt at the time. Having nobody to turn to for advice, I called Harvey Wagley, president of United Letter Service. I had first met Harvey at the Schuss Mountain annual stockholders' meeting. He was a Schuss stockholder and ran a large mailing house called United Letter Service.

I had used United Letter Service for my first mailing, so I called Harvey for advice. Harvey was in his sixties, a tall thin man who talked loudly and who had started his large business in a small downtown office over forty years earlier. He was a genuine entrepreneur, self-taught and with a wisdom that comes only from years of experience and years of learning.

I explained my problem to Harvey and he made a few suggestions: "Why not a 400,000 mailing instead of a million, and if it doesn't succeed, well, you'll take a lot longer to pay me back. Just don't worry about it."

Since Harvey was also willing to pay for the postage, the major bulk of my expenses would rest with his company. I think he also knew that I'd eventually pay him back, and he seemed to take a great deal of pride in helping other entrepreneurs get into business.

I accepted his offer and proceeded to order the mailing lists, envelopes, and printing. I remember the big lump I felt in my stomach as I ordered all of this material. I was already conditioned to fear the worst, but thousands of dollars was a lot of money to be playing with.

United Letter Service dropped the mailing at the post office in early January, 1972, and I waited for the response. Ten days went by and Wendy and I made sure that everything was ready. We had calculators, stamps, a filing system, forms, and everything we could possibly need for what we hoped would be the big response.

I also had a contractor give me an estimate on what it would cost to convert my basement into a work area should I need more room than my garage and my upstairs bedroom.

Finally, the response started to trickle in, then pour in, then it literally started to gush in. There were more responses than Wendy and I could possibly handle—more, in fact, than I could possibly imagine.

I called up a temporary service for help and was sent three women to assist me. I also called the contractor and told him to finish the basement as soon as he could because it looked as if I'd be needing it soon. And finally, I called Harvey Wagley to assure him that he'd get his money back and I called my investors and told them the good news, too.

I now had a business. I finally succeeded in probably my biggest gamble to date, and once again I could feel comfortable that my mortgage would be paid and I wouldn't have to live in poverty—at least for a little while.

I was now using practically every room in the house to process orders. The only place I didn't use was our own bedroom, but with the other three bedrooms being used, along with the living room, kitchen and garage, Wendy was getting a little concerned.

Our home was no longer our home. It was a factory processing orders and shipping calculators. It was the start of a new and rapidly emerging mail order company.

Projecting our gains, it looked as if I'd be left with $50,000 from the results of our campaign. I found out that we were selling more calculators than Sears, which was also carrying the product, but because of its needs, Craig Corporation was not filling our orders fast enough. We were the first to introduce the pocket calculator in November, and we had convinced Craig that the calculator would be a real winner in January, 1972.

18) Our First Mail Order Ad

"The majority of men meet with failure because of their lack of persistence in creating new plans to take the place of those which fail."

Napoleon Hill 1883—1970, Author of Think and Grow Rich

The very first full page ad we placed appeared in the Wall Street Journal. And like many of my experiences, it wasn't easy.

I was rather surprised by the sudden drop in calculator prices from $240 to $180 and had heard rumors that a drop to $100 was possible in the very near future. Rumors spread that the new $100 price point wasn't too far off.

The problem in marketing a calculator through direct mail was the time it took to conduct a campaign. Sure, I had the mailing piece that worked and a good idea of which mailing lists would work, but to produce large quantities of envelopes and mailing pieces, have them stuffed and then wait for the post office to deliver them might take months. The fear of having my mailing piece ready for the mails and having the prices drop stopped me from continuing in what was starting to become a successful formula.

The next logical step was an advertisement in the Wall Street Journal. Here was a national newspaper that printed an advertisement a few days after receipt. It was the fastest, most efficient way to hit the largest number of middle-to upper-income executives—the same type of consumer that responded to my mailing.

The next problem was to translate that entire mailing piece—including the letter, circular, order card, and full-color image into an advertisement in black and white—one that would hold the readers' interest, explain the product, and close the sale.

I took all the elements of that mailing piece, used a different approach, and ended up with a piece of copy that included all the things a good direct mail piece should have. I reduced the size of the pictures and concentrated on the copy. My theory was that if a reader was interested enough in a product, he or she would read the entire ad. And if I could convince the prospect with simple, basic, honest language that what we offered was indeed a good product and value, then I could expect them to respond.

My theory was based on my experiences in the fifties. I remember when the new cars would roll out. At that time it was really an exciting event. Car styles changed rapidly and the car companies made such hoopla that autumn turned into an exciting period for car enthusiasts.

I also remember picking up those new car brochures that showed full-color shots of the cars but little descriptive copy. The copy was written to create a mood, a feeling about the car, but nothing more. I had often thought that Detroit had missed the boat. If I were to write a car brochure today instead of saying that a car had "rack and pinion steering," I would explain what rack and pinion steering was, how it worked, and why my system was better than anyone else's. Detroit missed providing a real consumer service back in the fifties.

Will people read all that copy? If it's kept simple enough, informative, and if there is a genuine interest in the product, people will read and read and read and read.

After two days of rewriting, I sat down at my photo typesetter and set the headlines while my wife diligently set the type on our IBM Selectric Composer. I then proceeded to make my paste-up for what turned out to be a four-column by sixteen-inch ad.

When I finished the advertisement, I called the Wall Street Journal and spoke to Loren Commotore, the salesman in charge of small accounts. I found out that in order to run an advertisement, I had to fill out credit forms and provide references.

While that was pending, I reserved the back page of the Journal. I knew that sometimes, when I didn't have time to read the entire issue, I would scan the front and back pages. So, I figured I'd have better response if I ran my ad on the back page.

We filled out the forms and waited for final approval from the Journal. The target date was approaching, but still no confirmation. Lauren then called me about three days before the ad was to break with the news that they'd need a check in advance. Apparently my credit lines weren't sufficient to allow a $10,000 charge. Loren had to rush out to my home pick up the check, and release the go-ahead to run the ad.

Meanwhile I was preparing for the response. I had the telephone company install three new lines, the lock company put deadbolt locks on all our doors, and I hired an armed guard to stand by just in case.

My garage was loaded with about 250 calculators, the cars were cleared out, and our garage shipping department was ready to go.

All the while, our basement was under construction and the phone company was pre-wiring it for up to twelve lines. We were already using practically every room in the house to process orders, type labels, and ship, so the place was really busy.

I also felt that it was time to hire a permanent secretary to relieve my wife of some of her responsibilities. I placed an ad in the local paper and, after talking to a dozen women, I selected Mary Stanke to work for us. Mary was looking for a part-time job—something from 9 A.M. to 3 P.M—so she could spend time with her two children who returned home from school around 3 P.M. I offered her $3.25 an hour to start and she seemed pleased and was going to start on February 28, 1972—the day our first Wall Street Journal ad was to break. Mary has worked with me ever since or over 43 years as of this printing.

Meanwhile Alex Molnar, the Craig representative, wanted to see the action when the ad broke, so I put him on a chair by a phone to answer the phone calls.

Two days before the ad broke in the Journal, a discount house in the East advertised in a small ad, “Coming Soon—Craig 4501 Calculator, Only $139.00.”

From the last minute pressures of getting everything ready to getting the confirmation from the Journal and seeing the discount ad, I’d say that this had to be one of the most tense times of my life. To top it off, my one-year-old daughter, April, fell down the basement steps the evening before the ad broke. As we brought her bloodied body to the hospital, I knew I was really being put through a test. April was okay and fortunately nothing serious happened. I certainly felt relieved for that.

That first advertisement in the Wall Street Journal was a real thrill for me. A few days after it ran, we began to get orders. The phones were busy, my staff was working hard, and Mary Stanke was darting from room to room coordinating the activity.

In just ten days I had made $20,000. Not only was the response fast, but it was heavy as well. I had never in my life made so much money so quickly. It was too good to be true.

I was about to run more ads when I got a call from Peter Behrendt, president of Craig Corporation. He told me that my advertisement caused his regular dealers to call his company and demand that they get adequate inventories of the calculator.

I was getting 50 percent of Craig’s production—more than any other dealer including Sears—and as a result of my ad, Craig Corporation would have to cut off our shipments and allocate a very small percentage to us.

I was really upset. Here was my big opportunity to take advantage of everything I had done to build for this moment—including creating the original demand for the unit—and now it was being taken away from me.

I had never been in a back-order position with the calculator and orders were still coming in with very little inventory to back it up.

It wasn't until April of that year that we finally filled all our back orders, but by then it was too late. Calculator prices had dropped to $129.95, and the chances of our company succeeding at $179.95 were slim.

We did try once again in a regional edition of the Wall Street Journal in April and got one order from the ad. It was time to go to my next product.

19) Providing a Service

"I began learning long ago that those who are happiest are those who do the most for others."

Booker T. Washington 1856—1915, Educator and Author

From 1972 through 1978, I concentrated on the new wave of calculators and digital watches. I concentrated all our advertising in just the Wall Street Journal and I concentrated on the very same format, advertisement after advertisement.

A few ads were extremely successful, others were average, and some were unsuccessful. I found, however, that all I needed were a few successes to offset my many failures so like the gambler who continues to roll the dice, I kept rolling, but the dice always paid off in the end. The ads that seemed the most successful were those in which I told everything about a product—even the disadvantages. Soon I discovered that honesty in advertising was the most effective tool I could use in selling a product. In fact, it was the same lesson I had learned from my teen clubs.

In April of 1972, just as we were catching up with our back orders on our first pocket calculator, we moved into the basement. The carpenters, the rug installers, the painters were all finished. Our staff was down to just Mary Ann Haire, our first temporary employee, and Mary Stanke, our first full-time employee. The big explosion was over. Our business had wound down considerably.

Operating out of the basement was really one of the most enjoyable phases of my business career. Mary Stanke would arrive at 8:30 in the morning, ring the bell, and go down the stairs to the basement. Mary Ann Haire would follow. And I'd roll out of bed a few minutes before 8:30 and grope my way down the stairs to my desk.

The basement was where we processed all our orders, accepted the returned packages, and handled the customer service functions. We commissioned a company to warehouse our products and ship from the labels we supplied. Things were really quite simple and quiet except for those occasional telephone calls from customers in a rush to get a product or two.

By February of 1973 calculator prices had plummeted to $69.95 and the public was really confused. I knew they were because I would often get calls from people asking all sorts of questions, worried if we were in store for another price drop and wondering which calculator to buy.

So I took out a large ad that ran on the back page of the Wall Street Journal entitled The Truth About Pocket Calculators." There were no pictures, no subheadlines—just 3,000 words of very informative copy. The purpose of the ad was to inform and educate the consumer on how to buy a pocket calculator.

I talked about features, the floating decimal, the constant key. I discussed prices, where the units were manufactured, and even predicted the future. Then I honestly told consumers where they could buy calculators and gave them three options: department stores, discount stores, and mail order companies, giving the advantages and disadvantages of each. I ended the ad with "See our other ad in this issue of the Journal." The other ad showed five calculators that we were offering—all priced very competitively.

After the ad broke we were literally deluged with mail praising us for the public service we had provided and including orders for calculators that, within a few weeks, reached a sales volume of $250,000. We got a tremendous number of letters that asked us questions. After all, the advertisement clearly gave consumers the impression that we were experts and they came to us in droves with their questions.

There was so much mail that it was delivered in sacks and we spent many hours late in the evening sorting it and answering the huge response.

It was during that promotion that I realized the reason for the success of most businesses: simply that a business provides a service, and the more service it provides, the more responsive the market. Consumers appreciated the service I provided and they responded. All successful businesses owe their success to this very simple principle.

During 1972 and 1973, we got calls from our customers asking if we could ship our calculators to them that day. They were in a rush and didn't have the time to fill out the order form, put in their credit card number and then sign their name. Signing their name was an important part of the process as it was clear in our contract with the major credit card companies that the customer had to sign the order form for a mail order or the order was not valid. In short, it was not allowed to accept an order without a valid signature.

But I felt really bad for the customer and wanted to help. So I put the rules aside and took a chance and signed the coupon myself to make it official and then shipped out the calculator. I monitored the sales and found that nobody tried to cheat me by claiming that they had not authorized the purchase. In fact, I didn't get a single loss from providing this service.

After about a year of doing this, I decided to get a few toll-free numbers from Bell Systems—the company that was responsible for issuing toll-free numbers—and at the top of my coupon, in very small type, I put, "Credit card buyers call toll-free" and I listed my toll-free number. It was October, 1973 when that first ad broke in the Southwestern edition of the Wall Street Journal. I remember going into the basement and the phones were already ringing off the hook. By noon we had taken enough orders to realize a profit, and the sales continued to pour in.

In addition to the sales that poured in all day, we were able to determine the very first day that we had a profitable ad—something that saved us a few weeks that we normally needed to determine if an ad was profitable. And we could immediately start placing the ad in other editions of the Wall Street Journal.

I was elated with our new-found marketing tool. Yet I was also aware of the fact that the credit card companies could pull our authority to use their services at any moment if they realized what we were doing.

I continued to run ads using a coupon and that single line in small type. My competitors with whom I was always friendly would occasionally call me and ask me how I was doing and if I had a high "rip off rate." In other words, how many bad orders did we receive? I didn't want to lie. However, this was the greatest concept ever in direct marketing and the last thing I wanted was a competitor to copy our success. "You wouldn't believe the rip off rate," I would say and they thought I meant that it was high when in essence it was nonexistent. And still, nobody would copy us.

We used this method for almost a year. And then we were contacted by Bell Systems—the company that issued toll-free numbers. They asked me if they could feature our company in a large ad in the Wall Street Journal to promote their new toll-free service.

"But what about the credit card companies?" I inquired. "What we are doing is not quite encouraged or even allowed."

The Bell System manager with whom I spoke told me that I didn't have anything to worry about. "They are changing the rules to allow phone orders thanks to your efforts, the absence of your "chargebacks" (disputed charges) and the activity we have been monitoring from your phones.

The ad broke, our competitors jumped on the bandwagon, and soon this new service was responsible for a rapid growth in the catalog industry, the establishment of call and fulfillment centers and the overall expansion of the direct marketing industry.

Providing a service to our customers—that of taking a credit card order over the phone—helped to catapult us to become a major force in the direct response industry. It also pointed out that for every problem, there is an opportunity. The problem was trying to fill orders from customers who needed their calculator right away and the opportunity was to open up a new method of order taking that lifted the entire direct marketing industry to new heights.

As I tell my audiences, if you want to be successful, you learn all of the rules and you follow them one by one. If you want to be super successful, you learn all of the rules and you break them one by one.

Your sales budget too small to reach across the U.S.?

WATS changed all that for JS&A National Sales Group

Joe Sugarman's company was selling mini-calculators. Then Joe wrote some hard-sell ads and got an 800 number customers could call for more information or to place an instant order. Things began to happen fast and soon Joe was running his ads in the *Wall Street Journal*, *Playboy* and *Time*, always including the 800 number. Sales quadrupled! Joe got so many calls, he had to add 15 operators to handle the business. WATS can change things for you, too. But first, you need to tell our WATS expert what needs changing. For more information and literature, call toll free from anywhere in the U.S. (except Alaska and Hawaii) 800-821-2980. In Missouri, call 800-892-2217.

WIDE AREA TELECOMMUNICATIONS SERVICE.

WATS can change all that.

This was the first ad we ran using a toll-free number to take credit card orders over the phone even though it was illegal to do that at the time. It started a revolution in direct marketing.

You own a portable calculator. It has become part of your right arm. It's time to....

Announcing the new APF Mark VI portable memory calculator with the world's most complete feature package.

NATIONAL INTRODUCTORY PRICE

$89^{95}

RETAIL $129.95

UP-DATE

(TO A MEMORY UNIT)

Only the man who owns a calculator can ılly appreciate all the features and value of the ɔtally new APF Mark VI. And for the man ıinking of buying his first unit—your timing perfect.

APF built the Mark VI to accommodate ʳery important calculator feature in the most ʳactical size. The results combine the newest ıemory technology and every desired feature ı one classic calculator value.

CHAIN MEMORY SAVES TIME

Store the answers from any calculation in a ıemory bank and automatically obtain the ɔtal of those answers. Chain memory then ermits you to recall the total stored in the ıemory and use it in further chain calculations r as a constant . . . all without disturbing your riginal memory total. It's the ultimate achieveıent in memory logic.

CHAIN MEMORY OPENS NEW POSSIBILITIES

You can now figure out invoice extensions ıd add or subtract percentage discounts from ɔur total in a few easy steps. You can compute ɔmpound interest, cost analysis, expense reɔrts, stock and bond investments—easily and ɹickly. You'll be amazed at the savings in me. There are no numbers to write down and ter re-enter and you enter the minimum nount of data thus avoiding the chance of rror. It's like working with two calculators.

NEW PERCENTAGE SYSTEM

The new Mark VI percentage system lets you ɹtomatically add or subtract a percentage hile still reviewing the percentage amount. or example, to add 5% sales tax to a $50 purıase, enter 50 then the plus key, the number and press the percent key. $2.50 is displayed. ow press the equal key, $52.50 is displayed. ı short, you are able to automatically review ıe percentage amount and by pressing one ɹtton, add it to your total. On a conventional ılculator it would have taken eleven entries to btain the same answers.

SUPER LARGE DISPLAY

The large 8 digit green display with zero ıppression also has a negative balance sign, an verflow sign, a low battery indicator plus a ıemory indicator to let you know when you've ɔt something stored in memory. The display so has a 25 second battery saving fade-out. If ou forget to turn your unit off, it will autoıatically conserve 95% of its power.

FOUR FUNCTION CONSTANT

There's a separate four function automatic ɔnstant for addition, subtraction, multiplicaon and division. The constant is automatic. here is no constant switch to turn on and later ɔrget to turn off.

MULTI-PURPOSE KEYS

Three keys serve dual purposes. The MR key Memory Recall) not only recalls the total in ıemory but when you press the MR key and ıen the clear button, your constant appears n the display. The Clear button also acts as a lear entry key and the equals key automatiılly locks in the constant.

MANY MORE FEATURES

The APF Mark VI also has algebraic logic ʳou enter the negative sign before the number ou wish to subtract as you normally think), full floating decimal and a limited sign change ıature (you can change the sign of numbers ıtered before you press the equal button).

DESIGNED FOR YOUR DESK OR YOUR BRIEFCASE

The Mark VI complete with batteries weighs only 12½ ounces and measures 1½" x 4½" x 6"—just perfect for your briefcase and large enough to make a great all-purpose desk unit. Or give this unique unit as a gift. Its value, features and appearance make it one of today's great product discoveries.

COMPLETE AND SOLIDLY BACKED

Each unit comes complete with 4 AA penlight batteries, an AC power supply, a black soft imitation leather carrying case, and detailed instructions on how to obtain the maximum use from your unit. There's also a one year warranty backed by JS&A. If anything goes wrong with your unit during the first year JS&A will replace it with a brand new unit. After the warranty period APF will repair your unit at any one of their national service-by-mail facilities. Although the Mark VI is built to last, it's still good to know that the manufacturer is service conscience—a very important consideration when you purchase any calculator.

EXPERIENCED MANUFACTURER

APF may have even built your unit. APF is one of the nation's largest manufacturers of private label calculators—calculators labelled with other company's names. They have recently decided to establish their own brand name identity similar to the Bowmar and Texas Instrument trend. So, if you've never heard of them, you will soon. APF is a financially strong public company eager to establish a reputation as America's value and service leader.

A NEW WAY TO BUY

The best way to buy a calculator is to first use it. JS&A's concept of a two week trial period gives you the opportunity to use the APF Mark VI in your home or office under your everyday conditions—not showroom conditions. After two weeks of actual use, you decide whether or not you want to keep it. If you decide to keep your unit, you have the first-hand knowledge that the Mark VI fits your requirements and the peace of mind in knowing that you've made the right choice. If you decide to return it, there's no obligation and you'll receive a prompt and courteous refund. In fact, we go one step further. To practically eliminate any inconvenience to our customers we will pick up your unit in practically all but the Western States, at our expense, right at your door. JS&A customers are the most pampered in the nation. They have come to expect good service, honest value and the opportunity to be the first to purchase the really exciting new products of our decade. Order your Mark VI at no obligation today.

Credit Card Buyers—Call (800) 323-5886 if you wish to phone in your order.

Illinois residents call collect.

HANDSOME STYLING

The handsome Mark VI is slightly angled to accommodate desk-top viewing. Its full-thrust keyboard and well-spaced keys make blind entry a breeze.

ORDER FORM

Please rush me_____APF Mark VI calculator(s) at $89.95 each complete with batteries, AC adapter, carrying case, instructions and one year warranty. I understand that if I am not completely satisfied, I may return my purchase within two weeks for a prompt refund.

Enclosed please find my check for $______ which includes $2.50 postage & handling.

*Illinois residents add 5% sales tax.

Mail all orders to: JS&A National Sales Group 628 Michelline, Northbrook, Illinois 60062

☐ Please charge my Master Charge, (also include four numbers above name) Bank Americard, Diners Club, or American Express (be sure there are 13 digits) credit card account:

NO. ______ EXP. ______

SIGNATURE ______

NAME ______

COMPANY ______

ADDRESS ______

CITY ______ STATE ______

ZIP ______ PHONE ______

The JS&A National Sales Group is one of the leading national distributors of electronic calculators and other consumer and business related electronic products. Despite our size we insist upon complete customer service and satisfaction. Our descriptions must be accurate, our products must represent good value and you must be completely satisfied. You deal with people (not computers) and you receive answers to your letters and prompt refunds if you so request. The names of our customers are kept confidential and not sold for mailing lists. Our insistence on the highest standards of customer service is your assurance of complete satisfaction.

NATIONAL SALES GROUP
628 Michelline, Northbrook, Ill. 60062 (312) 498-6900

October, 1973

20) The Watergate Scandal

> ***"If people knew how hard I worked to gain my mastery, it wouldn't seem so wonderful."***
> *Michelangelo 1475—1564, Painter, Sculptor and Architect*

The Watergate scandal made quite an impact on our nation. It also made quite an impact on Joe Sugarman. As an involved American, I had three experiences worth relating about this very historic period.

The first took place in 1972—well before the election that November. A lawyer I met through one of my political advertising accounts had a serious problem and asked if I knew anyone who could help him.

Very simply, he needed someone to bug his law partner's phone because he suspected that his partner was cheating him. The lawyer did not know that I had actually done that type of work while I was in the Army. I told him of my experience and I explained to him that although I could probably do the job, it was illegal and I would rather put him in touch with someone else. I had just started my successful new business in my basement. I was quite busy, and besides, I didn't want to violate the law.

The lawyer, whose name I won't mention for obvious reasons, agreed to have me find somebody for him and I looked in the telephone directory for a store that sold an unusual German tape recorder called a UHER. This was the same type of recorder the intelligence community used to record signals from their eavesdropping devices. The stores that sold these devices were good places to find the name of a detective or a "manufacturer" of bugs. Incidentally, the UHER was the same tape recorder that caused that 18-1/2-minute gap in President Nixon's Watergate tapes.

After a personal visit to the tape recorder store, I was able to obtain the name of a character who actually made the bugs. I went over to this sleazy operation on the first floor of an apartment building on Chicago's north side and talked to him.

At first he was cold and brief with me, but using intelligence-type talk, I soon convinced him that I was for real and he finally opened up bragging about what a great job he did and telling me that half the bugs produced and planted in Chicago were his. He was so open and such a braggart that quite frankly I didn't believe him.

Anyone operating in such a shady illegal business would certainly keep his activities quiet, but not this character. I became concerned about having him plant the bug for my lawyer friend for fear he'd brag to some undercover police officer.

The character, whom we'll call J.D., agreed to meet with my friend and plant the bug. I arranged the meeting, warning my friend that I was not impressed with J.D. but felt that we couldn't be too choosy. He was free to work out his own deal and free to assume his own risks. My friend thanked me.

That day I had read about the Watergate break-in at the Democratic headquarters in Washington. When I called J.D. to give him the meeting address, he started bragging to me that it was his bug they found at the Watergate Hotel.

"Sure, J.D., you really do get around," was my sarcastic reply.

My second Watergate experience started when it was revealed that Nixon recorded his telephone conversations. The newspapers played up the story so much that it even gave credibility to the act of tape recording phone conversations. The reasoning went if Nixon could do it, so could any American.

So I quickly sourced three different tape recorders and three different telephone pick-up devices. The phone pick-up devices were nothing elaborate. You just attached them to the tape recorder and put a ring-shaped device around the earpiece of the phone. This would let you record phone conversations legally since it was clearly explained that Nixon did not violate the law. As long as one of the two parties knew the conversations was being recorded, it was legal.

I wrote an ad entitled, "Tap Your Phone" clearly explaining that President Nixon had made recordings of phone conversations an accepted practice. I urged businessmen to consider the recording of phone conversations as another form of business record-keeping and then offered the three recording system options in the ad.

The ad ran and it wasn't successful. We sold only a few units and did not even break even. Worse, however, was the reaction at the Wall Street Journal. They refused to run the ad again and threatened to drop us as an advertiser if we ever wanted to run anything like it again. If that wasn't bad enough, I got a call from the FBI. They wanted to talk to me.

When the agent arrived, I escorted him into my basement, we sat down, and we chatted. He explained that his primary interest was in determining if my equipment could be used for surreptitious recording, which is illegal. I assured him it wasn't and explained the premise for my advertisement.

The agent was quite reasonable and could see from my basement operation and our other advertisements that we were a reputable company and that our products were not violating the law but simply capitalizing on some Watergate publicity.

As we talked, the topic turned to Watergate and I asked the investigator if they knew who had made the Watergate bug. If you'll recall the story, it was the bug that actually started the Watergate scandal. The bug went bad and prompted the conspirators to replace or repair it. It was then that they were caught.

The agent said, "We know exactly who planted the bug."

I asked, "If I tell you his initials will you tell me if it was the same guy?"

The agent agreed and I said, "Was it J.D.?"

The agent nodded his head. "Yep, he is the guy," and then mentioned his actual name.

"Why wasn't he arrested?" I asked. The agent explained that the FBI had more important things to do, although I suspect that J.D. probably bragged to them in return for immunity. Maybe the FBI didn't care but, regardless, the same guy was working for my friend.

Later I checked with my friend and discovered that indeed he, too, had problems with his bug, but eventually it did work and he got his information. Thank goodness he wasn't caught.

I mentioned earlier that I had three experiences with the Watergate scandal. Unfortunately, the last one cost me a lot more than the first two.

It was May of 1973 when I traveled to Los Angeles to meet with a supplier. He had invited me to stay at his home and watch the Chicago Blackhawks play in the Stanley Cup finals which were blacked out on Chicago television.

My supplier's name was Howard and the first time we had done business was in 1972 when I introduced his product in a major advertising campaign. I eventually found out that Howard was not totally honest with me and that he had shipped me defective merchandise that caused a heavy return rate and eventually a large loss for my new company. JS&A had subsequently developed a very strong quality control prescreening system.

Howard was inviting me to Los Angeles to explore the possibility of buying all his remaining inventory and to let me see a few new ideas he had. I also planned to see a few more of my suppliers during the trip.

Howard was an enthusiastic, intense, fast-talking ex-New Yorker who seemed to have unlimited energy. I always marveled at his enthusiasm and drive, which caused me to overlook his worst character trait—his dishonesty.

Howard and I had dinner at his home, and then Howard and I retired to the living room of his two-bedroom apartment.

We were relaxing and watched the NBC national evening news to hear the latest Watergate developments. These were sounding more and more like a daytime soap opera. Every night, a new discovery, revelation, or indictment was announced, and the continuing story was now dominating the news.

That evening, however, seemed to be the most depressing. It was

Chicago Daily News

May 22, 1973

Norman Mark

Now you, too, can play the Watergate game

Like many Americans, Joe Sugarman and Howard Mercer are trying to find a brighter side to Watergate.

The Watergate Game

About two weeks ago, Joe, who sells pocket computers and other gadgets from his Northbrook home, was visiting Howard in Redondo Beach, Calif. (Howard, incidentally, is suing American Telephone and Telegraph on grounds that the phone company is harassing him for selling an automatic telephone dialing device.)

The two men watched the Black Hawks lose the Stanley Cup playoffs on TV. Then they became even more discouraged when NBC News later revealed that top Nixon administration officials had been indicted,

Like most good Americans, Howard and Joe immediately went out for a hamburger and began talking about Watergate. Howard said, "There has got to be something funny in this." Joe suggested they create a Watergate Game.

An anonymous lady at the next table giggled when she overheard Joe's idea and, thus, a new industry was born.

BY 4 A.M., "THE Watergate Scandal: a game of coverup and deception for the whole family," had been created. Within a week, investors with $250,000 (presumably delivered in cash in attache cases), were backing the game. A public relations firm was hired, an advertising agency became part of the team, a sales organization with 60 men began scouting drug stores and supermarkets, 5,500 square feet of warehouse and office space in Elk Grove Village was rented, five major playing card manufacturers agreed to print the game, and a computer firm was lined up to do the billing for a new company, American Symbolic Corp., which will market the $2.99 card game.

On June 11, when some 15,000 stores should be carrying the game, Joe and Howard will begin advertising on the Tonight and Today Shows, local evening newscasts and even All in the Family. Meanwhile, Joe and Howard are about to set off across the country to do TV interviews about their game.

(Joe insists he has done work for the CIA, the FBI and Army intelligence, which after all may be part of his cover for producing the game.)

Having revealed all the above (I granted neither Joe nor Howard even limited immunity), we began the game. The instructions say it is to be played on dark street corners in the early hours of the morning, but we played in a recreation room of a north suburban home. It wasn't very clandestine.

The instructions also say that players are encouraged to destroy important cards in the 54-card deck, but we never did that. I presume that was entered into the record to spur sales.

IN THE GAME, THE cards are dealt and one person becomes the accuser. He puts a card face down and supposedly tells everyone what it is. Everyone else also puts down a card; then, the accuser must guess which person, if any, is lying and has not matched his card.

If the accuser is wrong, he must take a penalty card. For instance, when I put my White House Aide card down, I accused Howard of lying. He wasn't; so I took a penalty card that indicated I committed perjury, losing 125 points for me. (A Big Contributor penalty card loses zero points, just as in real life.)

There are two wild cards, one of them titled "Attorney General's Wife." (The game is so secretive that this card is not mentioned as a wild card in the instructions.)

When the game is over, the instructions advise players to destroy the scraps of paper with the scores. (The game comes complete with cards, but with no paper shredder, a major oversight.)

The instructions conclude that the "game is not recommended for those who believe in fair play, honesty and the American electoral system."

Howard, 29, said that, "like most young people, we tend to be liberal." Joe, 35, didn't think that was the motivation for creating the game.

But then maybe both were just playing a game.

Newspaper columnists had a ball describing the game. Here is but one example.

announced that John Mitchell and John Ehrlichman had been indicted in the Watergate scandal—an indictment that truly shocked the nation. "What next?" I asked, as Howard just sat there in silence.

"I don't know," was his reply. "It just doesn't make sense anymore."

"Ya know, Howard, the timing's perfect for a Watergate game," I said. "The rules could be a riot."

Howard jumped up. "Wow, what a great idea! Sure, a Watergate game! Brilliant idea! Let's do it."

And so the Watergate Scandal game was born that May evening in Howard's apartment in Redondo Beach, California—a suburb of Los Angeles.

Howard and I stayed up until late in the evening working on our plans. I developed the game, the rules, and the instructions while Howard drew up the marketing and public relations plans. We were to be partners and my job was to get the cards produced while Howard lined up the sales.

The game was quite clever. The box it came in proclaimed, "A game of cover-up and deception for the whole family," and consisted of cards with such names as Phone Tapper, Campaign Chief, Hired Saboteur, Presidential Advisor, and Attorney General. The wild card was the Attorney General's wife who at the time was very outspoken.

The object of the game was to cover up and cheat, but if you got caught, you picked a penalty card that assigned you a number of points. The more points you received, the bigger the loser you were. Penalties included one hundred points for being indicted, fifty points for being exposed by the press, and no points for being a big contributor—just as in real life.

Some of the lines used in the instructions included: "This game may be further enhanced by playing it in such places as under a table, behind closed doors, and on dark street corners. Although the game is not intended for gambling purposes, passing the buck is perfectly O.K. Players have been known to bribe the dealer, stack the deck, remove and destroy important cards, and 'bug' other players."

My first job was to get somebody to print a few thousand decks right away. When I arrived home, I worked through the night to do all the artwork and typesetting for the card game, the box, and the instructions. Meanwhile Howard started contacting a public relations firm, lining up the publicity appearances and a national TV tour for both of us.

I located a card manufacturer, convinced him that we needed the cards quickly, and he cooperated. Within ten days we had performed a miracle. Not only did we have the cards, but we had the box as well. Meanwhile the PR firm arranged a big press conference for us at the Watergate in Washington where we were going to unveil the game for the first time.

Before the press conference, Howard called me all excited. "Joe, they're going crazy over this idea. Everybody wants to buy the game. The stores are clamoring for it. We've got to produce a million if we're going to capitalize on this fad!"

A million?" I asked. "Who's going to raise the money to pay for a million? Besides, that's too many games to start with."

"No, it isn't, Joe. I can sell a million just here in California. They are all going crazy for the idea," replied Howard.

"But, Howard, if they're going crazy, where are the orders?" I asked.

Howard proceeded to explain that the orders take a few weeks to issue and assured me that everybody promised him that he would have more orders than he could fill. He insisted that we didn't have time to waste and had to proceed with the production of the game if we wanted to capitalize on the Watergate news that were making headlines daily.

The game would sell for three dollars and cost distributors approximately $1.25. It cost us about 50 cents per game, so we stood to do quite well if we sold a million. But I still had my doubts.

I told Howard that I didn't want to risk any more of my capital. I had already paid out $5,000 to get the first batch of cards and boxes printed and didn't want to risk any more money until I knew for sure that the game really sold.

Howard suggested I contact my original JS&A investors and have them available for a sales presentation he would make in person. He would pass through Chicago on the way to our press conference in Washington and would talk to my group.

Howard came to my home and we held the presentation in my basement. I introduced Howard to my investors and he gave one of the most exciting presentations I have ever heard. It was so good that I, like my investors, ended up pledging money to produce a compromise 400,000 games without seeing one order and without talking to one buyer.

We all realized that Howard did not have a single penny in the deal, but his excuse was that the major effort he had to make was going to cost him a fortune in travel expenses. So nobody pressed the issue. In fact, we actually advanced him all his travel expenses.

My investors had trusted me before and had received a good return on their investment. They felt that with dynamo Howard and my creative talent they couldn't lose.

Howard and I flew to Washington and held our press conference. The turnout was great. Reporters received copies of the game and photographed a few models actually playing it. The publicity made everything from the Wall Street Journal to Time magazine, and radio stations and newspapers were calling us from around the country for interviews.

My big job was production. Working around the clock, I got not only the production organized but the packaging, the point-of-purchase displays, and the warehousing. It was a very difficult job with each project presenting its own set of problems.

Finally the games were in production and Howard arranged a tour for me. I was to appear on a number of TV shows in the Midwest while Howard would appear in California.

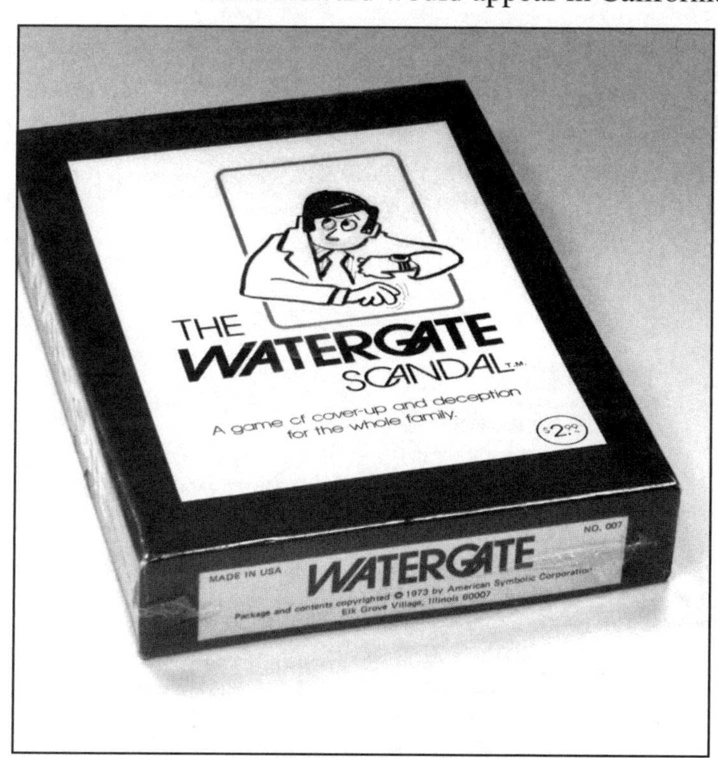

The Watergate Scandal game sold for $2.99.

My first TV show was a disaster. The TV reporter started out the interview with the question, "Mr. Sugarman, how can you make fun of a serious thing like Watergate?"

I replied, "America needs to laugh at itself, to poke fun at itself. We need to laugh at a time like this."

But then, to my amazement, the reporter retaliated, "But surely Mr. Sugarman, making people laugh is one thing, but capitalizing on the misfortune of others is a disgrace. You say America needs someone poking fun at its politics and making money off the problems of others. No, Mr. Sugarman, you should be ashamed of yourself."

The reporter then started a tirade about the seriousness of the problem and urged the listeners to express their views on the telephone. Every one of them made me feel like crawling into a hole.

"I'm sorry," the reporter said. "I really feel it's my duty to tell it like it is."

I called Howard that night as I lay in bed wondering what went wrong. Howard still had no orders, but he said he would have some

THE NEW YORK TIMES, THURSDAY, MAY 24, 1973

SHOP TALK

For $3 You Can Have Your Own Watergate 'Game Plan'

The Senate investigations into the Watergate scandal may be grinding out slowly, but two enterprising men are already capitalizing on the nation's current fascination.

Howard Mercer, a former Los Angeles disk jockey turned inventor, and Joe Sugarman, a Chicago advertising executive, have dreamed up the "Watergate Scandal Game." Any citizen with $3 in unmarked bills may buy it to play at home with friends or loved ones.

The object of the game—actually, it's no more than a deck of cards marked with such designations as Phone Tapper, Presidential Advisor, Big Contributor, Attorney General or Attorney General's Wife—is to lie, cheat, cover up and, if possible, even bribe the dealer. When a player is proven a liar, he must take a penalty card and a certain number of points is subtracted from his score.

The game's inventors have been especially tongue-in-cheek about penalties. A Big Contributor is fined nothing; being asked to resign costs 10 points, while being fired is 25. Penalties go up from 50 points for exposure by the press, to 200 for a prison sentence.

Cards are kept face down on the table and players may lie their heads off. The point is not to be caught red-handed by the Accuser, or player to the right of the dealer. He may also lie, but not be exposed.

The game should be in stores in about two weeks.

AMERICAN NOTES

Cashing In on Watergate

It was only a matter of time—and not much time—before various entrepreneurs began flooding the market with Watergate games, gadgets and paraphernalia. Those who like to relax at home with a good scandal can test their aim at a Watergate dart board, or brood over a Watergate jigsaw puzzle, or even write their friends on Watergate stationery. Or they can listen to a recording of the first (but undoubtedly not the last) country-and-western Watergate ballad, *At the Watergate (The Truth Come Pourin' Out)*. Sample lyric: "If you're wonderin' why they wouldn't blow the whistle, it's no mystery/ Lots of cash and lots of hints of Executive clemency."

In the Washington *Post*, Columnist Tom Donnelly reported coming across *The Watergate Cookbook*, written, he said, by people "deep in the soup" and featuring recipes for "purée of scoundrel, hush-money puppies and tongue à la Martha." Donnelly was only kidding; there is no such cookbook—not yet. But Howard Mercer, an inventor, and Joe Sugarman, an advertising executive, have created a slick card game called "the Watergate Scandal: a game of cover-up and deception for the whole family." The pious instructions read: "To win: nobody in the Watergate Scandal wins. There are just losers. Once the cards are dealt, however, the object of the game is to lie and cheat as much as possible."

Says Kirby Anderson of Cambridge, Mass., whose Urban Systems Products once marketed the Godfather Game and the Howard Hughes Game but has decided against Watergate: "The overall connotation is really kind of sickening."

THE PUZZLE OF WATERGATE

a jigsaw puzzle that will bug you

THE NATIONAL OBSERVER

June 2, 1973

Last year it was the "Godfather Game." This year? Uh-huh. Former Los Angeles disc jockey **Howard Mercer** and a Chicago advertising executive, **Joe Sugarman,** have devised "The Watergate Scandal Game." The game is no more than a deck of cards with designations such as Attorney General, Attorney General's Wife, Big Contributor, Phone Tapper, Presidential Adviser, and so on. The point of the game is to lie, cheat, cover up, and bribe the dealer. To be caught means being fined, unless you're a Big Contributor, for whom there is no penalty. The penalties include 10 points for resigning, 25 points for being fired, 50 points for exposure in the press, and 200 points for going to jail.

We got lots of publicity from our announcement of the game.

soon. He didn't sound too enthusiastic, but we were already committed and I knew Howard would come through.

My next interview was in a different city and also on TV. This reporter was a woman, considerably more friendly, and I was confident the interview would not be as bad as the last one. There were no phones in the studio for audience response. Prior to the show the reporter sympathized with my entrepreneurial spirit and was amazed at the short time it took to bring the product to market. But then the red light went on and the interview began.

"Mr. Sugarman, how could you make fun of a serious problem like Watergate?"

Not too worried, I answered, "America needs to laugh at itself. We need to make light of our serious problems. We must be able to poke fun at even our most serious misfortunes."

Suddenly, as if transformed into a witch, this friendly reporter proceeded to tear the game and me apart, live before a large St. Louis audience. I turned red, sweat forming on my brow, as I tried in vain to present my position. After the interview, this monster of a reporter turned back into that sympathetic lady. But it was too late.

I tried reaching Howard again that night. His wife answered the phone and I asked for Howard. She cupped the phone but I could hear her yell, "Howard, telephone."

"Howard replied, "Tell him I'm not home," which I heard even through the cupped phone.

"What?" I said. "Tell Howard I just heard him say that and I better talk to him." But Howard refused to come to the phone. I knew something was wrong.

I had one interview left and I was determined to finish it and immediately return home to find out what was going on. The TV reporter sat me in a chair on a talk show set, the red light went on, and we were on the air.

Mr. Sugarman, how could you make light of such a serious subject like Watergate?"

I looked at the reporter, paused for a moment and said, "I don't know. I'm embarrassed to be associated with this dumb game and I'm truly sorry I ever got involved in this thing in the first place. It's a stupid idea, and as far as I'm concerned, it was a big mistake."

The reporter looked at me dumbfounded. "But, Mr. Sugarman, don't you think Americans need to laugh at themselves, need to poke fun during serious times like these?" And he proceeded to try to convince me on the air that what I was doing was indeed good for all Americans.

When I got back to my office, it didn't take long before I realized Howard would no longer be reachable. I did manage to find out that none of the stores would handle the product because it was too controversial.

Once again I was stuck. But we tried to sell the game ourselves with very limited success. We did manage to sell 10,000 games to Canada. We exported 40,000 games to Australia. But in the United States, because we couldn't get distribution and because we couldn't even advertise the game in many magazines, we only sold about 5,000 games.

The 300,000-plus games took up a huge space in our warehouse. I had lost, my investors had lost, and only Howard had come out ahead. Not only had he not put up any money, but his travel expenses had been far less than the advance we gave him.

I was so disappointed with the experience that I have not played the game since then. And, rather than transferring the games to the same warehouse where I kept my Batman credit cards, my Teeny Boppers and Mad records, I just gave them to my investors to liquidate as they saw fit.

I did keep three games. I thought that one of these days I could contribute my failures to the Smithsonian and I certainly wanted to include my latest example.

If I had just concentrated on JS&A and not gone off on another tangent, I would have been way ahead. Hadn't I learned my lessons by now?

21) Out of the Basement

You can have everything in life you want, if you help others get what they want.

Zig Ziglar, Author

I concentrated our advertising in the Wall Street Journal, running very large advertisements that extolled the virtues of my calculators with interesting pictures and extensive copy.

I'd rarely have less than 1,000 words in each ad, and I'd write the copy as if I were a salesman trying to sell my product to a very bright consumer. I respected the intelligence of my readers, so I avoided the stereotyped hype and advertising clichés, I tried to present as much consumer information as possible and I presented this material with respect for my customers' judgment. This respect came across in my ads and consumers responded.

We also created the image of a very large company. Our ads were professional-looking, with no screaming headlines or exaggerated graphics. We consistently maintained this approach so that we soon had good recognition from Journal readers.

By concentrating on the Wall Street Journal, we also became one of their top ten advertisers—right up there with IBM, AT&T, and General Motors. In fact, examining the list of the top ten advertisers, you'd be convinced that JS&A was either a billion-dollar corporation like the rest on the list or, at a minimum, a company with a large corporate headquarters. Yet here we were—the four of us—Mary, Mary Ann, Wendy and I—operating out of the basement of my suburban home in Northbrook, Illinois.

In fact, Wendy wasn't even working full time. She had to look after April who at the time was not quite two years old and was always getting into trouble.

Chicago executives reading the Wall Street Journal would often call us on the phone and ask if they could come out to our corporate headquarters to pick up a calculator directly instead of buying it through the mail.

Rather than lose the sale, we encouraged customers to visit us. Many times I would look out the living room window of my home and see a very well dressed executive, sitting in his car, looking at the address in the advertisement and trying to convince himself that this home was the international headquarters of the huge JS&A empire.

I'd even see some customers sit there for five minutes trying to get up enough nerve to step out of their cars. When they eventually did, the typical customer, newspaper ad in hand, would walk up to the front door and ring the bell. Wendy, who would be carrying April, would answer the door and April usually chose this time to be screaming her lungs out.

Embarrassed and disoriented, our customers would walk down the stairs to the basement and I would end up selling them a calculator. They never failed to leave our home quite surprised. They expected, at a minimum, a skyscraper, and they saw a basement. They expected a huge organization and they saw four people and a screaming baby.

And they talked about it when they got back to their corporate worlds. As word spread, people were soon visiting us out of curiosity, and by mid-1973 there was so much traffic in our basement that we couldn't get much work done. Some of our neighbors were beginning to wonder what was going on, since the front of our house was turning into a parking lot.

There were also people who stopped by before they went to work —some at 6:30 in the morning. Wendy and I didn't appreciate that. Then there were those customers who would stop by at night—sometimes as late as 10:30. Wendy and I didn't like that either. And of course, there was the constant fear that one of our customers was really a professional burglar casing the place for a robbery.

As the traffic grew and the inconvenience mounted, I decided it was time to find a new facility. Just a few blocks away from my home, George Olson, a local real estate man, had converted an old gas station into a modest one-story office building.

The building had a thousand square feet, which seemed huge when compared to our basement which was half the size. And we had to pay rent—six hundred dollars—which seemed like a frightening burden, especially since we had to sign a three-year lease.

I had never had overhead and six hundred dollars a month really bothered me. I feared that my little business would burst its bubble and I'd be stuck with the rent if, one day, times got rough.

But on January 1, 1974, JS&A moved its entire operation from the basement of my home to the corner of Sanders and Dundee roads in Northbrook. I now had overhead and the realization that I had a business with enough space to grow.

22) The Big Jump

"The more tranquil a man becomes, the greater is his success, his influence, his power for good. Calmness of mind is one of the beautiful jewels of wisdom."

James Allen 1864—1912, Author of As A Man Thinketh

Within a few months after we moved into our new offices, I hit upon a very successful ad that I felt was worth advertising nationally in hundreds of magazines and newspapers. The response was so strong that we increased our staff from two people to fifteen and quickly grew out of our thousand square foot space.

The ad that proved so successful was for a liquid crystal calculator, one of the first liquid crystal calculators on the market. Called the Data King 800, it had great features and a good price, and we presented it in a very exciting and forceful manner. But what really made it a big seller was a small paragraph that appeared in the ad:

"Want to exchange your old, outdated calculator for the Data

Four of the 20 operators taking credit card orders over the phone. Our phone lines were always jammed.

King 800 without losing too much money? We've got a way. After you are absolutely satisfied with your Data King 800, send us your outdated unit. JS&A will then send it to a deserving school, nonprofit organization, or charitable institution which in turn will send you a letter of appreciation and a certificate acknowledging your contribution. Then use that contribution as a legitimate deduction on your income tax return. You'll be helping somebody in need while justifying the purchase of the latest calculator technology."

People were so impressed with the service we were providing those needy institutions that they responded in great numbers. Not only did we do well on the campaign, but we helped a number of needy institutions that really appreciated our efforts.

The program netted close to one half million dollars from that single advertisement and represented more money than I thought I'd ever see in my lifetime. That single advertisement changed the entire nature of our business. We now had the staff and the capital to expand and grow.

Our WATS 800 lines had increased from two to six and our cramped operation looked exactly like a bookie joint if you happened to be stopping by to purchase a calculator.

We were so jammed that we knew we had to find newer quarters —a place that gave us an opportunity to operate comfortably and also permit us to grow if we needed more space.

I found a new building in the industrial park a few miles from my home and moved in my fifteen employees and all our furniture. The 6,000 square foot facility seemed huge, but it didn't take me long to fill it up. I bought the piece of property next to the office site and built a warehouse, and we used our previous office site as a retail showroom for the remainder of our 3-year lease.

23) Famous JS&A Customers

"It is our attitude at the beginning of a difficult task which, more than anything else, will affect its successful outcome."
William James 1842—1910, Psychologist, Professor and Author

One of the many thrills of running a well-known national mail order company back then was the very famous clientele that you attracted throughout the years.

When my secretary buzzed me to tell me that Robert Redford was on the phone or Spiro Agnew wanted to talk to me, it no longer seemed unusual.

We had many famous customers, including country and western singers, movie stars, comedians, politicians, newscasters, TV personalities, and many stars of the past.

One of the most exciting orders I received came in 1976. As I passed near the mail desk, one of the young ladies called out to me, "Mr. Sugarman, look who just ordered from us."

I looked at the order and it was from Frank Sinatra. Sinatra had sent us a check accompanied by a letter ordering one of our products.

That very day I was expecting two friends I hadn't seen for a long time. I really wanted to impress them, so I borrowed the Sinatra check and letter.

To understand why I wanted to impress them, you'd have to understand my friends. They were the type of guys who always had to be one up on you. If you bought a new car, they would always talk about a faster, better, or more expensive version of the same model that one of their friends owned. I can remember telling them one year that my next-door neighbor had just installed an underground sprinkling system only to have one of them blurt out, "I know somebody who has a waterfall."

"Who cares?" I would always think, but I could never come up with any real rebuttal to their nonsense.

The Sinatra order, however, gave me a great idea for a practical joke. I was sure my friends would be impressed with my new offices, but I knew they wouldn't admit it. What I wanted to do was really shock them so they couldn't come up with their usual, "That's nothing, Joe," routine.

So I told Mary Stanke to buzz me three minutes after they entered my office and tell me over the intercom, "Mr. Sugarman, Frank Sinatra is on the phone and he'd like to talk to you." Meanwhile, I placed the Sinatra order in the center of a pile of other papers at the side of my desk.

True to form, my friends sat down in front of my desk and proceeded to be unimpressed with our offices or the level of success I had achieved.

Joe, you should see the other offices I just visited yesterday," said one of them in an effort to minimize his impression of our place.

Suddenly, Mary buzzed me on the intercom, "Mr. Sugarman, Frank Sinatra is on the phone and he'd like to talk to you."

I reached for the intercom, "Mary, tell Frank that we got his order and we'll get it out as quickly as possible. Also, tell him I'm in a conference and I can't talk to him right now."

The expressions on my friends' faces were a real delight. Their mouths hung open as they stared in disbelief. Finally one of them waved his hands vehemently and said, "Joe, talk to him please talk to him."

"No, I won't," I said. "You're more important to me than Frank Sinatra."

It didn't take more than a few seconds after that comment for one of my friends to say, "Aw, Joe, that wasn't Frank Sinatra; you're playing a practical joke on us."

"Just one second," I retorted indignantly. I then started searching through my stack of papers looking for the Sinatra order and taking my time in the process.

Finally, I found the order and the check and flipped it to the other side of my desk as if insulted that they would accuse me of trying to deceive them. "Here, take a look."

They examined the letter and the check and noted the current date and sat back once again in disbelief. My practical joke had totally disarmed them. There was nothing they could say to top the mere thought that they were more important to me than Frank Sinatra.

Just before they left, I told them the truth and we all had a good laugh. And the story normally would have ended there except for an episode that took place the following day at exactly the same time.

I was sitting in my office when Mary Stanke buzzed me on the intercom, "Mr. Sugarman, Marlon Brando is on the phone and he'd like

Frank Sinatra
Marlon Brando
Spiro Agnew
Dean Martin
Steve Jobs
Robert Redford
Steve Wozniak
Sammy Davis Jr.
Elvis Presley
Johnny Mathis
Nat King Cole
Lucy Arnaz

Our list of customers reflected many of the celebrities of the time.

to talk to you."

I reached for the intercom and replied, "Mary, my friends are gone."

Indeed, it was Marlon Brando. And we talked for about half an hour about a few of the products we were marketing.

Even when I meet some of these personalities in person, I often discover that they've bought my products years ago.

I had the opportunity to meet Pat Boone at his home one day, only to discover that the watch he was wearing was ours.

Politicians, top corporate executives, and international statesmen used to buy our products. As I mentioned in the beginning of this chapter, it was not surprising to be buzzed on my intercom and hear the name of a famous personality.

The mail order business is one of the few businesses that could cater to such an impressive list of customers. And it certainly adds a degree of excitement to our order-takers' lives.

24) The Growth Continues

"Successful people make decisions quickly and change them slowly if and when at all."

Napoleon Hill, Author of Think and Grow Rich

JS&A grew and grew. I continued to do all the copywriting, as I always did. I'd set the headlines on my photo typesetter and Wendy would set the body type on our IBM composer.

While in the new building, I purchased a new computer, computerized microfilm systems, and acquired every conceivable modern piece of space-age office equipment to make our operation more efficient.

And we continued attracting the most advanced products and building our success and reputation in the process.

Despite our success, I always made it a point to treat all our suppliers and friends with the same respect I had always had for them. Success did not change us. We constantly strived to provide good service and maintain a high degree of honesty and integrity.

One of the reasons for the success of my business was the effort expended by each one of my employees. They learned to respond to every problem by turning that problem into an opportunity to show our customers how we cared.

Mary Stanke is the most brilliant example of a dedicated employee. Trained as a secretary, she worked for Chrysler Corporation for a few years. She then retired to raise her two daughters while her husband handsomely supported his family as a foreman at a Chicago printing company, Rogers Park Press.

When Mary first started she was earning $3.25 an hour. Today she has become the President of JS&A and BluBlocker Corporation and makes a handsome salary.

Her rise through JS&A was not surprising. She worked whatever hours were necessary to get the job done. She was honest, so I could trust her to look after the books and my interests, and she made sure the business ran smoothly even while I was out of town. Actually, it ran better when I was out of town.

What was even more remarkable was how she was able to dedicate herself to her job and yet raise her two children, feed her family, and be a good housewife as well.

Mary also looked after my interests. She warned me about a few people I should have avoided, and she was always right. She adapted to every new level of growth, learning new skills and creating new systems.

If Wendy was the secret to my bouncing back, it was another woman, Mary Stanke, who was the secret to my successful bounce upward.

Mary never had to ask me for a raise. I have always paid her more than she expected and supported her decisions which often were exactly those that I would have made anyway.

Building JS&A was not easy, but with the support of Mary and a staff that followed her example, it is not surprising that JS&A grew.

For every product we advertised we learned that regardless of how we prepared, things could go wrong.

Either we were back-ordered on a product or it arrived defective and we had to return entire shipments. Some of our suppliers went bankrupt and many broke promises to us, causing us to look bad to our customers. The problems associated with our successes were endless with countless disappointments and a stream of unexpected setbacks. But we never gave up and always looked at the yearly balance sheet of our company and saw how we grew an average of 40 percent a year, year after year.

We answered all our correspondence, dealt with customers honestly, and treated every complaint as if it came from a next-door neighbor. My early experiences taught me how important service is in building a company.

We weren't perfect and occasionally we made mistakes, but whenever we did, we admitted it and corrected it in a responsible and prompt manner.

I also learned that whenever I dealt with honest suppliers, they responded responsibly whenever problems arose. Whenever I dealt with dishonest suppliers, they disappeared when problems arose. Problems were always a fact of business life, but I learned quickly how to choose a product. First choose an honest supplier.

JS&A had grown into a highly respected small business with sales of twelve million dollars, a staff of sixty people, and a reputation of service and honesty in all its dealings.

By the summer of 1978, the company was prepared to launch its biggest advertising drive in its continued growth. We were on the way to introducing the most exciting new products in our young history, with a new computer software program and a series of new innovations that would catapult us toward becoming a fifty million dollar-a-year company. The years of hard work were really starting to bear fruit. And then something happened that I didn't expect. When you are successful, you attract a lot of false friends—people who claim that they will do anything for you. And I attracted many of them. I never really knew who were my true friends.

My case was so complicated that I published a comic book which I sent to my 20,000 supporters.

One day, I thought to myself, "I'd love to be broke again and find out who my true friends really are."

A snowstorm hit Chicago dropping 26 inches of snow. Our computer malfunctioned, and the company responsible for repairing it couldn't make it to our office because of the weather. Half our employees were stuck at home. We couldn't even get a plowing company to clear our parking lot. Frustrated I went out and bought a full-sized plow, and one of our employees who knew how to use the plow cleared our place from all that snow.

It took a few weeks to get back to full speed. And in the process, we informed our customers of the delay, offering them a full refund if they wanted one and providing our usual excellent customer service.

One of the letters was received by a customer who also worked for the FTC (Federal Trade Commission), the government agency responsible for policing, among other things, advertising claims. They came to our offices requesting the notice we send out when our shipments are delayed. We cooperated fully with them and showed them the praise we received daily for our customer service. But they didn't care. The FTC had just passed a rule (not a law) that required exact wording on a delay notice. Our delay letter was more consumer friendly, but because we did not have the exact wording required in the new rule, they were going to fine us $100,000.

My reputation and my company's reputation was being attacked by the FTC, and although we tried to reason with them and show them what a good company we were, they wanted to make us an example to all the other mail order companies. Rather than cave into their demands which seemed like blackmail, I took out a major ad campaign telling my story and requesting an oversight hearing in Congress to investigate the FTC and their tactics, many of which I don't have the space in this book to cover.

People were so touched by what I was going through that they were sending me contributions—all of which I returned. I was determined to win this without any help except for the letters to Congress that I asked people to write.

I got my oversight hearing in Washington which turned out to be a scam. I eventually paid them over time a settlement that was more than the original demand. I had lost millions, my company was on the rocks, and everything I had built up was lost. I had to sell my office building and other assets to avoid bankruptcy. I learned a lot from my fight with the FTC and I also learned a lot from my mail order business.

25) My Mail Order Lessons

"We Make A Living By What We Get, We Make A Life By What We Give."

Winston Churchill, British Prime Minister

The mail order business was like a rapid series of learning experiences.

When I started in business, my ad successes were about eight to two. For every eight failures, there seemed always to be two advertisements that were successful enough to make up for the eight that weren't. And the eight that weren't gave me a real education.

I learned a great deal about people. I could tell within a few moments of meeting someone whether I was going to be successful in working with them. Through all my failures I discovered that certain actions by my suppliers and the people I did business with were going to lead inevitably to these suppliers' success or failure.

Once I realized the subtle things that seemed to force people to succeed or fail, I started to develop a set of philosophies and began using these philosophies.

So accurate are these philosophies that I can often predict the outcome of my actions even though the outcome is contrary to what everybody would expect.

My success rate improved with experience to a point where I rarely failed.

The mail order industry and the rapid sequence of failures and successes were a proving ground for my Success Forces philosophies. Sure, I had laid the groundwork before I had run my first advertisement, but it was my business experiences that confirmed these philosophies.

The Success Forces have become so important to me that I have learned to follow them closely, for I know that I will continue to succeed despite myself if I follow them.

The Success Forces philosophy is not something you can feel, see, or measure. It nevertheless is a real force that exerts an energy that when followed will force you toward success.

Simply knowing these forces will be an excellent starting point. Then you can observe the results when you follow the force versus when you don't. Only then can you prove to yourself how effective my Success Forces really are.

In the following section I will describe my Success Forces in detail. The first section of this book was designed to give you more of an insight into my evolution—of the failures that taught me what didn't work and the successes that taught me what did.

This next section will present the very basic forces that I am convinced will work for anyone. They are not complicated. In fact, they are rather basic—but they are incredibly powerful if you believe in them and use them.

SECTION II

INTRODUCTION

The Theory of Success Forces

For every action you take, a force is created, and this force will either steer you toward success or toward failure.

I am also convinced that there are seven very important Success Forces that, if understood, will bring you success—often despite yourself.

My very prosperous Chinese friends have a philosophy that seems to tie in very closely with mine. They feel that there are existing forces in nature that guide your destiny. If you are honest and honorable and follow the natural direction to which these forces point you, you will succeed.

These forces aren't meant to be spiritual or mystical, but rather the very subtle effects of your actions. If you find it hard to visualize the concept of Success Forces, picture a scale with one tray on each side balanced at a point in the center. Put weight on one side and it is forced down while the other side is forced up. Add enough weight on the side that's high and it will eventually sink below the other side. So it is with Success Forces. Take actions that add force to the success side of your scale and you create a force that brings success. Take actions that result in the opposite and the results are just the opposite.

What makes me an authority on success? That's why I included a biographical sketch of my life in the first part of this book. I have been on both sides of the scale enough times to know what works and what doesn't. If all I knew was success, I doubt I would have been able to discover the real Success Forces and then personally witness them working.

You might look at Success Forces as karmic in nature. In fact, when I wrote the first version of this book some 33 years ago, I didn't even know what karma was, nor many spiritual philosophies that I follow today. I'm amazed with all that I've learned since I wrote the first version of this book.

SUCCESS FORCE 1

Always Be Honest

Honesty is the strongest and most powerful Success Force.

Now you might have expected something more dramatic than honesty to lead off this section of my book, but if you'll follow my logic, you'll discover just how powerful honesty as a Success Force really is, and then we can build from there.

First, let's discuss the misconceptions. Some people feel that in business, to come out on top, you sometimes have to lie, cheat. and bribe. And you might have thought that the poor, naive. honest person doing business with someone who is unscrupulous is really at a disadvantage. These are misconceptions.

Honesty will put you right on top. No matter whom you confront, no matter what situation you find yourself in, honesty does work. And it works, as you will see, so effectively that your whole perception of dishonesty is bound to change.

In business, whenever I see anybody do anything dishonest, I tell my staff, "Don't worry. They won't be around very long." I say this with such confidence that Mary Stanke once asked me why I was so sure.

I couldn't tell her why, but I told her to keep an eye on three companies and two individuals and track their paths. "See where they go and how quickly they fail."

One by one, she tracked them and they each followed my predictions. How could I predict the future in this regard so accurately?

I can remember an experience with a non-profit organization's magazine in 1978. We had been advertising in this fraternal magazine for almost five years, and we were scheduled for a new digital watch advertisement in their November issue.

At the last minute, the magazine's publisher called Mary Stanke and canceled us from the issue. I didn't usually work personally with the magazines we placed ads in, but I felt I needed an explanation. What went wrong?

So I called the publisher whom I had known for five years, but I couldn't get an explanation from him that made sense. He couldn't give me any straight answers.

It wasn't until that issue finally came out that we saw why. One of our competitors was running a digital watch ad in that issue and on the same page where we had planned to run our digital watch ad.

Was the publisher bribed to cancel our ad and put our competitor's ad in? I don't know. I did know that the advertiser who had taken our ad placement had a bad reputation. Was I upset? Not at all. It was an indication to me that both the advertiser and the magazine were dishonest and would eventually pay their dues. As it happened, the advertiser eventually went bankrupt, leaving the magazine holding the bag for a great deal of money. We stopped advertising in the publication which deprived the magazine of at least $100,000 in advertising revenue. We discovered a few new fraternal magazines that worked very well for us—ones we might not have discovered had it not been for the rejection we got from the magazine that treated us so badly.

I have observed enough dishonesty to know that there is a very strong failure force associated with it. More importantly, however, is that there is a very powerful Success Force created by honesty. Without a doubt, the more honest you are, the more successful you will ultimately become.

Let's acknowledge a few facts about honesty. First, it's relative. What is honest to you might not be to somebody else. And then there's the degree of honesty to be considered. Honesty to an extreme may be both impractical and lacking in common sense. Driving ten miles to return a nickel to a customer you overcharged might be impractical and ludicrous, even though it is honest.

Each time you are honest and conduct yourself with honesty, a Success Force will drive you toward greater success. Each time you lie, even with a little white lie, there are strong forces pushing you toward failure.

With this in mind, each time you have a choice to be honest or dishonest and you choose to be honest, your chances of success are greater.

The force may not work right away. As a matter of fact, it may not show up for months. It may be very painful to tell the truth, and you may even question how telling the truth in a painful situation will result in your eventual success. But it will.

The more painful it is to tell the truth, the greater the Success Force you create. How do you get this Success Force to work for you and how do you know if it does indeed work? That will come from your own personal experiences. The simple fact that you are aware of honesty as a powerful Success Force will help you discover this important principle.

I will cite just a few observations that I have made, although they are not as convincing as having you discover for yourself just how effective honesty can really be in bringing you success.

At JS&A I've always insisted on honesty as our number one policy. We treated our customers with respect and we had a cardinal rule that all questions, when asked, were answered honestly.

We also conduct our business relationships with honesty. If we ordered 1,000 calculators and the manufacturer shipped us 1,020 by mistake and billed us for only 1,000, we let him know and paid for the 20 extra pieces or returned them.

No employee could be fired for telling the truth at JS&A—no matter how embarrassing. All of our advertising was first checked by the manufacturers and then by our lawyers. Every statement was checked thoroughly. If there was an exaggeration, it was toned down to reflect the truth. Every fact had to be accurate. But if by chance we made a mistake in an advertising claim, we always admitted it, corrected the mistake, and advised our customers.

If one of our customers was treated poorly and it was our fault, we admitted it and corrected the matter to the fair and just satisfaction of the customer. We also hired very honest people.

Quite often I've known people who are willing to swing a dishonest deal, make a fast buck and disappear. They never really make it, despite what you hear. In my experience in business, every dishonest businessman is eventually found out and travels under a dark cloud. He doesn't see the cloud, but everybody he deals with does.

Sure, the dishonest individual makes a fast buck, but he pays for it over and over again in the long run. Remember, he's constantly creating negative forces—the opposite of Success Forces.

There are indeed some people who are dishonest and seem to get away with it. But do they? I know a rip-off artist who cheated thousands of consumers and supposedly got away with it, making millions of dollars and driving around in a Rolls Royce.

But that's from the outside. His family life failed, he had major health problems, and he experienced real heartbreaks and failures. I contend that dishonesty will create a failure force that often manifests itself in other ways—often not apparent to the outside observer.

But if you're in business and you agree that honesty is the best policy, how do you avoid being "taken" and still keep this powerful force working in your favor? What is the key?

The key is to protect yourself. By protecting yourself, I mean dealing with honest people to start with. When you deal with honest people, chances are you'll work better together and you'll have trust in each other. You'll spend less time worrying about each other's motives and more time on how you can both succeed. There will be less time-consuming politics, and you'll feel free to move on the other person's word when delay can mean a lost opportunity.

When you deal with honest people, it is a great pleasure and it is enjoyable; great things get accomplished in a very short period of time. Contrast this with a dishonest relationship. You're constantly cautious. You're spending more time protecting yourself than you are devoting yourself to your business. You sign detailed contracts that in a dishonest relationship don't mean much anyway.

That's not to say you don't sign contracts with people you feel are honest. Quite the contrary. An honest person may be very honest, but he may have a poor memory. Sign contracts or at least exchange letters. Do something to document your decisions and understandings.

When I first meet somebody, I try to find out if they're honest. If I feel they are honest and I can trust them, we can develop a good business relationship. That's how I pick some of my products. I first pick the people.

When a manufacturer would present a product to me at JS&A, it didn't take too long before I discovered whether the guy was lying to me. When this happened, his chances of having me market his product were very slim.

Once a gentleman presented me with a product and volunteered the price he was allegedly paying for it from the Far East. It just so happened I knew what that particular product cost from the Far East (which was considerably less than what he told me) and exactly what he was paying for it. He had no idea that I had that information and because of that, I knew he was dishonest.

Now you might say, "Well, that's the way you do business. You use a little white lie every once in awhile."

Not true. I would rather he had said nothing than lie to me. How do I know if his next statement will be true? If he volunteers a dishonest statement, how can I rely on any answer he'd give to my questions?

I was very reluctant to deal with this man. Deep inside I really didn't want to do business with him. If he had been honest, he could have walked away with a sale for his product. But he walked away with nothing, and the funny part is that he doesn't know why.

There are so many ways to distinguish the phonies from the honest individuals. Just ask enough questions and they'll dig themselves into a hole.

Honesty has to be worked at. It's not easy because sometimes it seems that the easiest thing is to tell a little white lie to avoid embarrassment. But don't do it. Every lie brings into existence a negative failure force and every honest answer a positive Success Force.

Now I'm not perfect either. I have made statements that have come back and hit me like a boomerang.

Even though I work at being honest, I do slip. It's human to err, but I've also seen these slips come back and haunt me with a negative failure force that makes me regret any dishonesty—even a white lie.

If you can use honesty as your guiding philosophy, you'll be amazed at how powerful it is. I find that honesty is a strong and effective force in advertising. I always bring up a negative feature of a product and I avoid exaggerating any of the positive features of whatever I sell. My customers sense this honesty and know they are dealing with an honest company, and they therefore respond.

Whenever I try to cover up a small flaw or fault in a product, it haunts me, and I've never succeeded. Whenever I have been frank and honest, I've been my most successful.

Honesty is a very powerful force. It may be the rougher road to take. It may be a little embarrassing at times, but if you use honesty as the cornerstone of the Success Force philosophy, you'll never go wrong.

SUCCESS FORCE 2

Learn From Your Failures

One of the most powerful Success Forces is failure. Every time you fail you create a positive force for success.

To explain how this force works, let's examine a baby when he takes his first steps. What happens? He falls. So he tries and tries again. Finally, after many failures, the little toddler starts to walk—wobbly at first, but he is walking.

The baby at first failed to walk, but each time he fell, he learned something. From all his failures, he was able to learn enough to balance and walk without falling.

I contend that this process works throughout one's entire life. We learn from our failures. Pile up enough failures and success is a sure bet. But most of us don't like failure. In fact, we avoid it at all costs, even if it means missing out on an opportunity.

I am firmly convinced that learning from failure is such a powerful Success Force that it gives me the reassurance to try almost anything, for I know that even if I fail, it will create a force for success later.

Take action, learn from your failures, bounce back and know that every failure brings you closer and closer to success.

When I was twenty years old and working in New York on Spectra '59, I had already experienced many failures in life. I had a philosophy in 1959 that I continue to believe in.

Every time I failed, I said to myself, "Well, I'll put it in my back pocket and one of these days when I need it, I'll reach in and take it out." I meant, of course, the lesson that I had learned. In today's computer jargon, I might have simply said that I was "storing my experience in my hard drive."

The Chinese have a theory which they express about failure and success. Simply stated, it says that no matter what course of action you take, whether you succeed or fail, it is more important that you at least act in an attempt to succeed or fail. They believe that if you take action, in the long run you will succeed, regardless of how many times you fail. They view "not taking action" as a much bigger disgrace than failing.

Certainly among the most interesting aspects of my life is how many times I have failed. Whenever I give a speech, I always start off with a story about a few failures I've had that might interest the audience.

Then I tell my audience, "I'm here today not because I'm a huge success but because I have probably failed more times than anybody in this room. But from all of these failures, I have learned things and from the things that I've learned, I have been able to succeed."

If my premise is correct, it's just a matter of time until those failures start to add up and create a tremendous force to succeed. But there's a problem. Who likes to fail?

Most of us go through life with big egos and try to avoid failure. However, you must realize that failure is one of the Success Forces, and to get the "opportunity" to fail is also to be able to increase your opportunity for success in the future.

I was supposedly an expert at picking products to market through my company. Yet the truth is that every product I thought was going to be a huge success turned out average at best, and many products I thought were average or below turned out to be super winners. And the story is the same for all my endeavors. Every time I thought I was on the way to great success I was disappointed, and every time I least expected it, I scored big.

There's an interesting conclusion here. If all I ever did was attempt those projects I was convinced were sure winners, I would have achieved only average success. It was my acceptance of possible failure that let me attempt those seemingly average or losing opportunities that eventually led to great success.

If you then realize that failure is indeed a force—more powerful than success—then you'll understand one of the truly powerful forces that works in your favor each time you experience it.

But there's a key. Just as "protect yourself' was the key to honesty, the key to failure is to "bounce back." Look at the failure as a learning experience. Learn from your failure those things that are worth putting in your back pocket and then tackle the next project.

I have a philosophy that makes it very easy to accept failure. I say that everything happens for the best even if you don't think so at the time. And further, I am never attached to any outcome. If it turns out to be a failure of some sort, so be it. I know deep inside that this will be for the best although I may not realize it at the time.

Learning from your failures creates a great Success Force. So realize quickly the lessons learned, realize that failure isn't so bad after all, and, above all bounce back.

The problem with most people is that they don't learn from their failures or they give up. Failure is only as powerful as what you get out of it. By understanding just how powerful it can be and accepting it as a Success Force, you will gain more courage to attempt new and different things.

Many of the success books talk about persistence as the ultimate way to achieve success. Isn't persistence really a way of saying, "I've failed but I know why I failed; I've learned something new, and I must continue until I succeed."

Not many people are willing to give failure a second opportunity. They fail once and it's all over. The bitter pill of failure—often combined with embarrassment and deflated egos—is more than most people can handle.

I have failed so many times, even during my supposedly successful years with JS&A, that I am convinced of the power and the impact failure has as one of the Success Forces.

I'm not suggesting that if you want to go out and achieve success, you should go out and try to fail. I am saying that you should attempt things in life with the attitude that if you fail, you should consider it a blessing—a Success Force that later will let you succeed beyond your wildest imagination.

In some countries, failure can be devastating. The aura surrounding failure in Japan, for instance, has caused many a businessman to commit suicide rather than face the disdain of his peers. On the other hand, failure does not have that stigma in America. The freedom to fail is one of our most precious freedoms and accounts for the great entrepreneurial spirit we nourish in the United States.

To fail and bounce back requires a lot of resilience. I don't want to give you the impression that failure was a pleasure for me. It wasn't. It was quite painful. I can remember working for a solid year only to lose every penny I had in a bad deal or in a promotion that didn't work. Remember my Batman credit card, my Teeny Bopper promotion and my Watergate game?—all painful and hard lessons. But I never gave up and I always bounced back.

Let's put this in the form of a metaphor. Everybody in life is given a pail of oysters. In one of the oysters is a valuable pearl. It is up to you to find the pearl by opening each oyster until you find it. But oysters are hard to open and if you're doing it with your bare hands, it can cut and hurt you. Too many people try to open just the first few oysters and when they don't find a pearl, they give up. "Too hard to open those oysters," might be the excuse. But in one of those oysters is a pearl and it might be the first one, the tenth one or even the last one. It is there for sure; you just have to be persistent and find it.

My failures weren't pleasant and I certainly wouldn't want to relive those days. I doubt anybody relishes those kinds of memories. But I do owe my present success to those earlier failures, the things I learned, and the positive Success Forces they created.

If you're willing to accept failure and learn from it, if you're willing to consider failure as a blessing in disguise and bounce back, you've got the potential of harnessing one of the most powerful Success Forces.

SUCCESS FORCE 3

Turn Problems Into Opportunities

A powerful Success Force can be created by the way you view a problem.

Problems, as well as failures, are negative things. But problems have a hidden ingredient that makes them very effective in creating a Success Force. The word is "opportunity."

Each problem has hidden in it an opportunity so powerful that it literally dwarfs the problem. The greatest success stories were created by people who recognized a problem and turned it into an opportunity.

If you can program yourself to view every problem as an opportunity, can you imagine what a powerful force you can apply to your life?

When the digital watch first came out, it had a high defective rate. At JS&A we looked at this problem as an opportunity to prove to our customers what a good company we were.

We gave customers loaner watches while we repaired their defective ones. We refunded their postage costs for mailing their watches to us.

We soon had many compliments on our concept. We received letters from customers who told us that they were so amazed at the service they received that they told their friends about it and their friends bought watches from us too. One man reported that he was personally responsible for the sale of a dozen watches, while another had convinced his entire company of the value we provided with our warranty.

We turned a real problem into an opportunity to prove our commitment of service to our customers, and the results were quite successful.

The digital watch story is only one example of how we took problems and turned them into opportunities. Whenever you have a problem, the best thing to say to yourself is, "Okay, I've got a problem but hidden in there is an opportunity. Where is it, and what is it?"

Sometimes you can't see it. It's well hidden. Other times, simply looking for the opportunity forces one to pop out. Even the more difficult-to-find opportunities, those that you may not be able to see right away, pop up if you work at it long enough.

There is no exception to this rule. It works as surely as the other

Success Forces. Let the problem consume you and you get stuck. But take that problem, turn it around by finding the opportunity, and you create a Success Force.

Many things in life are similar to the problem-opportunity relationship. When found in the ground a diamond may resemble a piece of coal full of black carbon. But that ugly stone—when polished, cut, and placed in a setting—becomes the most beautiful gem in the world.

Look at how you take problems and turn them into opportunities as in the coal-diamond example. Your opportunities are camouflaged, just like the diamond. Spend a little time polishing or even looking at your problem in a different way, and you'll be amazed at how the opportunities pop up.

I'd like to offer a few suggestions on how to help you find that opportunity in your next problem. First, say to yourself that there is an opportunity. Without conviction, you'll never find it.

Second, restate the problem. Often just stating it differently will open up an entire new perspective that will produce a whole list of opportunities. Let me give you a little lesson in restating a problem.

Let's take the digital watch example. We could have stated the problem very simply by saying, "Providing service for digital watches is a problem."

Or, we may say, "Consumers are upset with the quality of digital watches and they are concerned about service."

Both of the above state the problem quite clearly and are accurate statements. However, let's restate our problem a little differently: "What can JS&A do to remove the problem of digital watch service? What would our customers appreciate about our servicing their defective watches?"

Already you see that by simply restating the problem, you get a totally different perspective. We went from a problem and then took it full circle to viewing the problem from the customer's perspective. That is exactly how we turned the service program into an opportunity. We restated the problem, and simply by doing that, we got a different perspective.

Another good example of turning problems into opportunities is the example of how we launched toll-free order taking. We had a problem—the desire to fill customer orders without a signature confirmation. We turned this into a major opportunity.

Discovering BluBlocker sunglasses is another example. In 1986, I was doing an 8-page insert for United Airlines, and one of the products I was to feature was no longer available as the company making it went bankrupt. I remember looking through a pair of sunglasses a friend of mine wore that had a story that seemed to be very compelling to me. I called up my friend. I had a problem. I had to fill a space in my insert. The opportunity was to get this new and exciting pair of sunglasses featured in the insert. The rest is history. BluBlocker sunglasses were a huge hit and it all stemmed from a problem I had with one of my suppliers.

Looking at problems from different perspectives and restating a problem from a different viewpoint often lead to discovering the opportunity present in every problem. With a little practice and a positive attitude, you'll always find that opportunity. It's always there.

Looking at your problems as just problems never brings success. Looking at your problems as opportunities will create a powerful Success Force.

SUCCESS FORCE 4

Focus Your Energy

If you've ever taken a magnifying glass on a sunny day and focused the concentrated beam of the sun on a piece of paper, you know the power of concentration. The paper will ignite in a matter of seconds. Without the ability to concentrate the sun's rays, the paper would never burn.

The same concept can also be described as one of my Success Forces. By zeroing in on a few targets and concentrating your efforts, you create tremendous forces that act to accelerate success.

Whenever I have focused on my business, it has brought me success. Whenever I go off on a tangent, I have often failed. If you already understand how I view failure, you can best understand the concept of concentration.

One of my suppliers, Texas Instruments, has found that at the beginning stages of a project, production is low and the cost per unit is high. As they learn from their failures, productivity is increased. This process follows a curve that Texas Instruments has been able to plot and calls "The Learning Curve."

In life we follow the same type of curve in all our endeavors. By concentrating solidly on one area, you eventually learn from your mistakes, and as you learn, your productivity increases. The more you concentrate, the more confined an area you put your energy into, and the less chance you have of failure.

You can't be everything to everyone. When you find something that works, continue to put your energy into it and watch your success grow.

Go off on a tangent and what happens? You enter a brand new learning curve. You make an entirely new series of mistakes and you experience a whole new series of failures.

Something else happens when you go off on a tangent. You divert your attention from your area of prime effectiveness. You lose on two counts.

By concentrating on a specific area and avoiding tangents, you create a tremendous Success Force. The more you concentrate, the better your chances of success. In my business, I started out by concentrating only in micro-electronic products. I concentrated my early advertising campaigns in the *Wall Street Journal* on big ads. I concentrated with the same format for my advertising. The more I found ways to concentrate myself, the easier success came.

Every time I took a departure or went off on a tangent, I paid the price. While successfully concentrating my efforts with JS&A, I was encouraged to take my first tangent with my Watergate game. Not only did I have to learn an entirely new business, but I was diverted from my very highly-productive activity with JS&A. The only redeeming value in the whole Watergate tangent was that I learned from the failure (Success Force Two), but I would have rather concentrated on my business. (Success Force 4).

Just as there is a secret to the Success Forces of honesty and failure, there is also a secret to concentration. "Don't go off on tangents." Tangents are dangerous. I learned how dangerous they are when I saw my father operate his business. He had a beautiful process camera manufacturing operation. He manufactured the cameras that printers used to produce plates, but as he succeeded, he thought he could build his empire by importing products from overseas and then by owning manufacturing facilities overseas. He soon overextended himself and ended up almost going under.

All his competitors in the camera business concentrated on making cameras and they prospered and grew. My dad's business floundered. I always felt that if my dad had concentrated on his camera business, he could have been wildly successful. I learned from my father. I learned what not to do. I learned what happens when you go off on tangents.

Decide how many things you can concentrate on and discipline yourself not to go off on tangents. You'll then discover that concentration is a powerful Success Force.

SUCCESS FORCE 5

Do It Differently

If you are one of those who remember JS&A's advertisements, you might have observed a number of companies who ran mail order ads that looked very similar to ours. They used the same type faces, the same layout, and the same photographic style that we did.

It would seem logical that if anyone were trying to break into the mail order business, the first thing he or she would do is to try to duplicate our successful approach, copy our product selection, and look like us.

I believe that every element you copy is a Failure Force. And every time you innovate or do something different, you create a very powerful Success Force. The secret, therefore, is don't copy.

Some of my biggest failures occurred when I simply tried to copy someone else's success and not innovate on my own. Copying has two strikes against it. In the first place, nothing happens as it should. Throughout my life, every concept I thought was going to turn out to be a huge success ended in failure, in great disappointment, or at best, in a modest success. And many marginal-appearing concepts turned out to be my real success stories.

And secondly, every success is comprised of several obvious elements and several billion not so obvious ones. The point is that in order to come near duplicating a success, you've got to duplicate its elements, the majority of which you may not be aware of. But even if you were successful, the most difficult element to copy is timing.

How can you possibly duplicate a time in space—a time when all other elements of the success were in just the right position to achieve success? Every time I have copied, I have failed. Every time I have innovated, I have, on average, done quite well. The more innovation, the greater the success.

During my days of handling advertising for the Schuss Mountain Ski Resort, a rock group that had played for me at Frank Bond's on a few occasions was to perform near the resort in nearby Traverse City. Traverse City had a beautiful 3,000-seat auditorium and had a small college that often used the auditorium.

The rock group, the American Breed, was to perform with a few other groups in a school promotion. The night of the concert, a winter blizzard hit and the American Breed barely made it to the show. The blizzard was so bad that the school considered calling off the concert but finally let it take place anyway.

Despite the blizzard, over 3,000 students jammed the concert hall and thousands were left outside to return home disappointed. The concert was a huge success.

Now I knew the American Breed very well. I knew the rock concert business, I knew the promotion business, and I knew how to advertise these shows.

So I decided to set up my own American Breed command performance in Traverse City to take place in May when the weather would be more predictable.

I planned two shows. My idea was to spend about $6,000 promoting the show to fill up the first performance and really do well on the second show.

I made professional radio announcements using professional announcers, and I printed beautiful posters. I hired a few students at the college to promote the show, hang up the posters, and publicize the event.

I handled the show so professionally and the American Breed was such a popular group in Traverse City that I was convinced we would have a huge success.

The radio spots, the publicity, the posters, and all our promotion came off without a flaw. And on the day of the concert the weather was perfect. Instead of 3,000 for the first concert, we got 150, and the second concert drew 175. I lost my shirt.

I mentioned the above example as an illustration of timing and copying. Obviously something was wrong. I could give you dozens of reasons why I failed, but the overriding single most important reason was because I was copying a previous success.

Each problem or each situation has its own set of circumstances that are unique to it. Trying to copy another success does not force you to look at those unique circumstances that may demand an entirely different approach.

There is nothing wrong with innovation tempered with a little copying. Take for example what Mark O. Haroldson did. Haroldson read a book written by Joe Karbo entitled *A Lazy Man's Way to Riches.* The book explained how to use mail order to acquire wealth.

Haroldson then wrote his own ad fashioned after Joe Karbo's ad using suggestions from Karbo's book. But Haroldson offered his own concept, which was a blueprint for growing wealthy from real estate.

His first ads describing his "wealth formula" drew terrific response and he launched a very successful mail order book campaign that earned him millions of dollars.

Haroldson was a good example of building on the success of someone else but adding his own innovation.

I'm sure there are stories that tell how somebody copied something and succeeded, and I'm sure there are cases where someone copied somebody else and the timing was in fact better than the innovator, making the copycat more successful than the innovator. But these stories are rare.

If you've ever followed the record industry, you see many good examples of copying. When the Beatles became popular, there were hundreds of rock groups trying to imitate them. Nobody succeeded like they did. And instead of copying themselves, the Beatles constantly innovated, producing some of the most original music of their time.

We've all heard of rock singers who had one smash hit, then followed it up with what sounded like a copy of the first hit. The second record never sells as well as the first.

When I see somebody copying me, I am never worried. I would be concerned if I saw somebody innovating and selling the same products I do. Then I'd have some real competition.

Frank Schultz sold grapefruit through the mail. He had been selling grapefruit using direct mail, but whenever he went to an advertising agency to produce an advertisement he could run in a magazine or newspaper, the ad they produced did not succeed.

Schultz attended my mail order seminar and wrote an ad. The ad was a huge success, and Schultz sold his grapefruit for ten years from that same advertisement. What he did was to take the same principles I use, but he innovated and produced what I consider one of the best mail order ads I've ever seen from any of my students, making millions of dollars in the process.

Copying seems like an easy way out, and I know that there are mail order books that preach copying as a way to success. But the only one making any money from those books is the author. His or her approach to success might be innovative, so the author is doing well, but their advice isn't very good.

You might wonder how you can innovate. For starters, just avoid copying. Then realize that an innovator is someone who does things others think can't be done or who does things few people have done before.

Unfortunately, there is no exact formula for innovation. And since everything might appear to have already been invented, innovation might just be putting together the same things in a unique way.

The important point is that copying often brings you failure while innovation or doing it differently is a most powerful Success Force.

SUCCESS FORCE 6

Clean Your Desk

One of the interesting things I've noted about successful people is how clean their desks are.

During my summer vacation breaks from college, one of my assignments while working for my father was to interview successful business executives who owned some of my father's printing equipment.

I was in charge of publishing a newspaper my father wanted to mail to his potential customers. It contained editorial material in addition to the usual hard-sell advertisements.

I felt that the readers of this paper would enjoy reading about successful printers who had purchased my father's equipment. I conducted at least ten interviews and observed a few things that seemed to be true about each company president.

At one point in his or her careers, each president had been told that his or her idea could not be done. And these presidents, convinced in their own minds that it could be done, took on the challenge to prove they were right. I have since learned that when somebody tells me that something can't be done, it should be a signal that there is a great opportunity if I can just prove that I'm right.

The second thing that all these people had in common was a clean desk. I wondered if these presidents did any work. And when I walked through their factories or printing plants, I was amazed at how clean and organized each of their facilities were.

Floors were clean, presses were polished, and files were neat. These companies gave you the feeling that they were very well managed and very efficient operations.

I always remembered my impressions from these interviews, and throughout my life I have always been aware of the role cleanliness played in a company's operation.

It was only when my company grew from a basement operation to a full-scale business in 1974 that I instituted many of my concepts on cleanliness and discipline.

We had grown so rapidly during 1974 that I had to resort to short cuts to keep the operation going smoothly, so the cleanliness and discipline I had believed in was postponed until we moved into our new deluxe office facility in Northbrook, Illinois.

Our office facility was a single-story 6,000-square-foot office building—a far cry from our previous 1,000-square-foot office. All fifteen of our group fit nicely into a portion of the space, and we purchased some new desks and chairs.

The building was built by a group of architects to reflect their creative ability. It was a spacious, high-quality building with eight-foot doors, a beautiful studio for me, beautiful lighting, and first-class treatment throughout. The impression you got from entering the building was unlike the one we projected in my basement or the corner store we had previously rented. We now projected the image that we were going to be around for a while and that we were a quality company.

But to carry that image forward we needed a clean-looking operation. Although we had more room and new desks, we still looked messy. At night papers were left in piles on the desks. There were labels, empty boxes, calculators—a variety of clutter that didn't fit the clean image of the building.

I remembered my previous newspaper interviews and subsequent observations and decided to implement a clean desk policy.

I insisted that all my employees clear off their desks before they left for home at night, and that nothing be left on their desks. This meant that even their in and out boxes had to be put away.

You can't imagine the complaints and moans I heard from my fifteen employees. But the main complaint was absolutely valid. They had no place to store all their papers.

I agreed with them and suspended the regulation until we could purchase additional file cabinets and desks to accommodate our workload.

When we received the desks and files, I once again announced my new clean desk policy. And once again my fifteen employees complained. Although we now had a place to put everything, we had no system of knowing what we had stored away. It was possible for a file to be stored and forgotten—one that required immediate action. Again my employees were correct. We indeed did not have the systems in place to handle the retrieval of files. and we had no auditing procedures to ensure that everything was indeed followed up.

Mary Stanke and I worked out procedures to ensure that everything that was put away at night could efficiently be brought out during the day.

Again, we instituted the clean desk policy and, surprisingly, with very few complaints. The employees now saw a much more efficient operation and felt considerably more at ease with the procedures.

Every night each desk was cleared and everything efficiently put away. If you walked into our offices at night, you'd think our Customer Service Department was an office furniture showroom. The floors were polished, the desks were clean, and everything was dusted and ready for the next big day.

There was no question in my mind of the efficiency of the operation. At the time, we had to handle hundreds of thousands of orders, pieces of paper and correspondence—and we handled them efficiently because of the systems we employed.

Was it the clean desk that did the trick? Was it the employees' feelings of organization that caused their efficiency to improve? The clean desks were really manifestations of discipline. They were the direct reflection of how efficiently our company ran.

I'm sure many of you with dirty desks may have a few valid reasons for keeping a dirty desk. You might work better with a cluttered desk. But remember that I'm not proposing that you work with a clean desk, just that you clear your desk at the end of the day. I work best on a large cluttered desk. But, at the end of the day, I put everything away.

You might be the type of person who works from eight in the morning until midnight and feel my concept may not apply to you. You're probably working too hard or you're not making good use of your time. You've either got to delegate or refine your entire operation. You've got too much on your plate.

In the past, the excuse I had been using for not clearing off my desk at the end of the day was that I was putting in enormous hours. I then realized that to keep a clean desk I would have to reduce my time. I was forced to think of logical steps to reduce my workload. In short, a clean desk represented a goal for me. If my desk remained cluttered, it was a negative signal.

I realize that cleaning your desk at the end of the day might sound like wasted effort, but it does work. It creates a Success Force to flush out the inconsistencies in your business efficiency. It forces you to organize your work, to organize your workload, and to put things in a proper perspective.

And it works, not just for me, but for many of the people who have heard my speeches.

People understand and relate to many of my philosophies, but the one philosophy that draws the most attention is the one on clean desks. I get letters from people who tell me how much cleaning their desk literally changed their lives and brought them success.

It's a Success Force that people can employ immediately to test my concept. Honesty, concentration, failure, and innovation are conceptual in nature, but clearing your desk can be done right after you close this book.

You may not have a desk to clean. Then how clear are the counters in your kitchen at night or your workbench in the basement or the top drawer in your bedroom dresser? They are all really reflections of the cleanliness and discipline you must have to be successful.

A desk is also a good early warning indicator. Let's say you do clean your desk and get things organized and you are quite pleased with your newfound organization. Then one day you leave your desk dirty and, before long, you leave it dirty again. This should be a signal that you're doing something wrong or that your sloppiness is a symptom of something else that may be bothering you. Fine. Start figuring out why.

It could be just laziness, but what is suddenly causing that laziness? Is it because you are reluctant to tackle a big job? Why are you reluctant? By getting to the root or nature of your problem, you can often solve it quickly and achieve success.

Every time you clean your desk at the end of the day, you create a Success Force. Every time you don't clean your desk, you create a failure force.

And if others around you get into the habit of cleaning their desks at the end of the day, you suddenly find yourself better able to judge a problem before the problem gets serious through this unique early warning system.

An army experience I once had explains this concept from a general's point of view. When I was in the intelligence branch of the army, I met a girl who was the secretary to my commanding officer. Andrea's father was a colonel.

I dated Andrea quite often and on occasion I would go to her house to pick her up only to end up waiting for a half hour while she finished getting ready. This gave me the opportunity to talk to her father who would often be sitting in his study.

One day we were discussing general staff inspections in which a general drives into a camp and conducts an examination of the camp's facilities, cleanliness, and staff.

What puzzled me about these inspections was that each general seemed to have a favorite thing he'd inspect. One general would pay particular attention to toilets. Each toilet facility had to be so sparkling that (if you'll excuse the expression) you could eat off the floors.

Another general might select beds as his favorite target. Each camp had to have beds made up so perfectly and tightly that you could bounce a quarter off the blankets.

This general's target was windows. The panes and the windows had to be clean and sparkling inside and out.

Interesting, however, was the fact that the generals let their particular targets be known well in advance of their visit. It seemed that everybody knew what to concentrate on to prepare for the inspection.

What puzzled me about the inspections was why the generals would let everybody know in advance what to do to please them. If I were conducting an inspection, I wouldn't say a thing. So I asked the general why he let his main focus be known in advance so that everybody could neglect the other things and concentrate on that one area.

"Simple," he replied. "If the troops know I'm keen on windows and I walk in and find dirty windows, I know immediately something is wrong and I really start examining other things closely. If the windows are clean and dust-free, I know things are, for the most part, in order. I can tell in a few minutes a great deal about the morale and efficiency of a base."

Using the general's example, imagine how the same principle can be used to judge your company's performance. If you let it be known that clean desks are your point of inspection, then a dirty desk would signal problems.

As long as the desks at JS&A were cleared off at night, I knew things were functioning smoothly. The minute I saw things left on desks, I got nosy and started snooping around. With a little effort I would usually find a problem, and once that problem was corrected, the desks got cleaner.

If you have the willpower to clean your desk at the end of the day, to organize your work properly and to put the work in a suitable container or file, you'll be well on the way to using one of my most effective Success Forces.

A clean desk, more than any other force, is easy to implement. Try it and see if it doesn't produce a very positive Success Force that you can usually measure within the first few months.

SUCCESS FORCE 7

Focus on Helping Others

There is a spiritual principle that states that whatever you focus on will expand. So if you focus on your business, your business should expand. If you focus on good health, you stay healthy.

I often share this principle with an audience at the start of my presentation. But then I play a little trick on them. I ask, “And what happens when you focus on money?”

The audience by this time thinks they know the answer and I’ll hear, “The money expands.”

“No, no,” I scold the audience, “Money is just a symbol for work and effort. You work; you earn money. If you focus on money, the work and the effort expand, not the money.”

And then I explain that if you want to make a lot of money, focus on helping others. The more you help others, the more money will flow into your life. Now you might think I’m suggesting you go out and become missionaries. What does helping others encompass?

It could encompass many things such as selling and delivering a good product through your company, always being open to help others in need of advice, sharing your knowledge with others, and on occasion financially supporting someone or something. You can contribute to your community by getting involved.

Let me give you examples from my life. I used to give seminars on direct marketing copywriting and marketing in general. I found that this exercise forced me to organize what I did in a way that I could teach the material and this consequently made me a much better marketer. In fact, I have often said that I learned more from the experience of giving to my students than they did, and I did this for more than 20 years.

My speeches were also a way of sharing my knowledge but they also inspired people to achieve greater success.

My books are another example. Through my books, I leave a legacy that will be available for years and years—probably long after I’m gone. And I share in my books all that I taught at my seminars and a lot more I didn’t teach. I don’t hold back.

BluBlocker Sunglasses was a good example of selling a product that helped others by protecting their eyes. But there was more than just selling. I also alerted the nation, and possibly the world, to the dangers of UV and blue light through my print ads and infomercials—something that few consumers knew about. And no other sunglass company pointed this out until we started our advertising campaigns. And for each new war America fought, we contributed 20,000 pairs of BluBlockers to the troops—the Gulf war, the Iraq war and the Afghan war and a few other times as well.

When people call me for advice, I try my best to help them or at a minimum tell them where they can get the information. And I too have my favorite charities that I have supported for many years. If I hear of an injustice and it will take some money to correct it, I'm one of the first to contribute.

Giving is very important. But just as important is receiving. You might be great at helping people and being very generous but you also must be open to receiving. It completes a cycle. Not being open to receiving blocks the flow in your life. I once had a doctor perform an adjustment to my shoulder for which he refused payment and did it as a kind gesture. I wanted to reciprocate so I offered him a book I had just written. He refused to accept it as the treatment was a gift from him. I told him that by refusing my gift to him, he is creating a block in his life that will affect his future success.

The doctor accepted the gift and told me a few years later that the insight he got from that unusual experience made a dramatic difference in his life. He had always been reluctant to accept gifts and in fact felt guilty but realizing the cycle that exists between giving and receiving, it truly changed his life.

In short, **the more you give of yourself, the more the money will flow to support your very existence.** On the other hand, doing things strictly for the money will render you poor in no time. Looking for that next get-rich-quick scheme will more than likely not make you rich.

Giving, helping others, and contributing to society are the true paths to wealth and one of the most important of all the Success Forces.

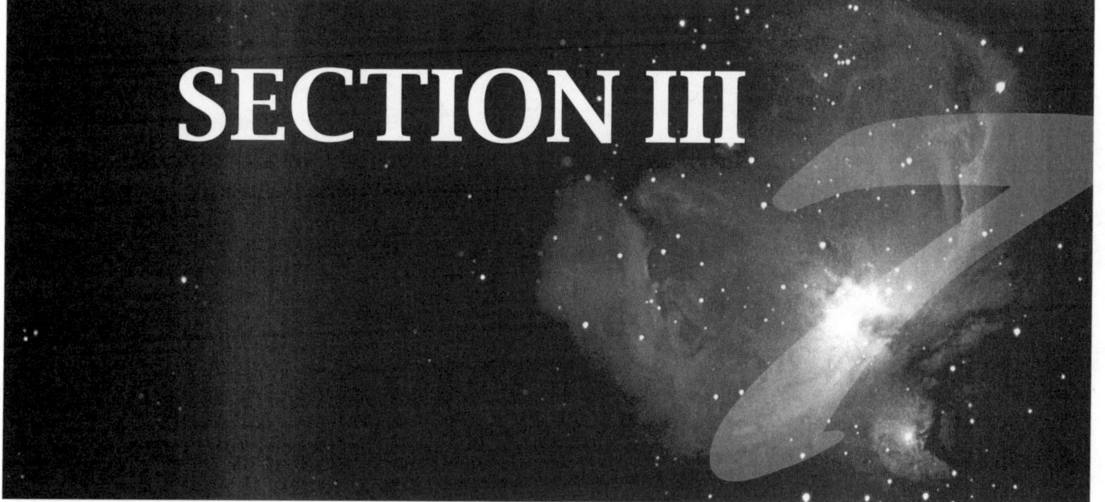
SECTION III

Success Philosophies

I have many success philosophies that go beyond the Success Force theory I've just presented.

I don't consider them in the same category as a Success Force. They do not have the same degree of effect on success that my Success Forces do. However, if you'll remember and follow them, they will also be helpful in guiding you toward success.

In this section of the book, I will take my success philosophies and explain them, using some examples from my personal experiences.

Some of these philosophies you may have heard elsewhere, but in those cases my interpretation of them may be different. Others may be uniquely mine—except that I'm always amazed when I read of someone who lived ten centuries ago quoting my philosophy.

If you combine my success philosophies with my Success Forces, you can't help but be positioned for great success.

Read this section carefully and study the examples. Refer to this section often. It will be a great help to you throughout your life.

1) Don't Let Ego Distort Good Business Sense

It's pretty hard to admit a mistake or a failure. We all have egos and whether they are big or small it still hurts our egos when we fail.

Your ego is one of your most important assets. It's a motivator that drives you on to bigger and better things. It keeps you going when times get rough.

But the important part about ego is knowing when to put ego aside and accept failure, or when not to listen to your ego when you have to make an important decision.

Whenever I have let ego distort good business sense, I have suffered as a result. Whenever I was able to control my ego, I succeeded. It's just that simple.

I have seen large corporations refuse to abandon a product line even though they were losing a fortune just for the sake of protecting their egos. Millions of dollars later, they finally decided to drop the line quietly, but it was really too late. They had lost their shirts.

Another example is a reaction to somebody competing unfairly with you. I have seen a company run an advertisement opposite me and offer the same product at a lower price. My ego was hurt and I wanted revenge. But it was really only my ego that was upset. Good business sense dictated that I continue the course of action that made good business sense instead of one designed to get revenge and satisfy my wounded ego.

Revenge is a good example of letting your ego distort good business sense. Revenge is destructive. Taking a solid, mature course of action is the best way to go.

Another example of ego is when I completed what I thought was a terrific ad only to test it and find out that the product was a marginal seller. I'm sometimes tempted to keep running the ad even though I know I shouldn't.

I see that often with inventors. They're so proud of their invention that they refuse to let common sense guide them.

Whenever an ad doesn't work, a product doesn't sell, or a product cycle has ended, I drop it. There is no room for ego to distort good business sense.

Using ego for positive advantage is, however, a very powerful force. It gave me the guts to announce a five-day $2,000 marketing seminar at my former Northern Wisconsin estate that quickly sold out. It drives me to create the very best mail order advertising I can produce.

Your ego is powerful. Used in a positive way with common sense, it works and it works wonders. Letting it distort good business sense can cost you a fortune and increase your chances of failure. Get to know your ego, and make it work for you.

2) Become an Expert

No concept is more powerful than becoming an expert in whatever you undertake.

If you own a store that sells leather goods, then become an expert on leather. Visit a tannery. See how leather is processed. Study the history of leather and how it evolved. Keep up to date on the latest leather technology and monitor your competition.

Having a thorough knowledge of a particular subject will open more doors for you and bring you greater success than you'll ever believe.

Becoming an expert has its limitations, too. I contend that you should become an expert to the extent necessary to fulfill your perception or goal.

If your plans are to sell leather, it might be a waste of your time to actually tan leather or learn how cattle are slaughtered before the hides are removed. There's a practical limit to how much you need to know.

I have sat in on seminars conducted at direct marketing conventions and cringed as the so-called experts told their audiences they shouldn't become experts. In the entire history of running my company and writing hundreds of advertisements, every one of my most successful ads resulted from my becoming an expert on the product—to a limit—and then writing the advertisement. I can cite two examples of this concept.

I was approached at the Consumer Electronics Show in June of 1975 and presented with a new product about to be manufactured in Hong Kong.

The product was presented to me as a miniature walkie-talkie. It measured only 1/2 inch by 1-1/2 inches by 5 inches, and it fit into a pocket, so it was a handy device, but I needed more information so I could explain why the unit was so small, how it operated. and what would appeal to the consumer.

I met with the engineers and they explained how sensitive the unit's receiver was, how well the transmitter performed, and how the integrated circuits functioned in the unit.

But something was missing. I still hadn't found the really exciting way to present the product until the engineers started to talk about the transmitter frequency. The engineer mentioned that it transmitted on the 27 megahertz frequency. I delved further.

What other products broadcast on that frequency?" I questioned.

The engineers told me that the CB bands used the frequency and 27 megahertz was in fact CB channel 14.

That was the grabber I was looking for. The CB radio craze was just beginning and the fact that the miniature walkie-talkie broadcast on channel 14 gave me my headline—"Pocket CB."

Sales soared. Unfortunately. the manufacturer had production delays, but when we finally delivered, the pocket CB turned out to be one of the most successful products in our history. Instead of selling a pocket walkie talkie, we tied into a national fad and called it a "Pocket CB." We eventually sold 250,000 units or retail sales of $10 million.

Another example of becoming an expert (to a certain extent) was for a new digital watch we were about to announce,

The manufacturer, Micro Display Systems in Dallas, Texas had given us their first watch to introduce one year earlier. The watch represented a breakthrough in digital watch design because it incorporated a liquid crystal display and a small night light. During the day you could read the digital display without pressing a button and at night you pressed the night light button to illuminate the display.

The new watch represented a major advance over even the previous model. It had a light that glowed automatically in the dark so there was no button to press at all—day or night. But how was I to convey this fact?

I started to become an expert. I talked to the engineers at length. Then I came upon an interesting fact when discussing the glow-in-the-dark light source.

It seemed that the light source used a material called tritium that, when combined with phosphor and instantly sealed, created a phosphorescent glow. I investigated further.

I then asked for a description of how the capsule was sealed only to discover that a laser beam was used. In fact, the whole process was impossible to perform until a laser beam process was developed for sealing the tritium/phosphor capsule.

That's all I needed to know. I used the headline "Laser Beam Digital Watch" and proceeded to explain how the new watch breakthrough was made possible by the use of a laser beam.

The watch sold quite well. In both of the examples above I became an expert. When I had just enough facts, the marketing solutions popped out.

Becoming an expert is a sure way to grow. I can remember an employee of ours who often complained that he had a lot of untapped potential that was going to waste. He wanted to get into some responsible sales position to sell our pocket CB unit, but he said he wasn't given the chance. But for someone who wanted to get into CB sales, he knew nothing about CB. If I had been him, I would have become an expert on sales and citizen band radios, devoured all the books on the subjects, and then approached us. Even after he did talk to us and I suggested that he should first become an expert on the subjects of CB and sales, he never did.

Joe Girard, the super-successful car salesman in Detroit, is no expert on cars. He found early in the game that he didn't have to be. He did, however, become an expert on motivation, service, and sales techniques, and he uses these skills with great success. If I were going to be an insurance salesman, I'd learn everything I could about sales, insurance, and people. The best sales reps who sell us products are those who not only are experts on their products but also know a great deal about our company and its needs.

The more you become an expert on a subject, the more information you have in your mental data bank and the more information you'll be able to recall when you need it.

I'd like to relate a true story about something that happened to me in high school that best explains why it pays to become an expert.

I was a junior at the time and a beautiful blond girl (in those days a blond was naturally blond) from California started attending our high school.

Betty Jane was so beautiful that even those handsome senior football players were too awestruck even to walk up to her and start a conversation. To watch her walk down the hall was an experience in itself. All heads would turn and everybody would stare. Girls would huddle and gossip behind her back. The poor girl was having a rough time blending in. That's for sure.

I had found out two things about her. First, she was from San Diego and secondly, she disliked boys who squeezed their toothpaste in the middle.

That afternoon I raced home and checked my medicine cabinet. Sure enough I squeezed my toothpaste from the end and not the middle. I indeed had something in common with her. But in retrospect, I realized that it would be difficult to develop a meaningful relationship over a tube of toothpaste.

But then I had a brainstorm. If I really wanted to get to know Betty Jane, what could I do? I had heard that she was from San Diego and used that as the premise of my new plan. I had deduced that anybody from San Diego living in the Chicago area would have to be homesick. What if somebody approached her who was an expert on San Diego or was also from San Diego? She would have something to talk about and would probably enjoy sharing her experiences and memories. So I proceeded to be that somebody.

I went to my local library and got all the books I could on San Diego. I wrote the San Diego Chamber of Commerce, the San Diego Port Authority, the San Diego Zoo, the San Diego Board of Education, and the San Diego Road Commission.

I then read everything I could on the city, its people, the schools, and its recreational activities. I even made a few long-distance calls, interviewed some people from San Diego, and after almost two months I became an expert on San Diego. I knew enough to discuss the schools, where the kids hung out, the latest fads, the places to go, the most popular drive-ins and movie houses, and even some of the slang. I was an expert in the true tradition of my concept.

And I also studied Betty Jane's movements. I knew that on Tuesdays and Thursdays at 9 A.M. she had a class near my locker, and that at 9:03 A.M. she would walk by my locker, usually alone, and pass within three feet of me.

So I planned to wait until she was a few feet away, whirl, and then start talking to her. I was not only prepared on San Diego, but I also had my timing down to a science.

I'll never forget that day. I dressed in my very best high school clothes. I had a clean slick haircut and was prepared for my pitch. I was ready.

From the corner of my eye I saw Betty Jane walking out of her classroom. I shut my locker door just as she was approaching. Then I turned, whirled around and said, "Betty Jane, I understand you're from San Diego?"

Betty Jane turned, smiled, and said, "No, I'm from Sacramento."

I don't remember what happened after that. It's a memory that somehow fades after the word "Sacramento," but it does illustrate my concept: become an expert—but make sure you have all your facts straight.

3) Never Give Up

One of the overriding reasons for my success is that I never gave up until I had no choice. Call it persistence or ego, but I never felt right unless I had given it everything I had. I was a fighter—not with fists and gloves, but with ideas, effort, and persistence. If I felt I had an idea that was good, I took it to its logical conclusion. I never gave up until the handwriting was on the wall.

Through all my failures, I always held the philosophy that even if I lost, it was an experience I could put in my back pocket and some day it would benefit me.

The real world is full of traps, failures, and disappointments. I often wonder if they're there to test us as we strive for success. If you can withstand these pitfalls and not give up, success often follows.

There's a thin line between my philosophies of "never give up" and "don't let ego distort good business sense." The best way to determine where that line is would be to ask yourself a question: "Do I feel there's still a chance for success and is it worth the effort?" If the answer is "yes," then don't give up. If the answer is "no," you're probably trying to satisfy your ego.

After giving a speech I always end with a story of a small college in Fulton, Missouri. The Fulton College officials were meeting to discuss the commencement exercise and whom they could hire to give the keynote speech.

After a bunch of names were thrown out, a young professor suggested Winston Churchill. After the laughter died down, the professor who suggested it said, "Hey, you never know. He might just accept."

The professor wrote Winston Churchill and within a short period of time, he got a letter back accepting the speaking engagement. Everybody was shocked but Winston Churchill had indeed accepted the invitation.

On the day of the commencement, the entire town of Fulton Missouri was decked out in signs welcoming the elder statesman. He drove through town and to Fulton College where they escorted him to the stage to sit in a chair until it was his turn to give his speech.

The college President was the first to speak. In his ten minute speech he told of the great achievements Churchill had realized in his lifetime and how thrilled little Fulton College was to have such a distinguished statesman as their commencement speaker.

Then the college President sat down and the Fulton mayor got up and gave the official welcoming address for about ten minutes. Then it came time for Churchill to speak. Churchill was very old at this time and he hobbled to the podium with the help of the mayor.

Churchill looked over the audience of graduating students with their caps and gowns and shiny faces. There was a slight pause and you could almost hear a pin drop it was so quiet as the audience waited in suspense for him to start.

Then he gave his speech—the entirety of which will long be remembered.

"Never give up, never, never, never give up." And then he walked off stage.

I often tell this story to point out the theme to my success. I've never given up.

4) The Truth Always Emerges

I once gave a speech in Mexico City at the Direct Mail Marketing Association's annual convention. One of the keynote speakers at the convention was Ben Bradlee, who at the time was Editor-in-Chief of the Washington Post. Bradlee gave the audience a little insight into the Watergate scandal and told how his reporters blew the whistle and exposed the whole thing.

But what I got out of his speech was something I've observed in my lifetime but was never able to put into words—namely, if you wait long enough, the truth will emerge.

Think about it. A weekly magazine report on an incident is often more accurate and truthful than a newspaper story on the same event. The newspaper can't afford to wait, so it publishes what it has as quickly as it can. It doesn't have the perspective of a weekly magazine that can take all the newspaper reports and paint a more accurate picture.

And take a report from a monthly magazine doing a story previously covered by a weekly news magazine. Very often it is far more accurate and expansive than the weekly magazine's report which was put together with all the data it could gather during that week.

The history books offer yet another version of the event. Presidents are often judged thirty or forty years after they die.

If somebody lies to me and I am unaware of it at the time, I eventually find out. The truth always emerges. All you have to do is have the patience to wait.

Please don't use this philosophy as an excuse to procrastinate, but when you are unsure of yourself, waiting sometimes flushes out all the facts you need to make a better decision.

Remember this philosophy. See how it has worked in history. See how it works in your daily life. Once you understand and appreciate this philosophy, you'll be amazed at how much better your decisions become.

There is a limit to how long you wait, however. I remember meeting Jack Tramiel who was at the time the president of the game company Atari. I asked him what his formula for success was and he replied, "I make a decision. It might be the right decision; it might be the wrong decision but I make a decision." So make that decision, but make it on enough information, and that often takes time to emerge.

But know that the truth always does emerge. And remember what true entrepreneurs follow: "Ready, Fire, Aim."

5) Life Is a Moving Target

We had an electronic game in our basement at our estate in northern Wisconsin called "Sea Wolf." It consists of various boats going across a TV screen at different speeds. You use a periscope with cross hairs to aim at the boats, and you press a button to release a torpedo that moves slowly through the waves before it strikes the target. Every time you strike a boat with a torpedo you score some points.

The faster a boat moves across the screen, the more points you earn when you hit the moving target. In order to do this, you've got to fire your torpedo well enough ahead of its projected course. A PT boat worth 700 points zips across the screen so fast that you have to fire within seconds of its appearance and well in advance of its projected course. A slow-moving freighter is worth only 100 points, but you have plenty of time to hit it almost dead on.

The game repeats the same cycle every nine boats. Once you realize this and can remember this cycle, you can improve your accuracy by anticipating the next boat.

The game, in my opinion, is a good analogy of life. In fact, at my seminars I urged my students to play the game. At the end of the course we discuss its significance and how life parallels this unique game.

First of all, life is a moving target. The Chinese say that the only thing constant in life is change.

If you'll view life as a series of moving targets, you will find that some targets move fast, requiring you to lead the target before you fire, and others require you to shoot straight ahead. For those fast-moving, hard-to-shoot targets, you score more points so to be very successful in life you've got to be prepared to try tougher challenges.

Life is really a series of targets. However, in life they may not look like targets, nor do you shoot at them.

To score in life you first have to realize that everything does move and relationships change. Knowing this, you can expect change and be better able to accept it.

The person whom you married more than likely has changed -- hopefully enough to complement your changes. Expecting this change can help you accept your partner.

Your business changes. Competition, technology, the economy, and consumer moods are changing all the time. Awareness of these changes and their direction will help you take aim.

"The world is a moving target and a computer helps you to take aim," was IBM's appropriate slogan to sell their computers. A computer condenses the time and the information you need to point your company in the proper direction. And pointed in the proper direction with the proper timing, your shots can score points you wouldn't previously score.

There is no great step-by-step procedure I can leave with you for improving your aim or to help you score more points. But you should be aware that change is a fact of life, and that life is a moving target. The faster the target, the more points you score if your aim is right.

6) Humility

One of the amazing things I discovered about success was that those people who are truly successful and have reached a high level of self-actualization are very humble people. The people who are failures are often the most arrogant.

At JS&A I discovered a little test that helped me separate the successful people from the failures. When people call me at my office, I am often busy in meetings or working in my studio, and I have my secretary take messages for me. I've asked her to take as much information about the call as possible so I can at least determine the priority of my calls when I have time to call back.

Whenever somebody calls and is arrogant, disrespectful, and discourteous to my secretary in an effort to get through to me, these people usually turn out to be failures in life. The contrast between the way they talked to me and the way they talked to her is almost funny. I have often overheard some of these conversations that sound as if they come from two entirely different people.

My secretary didn't know the name Charles Tandy, so when the late chairman of the board of the very successful Tandy Corporation, the parent company of Radio Shack, stopped through Chicago and wanted to see me, he was understanding and pleasant and calmly left his message.

As soon as I recognized the correlation between humility, failure, and success, I started observing those who had been disrespectful to my secretary. I made an effort to get to know them a little better. I also met with a number of people who were very courteous to my secretary.

From these observations I discovered that the truly successful people in life were genuinely humble. The truly arrogant and disrespectful individuals were often people who were failures. Their lack of humility may have indeed played an important role in their failure.

I also found a Chinese saying that says with humility you will never have to worry about failure.

All my life I have repeated time and again one philosophy about success—namely, that if I am fortunate enough to be successful, I will remain humble. For any truly successful person will tell you that it is only when you are indeed successful that you realize how important every person is regardless of his or her station in life.

7) The Power of Belief

My cousin, Dr. Arnold J. Mandell, is a psychiatrist who was once given a very interesting assignment while he was practicing psychiatry in California. He was hired by the San Diego Chargers football team to determine what it took to be a superstar and what personality traits were exhibited by players who played various positions.

He worked on his project interviewing many of the superstars, the wide receivers and several other player positions. Then he wrote a book called "The Nightmare Season" with his findings.

But what I got out of the book was how he described the two personality types it took to be a superstar. The first personality type was the deeply religious person who had great faith in a higher power. The second was a very egotistical player who believed in himself.

When I read the book, I realized something that was common to both types of players even if they seemed so different. That common element was simply "belief." Both players had strong beliefs. The religious player had a strong belief in a higher power whereas the egotistical player had a strong belief in himself. In both cases there was clear evidence of the importance of belief.

It has been said that belief can be a very powerful support for people. If you sincerely believe in something, it will happen. If you believe you will be successful, you will be. And if you believe you won't be, you'll be right as well.

I was able to get though some of the worst failures because I firmly believed I was going to be a success. Failure didn't faze me as much as it would have if I had not had that belief.

Belief is a very powerful tool in your arsenal to achieve success. Embrace it, use it and realize how powerful this very important concept is in achieving success.

8) Protect Your Health

I've noticed through the years that the most successful people are those who take excellent care of themselves. They have a good diet, they exercise on a regular basis and their lifestyles are usually void of smoking, alcohol and drugs. It makes sense. Here's why.

To be successful, you must also have discipline—most often in your work environment. And that usually translates into your personal life as well. Sure there are exceptions to this rule, but in general, if you examine the lifestyles of successful entrepreneurs, you'll find they are fit, look younger than their age, and are able to handle stress better than most.

Stress is a killer so you want to make sure you can handle the stress in your business environment and that you find ways to release any stress when it builds up.

Diet is extremely important too. When I was in my early 20's, I realized that certain foods were not good for me. So each year I would give up one food or class of food for the sake of my health. For example, I sensed that all colas were bad because of the sugar content. Even diet sodas I felt were bad. And I loved a good Coke with a pizza. In fact, without a Coke, a pizza didn't taste as good.

So one year I gave up all soft drinks whether diet or regular. That was it. And I vowed never in my life to take another cola drink. I never had a smoking problem and I never had a drinking or alcohol problem, so I never had anything addictive to give up. This would be my test.

Sure enough it was very difficult to give up that Coke. I was feeling those withdrawal pains. Pizza didn't taste as good. I really missed my favorite drink. But I stuck with it and ever since that day when I took my last swig of Coke, I've never tried a soft drink again.

So successful was that experience that I said to myself, what else can I give up? So I looked at my habits. And one of them was a cup of coffee in the morning, one at noon and a few more in the afternoon. So I made coffee my next target and gave it up for the rest of my life.

Then came salad dressing. I could give it up and all its calories and learn to experience the true taste of my salad without anything to enhance its taste.

I then realized the value or lack of value of pizza in my diet. Those bread crusts, the cheese, the condiments put over the dough—

none of that I felt were really good for me yet I loved pizza. One of my accounts in Evanston, Illinois was the Spot restaurant. They sold pizza and it was up to me to help promote their food. Nevertheless, I gave up pizza for the rest of my life.

Then came red meat, dairy and finally I settled on a mostly raw food diet with occasionally fish.

It's been a while since I've given up something although now I will be cutting down on anything with grain. In my research I've determined that grain is toxic to our bodies and not natural. Research is still going on about this but it would mean that the breakfast cereal, that slice of bread and even that chocolate chip cookie I enjoy will be off limits for me. I know what you're thinking. Pretty soon there won't be much food left to enjoy. Quite the contrary. I'm more than satisfied now with my food choices.

Finally, I take a blood test once a year. It's probably one of the most accurate ways I can really detect what is going on in my body. And I get the test under the sponsorship of the Life Extension Foundation who has an annual blood test sale once a year. After I take my blood test, I call Life Extension and one of their doctors goes over the results with me on the phone. Or I consult with my doctor or healthcare professional.

What else do I do? I also take vitamins and supplements such as a daily vitamin, fish oil pills, and a host of other vitamins recommended by my health care professional. You can keep your weight down. They've determined that people on a caloric restricted diet live longer lives and are less likely to get a disease. In short, you should immerse yourself in the latest health reports from several excellent sources on the Internet and adjust your diets with this new information.

I'm convinced that science is moving so quickly that within the next 10 to 15 years, we'll have the resources to live to 120 years of age without the usual diseases that often accompany old age. This is a further incentive to focus on your health now.

I credit my health status on the elimination of those foods that I recognized early in my life as being bad for my health. I also credit a healthy diet, supplements and believe it or not, one of the most important things, attitude. With a positive attitude, you'll live longer according to the latest research.

I also exercise on a regular basis. Once again, exercise improves your health. And it helps to keep your weight in check. I am the same weight as I was in high school.

I urge you to take a serious review of yourself and take the necessary steps to improve your health and well being.

Remember, you can have all the money and success in the world but if you don't have your health, you have nothing.

9) Cycles

I have built my success on a philosophy of cycle watching. I realized early that practically everything in life is cyclical. The stock market, consumer moods, economics, nature—everything rises and falls, usually in a regular rhythm.

I first became aware of this phenomenon when I took advanced physics in college. It was a very rough course but one of my most interesting. For the first time since I started school, all my previous math courses made sense. I was using advanced calculus, geometry, statics, and dynamics, and they were fitting together as useful tools to solve very complex physics problems.

But I also learned that in many a physics equation—whether it involved fluids, solids, gases, or whether it was discovered by a physicist 200 years ago or just recently—there was always the constant pi in the equation, or 3.1416. This number, when multiplied by the diameter of a circle, gave you the circumference of that circle.

A circle is in essence a cycle—one complete revolution. It led me to believe that all of nature is cyclical and has its peaks and valleys. But then I started studying other forms of nature.

I learned that many things have cycles in almost an uncanny and predictable way. For example, the eleven-year peak in salmon production and the seventeen-year locusts have specific cycles. Even the stock market and the economy have their cycles.

In my years at JS&A, I built my business on being able to sense the start of a cycle, follow it to its practical peak and get out in time to go on to another emerging cycle. I never tried to follow the cycle beyond its peak. Sometimes I was responsible for creating the cycle.

Every event in life is a combination of many cycles. Take my business, for example. During one year, more expensive items will sell best; during the next year, inexpensive items. There may be a lull in consumer confidence, but one product may be selling better than another. And the list goes on.

It was up to me to sense these cycles and somehow develop strategies to concentrate on the upward movements and to avoid those cycles that would be declining.

It is my opinion that thousands of cycles affect our lives every day. Being able to sense or detect these cycles is one of the keys to success. Many successful businessmen have a "gut feeling" for a situation. Some call it intuition.

Feeling the cycle is very often based on experience. And having enough experience, enough failures, and enough facts will help you.

We tend to avoid situations in life that are unpleasant to us and feel attracted to situations that make us feel good. It's the same principle with cycles. We are going to be attracted to making moves based on feeling good about the facts we know and the feelings we have about a situation.

Let me cite two examples of products that ran their cycles, peaked, and then flattened.

The printing calculator was a sensation in 1974 when prices dropped to around $100 and the market really opened up. Casio, a Japanese company, had presented me with a printing calculator they were planning to sell for $150.

I thought the item was good. It had an unusual printing head, had good quality and the unit looked good. But Casio saw that they weren't selling very well so they dropped their price to $100 retail at a cost to me of $70. The ad I ran for the unit was a huge success, tempered only by the fact that Casio couldn't supply us with enough of them.

In 1978, four years later, one of Casio's competitors, Canon approached us with a printing calculator. The printing calculator market was poor. I felt that the market looked as if a printing calculator might just make a comeback and be successful again. We tried a test and our hunch was correct. We sold 20,000 Canon printing calculators and revived the cycle in the United States for all dealers.

The telephone answering unit is another example of starting a cycle. These units were once popular, but sales went flat. I had a gut feeling that there could be an upswing in the market for this type of unit, so I selected the Ford Code-A-Phone which I thought was the best unit on the market at the time, and I ran it in an advertising campaign. We sold thousands of them for three solid years.

We had been responsible for starting cycles for calculators, pinball games, security systems, micro recorders, telephones. and a multitude of other products—which may explain why the retailing giants like Sears, Montgomery Ward, J.C.Penney, and all the discount chains carefully watched what we did.

I wrote the earlier version of this book on Maui, an island in the Hawaiian Island chain, in 1980. I had come to Maui to buy a condominium as an investment. I couldn't believe the prices. Things were way overpriced at that time. I realized I was too late. If I was thinking of getting in on this cycle, I was near its peak and not at its beginning.

As I write the revised version of this book, it is the year 2014 and prices have plummeted. Now might be the ideal time to buy a property on Maui. So I guess if you wait long enough you can catch the cycle and find an advantageous time to buy.

In fact, as a general rule, when you hear of a tremendous opportunity in which others have made a lot of money, it's often too late. The cycle is probably near its peak or on the way down.

Always look for the ground floor opportunity and ride the cycle up. It is the riskiest time, and when you look at the opportunity it will have the appearance of a deal that could go sour. But that's how I've discovered my greatest growth opportunities.

In the stock market, often when the market is at its lowest and the public is discouraged and everybody is dumping their stocks and the experts are claiming that the end of capitalism as we know it is near, that is often the best time to buy stocks. As a matter of fact, the success secret in stocks is in the buying. Buy low when everybody is running for the hills and you'll do well in the long run.

The start of a cycle is never obvious. It is only after you have discovered you were right that it becomes obvious. But recognizing the start of a cycle upswing in anything you do will add great benefits to your potential success.

There are cycles in your personal life, too. A friend of mine, Bernard Gittelson, wrote a book entitled "Biorhythm—A Personal Science" in which he explains that our bodies have regular cycles too. Some days we're up; other days we're down.

You may not subscribe to his theory, but it is a good study of how a series of cycles can affect your moods and your physical and mental abilities.

Having a keen sense for cycles comes from experience, awareness, intuition and gut feelings. And sometimes it is just a matter of observation over time. But by simply being aware of the role that cycles play in both our lives and in business, you will have a great tool to use throughout your life.

10) Strive For Excellence

In examining the lives of really successful people I have discovered another trait that seems to characterize their lives.

These people, when faced with accepting mediocre work, rejected it and spent the money and risked the time to produce the best possible results.

When Joe Siegel, formerly of the Franklin Mint, ran the company, if everything wasn't perfect, he'd redo it, often throwing away thousands of dollars of printing during a time when the mint couldn't afford it.

When I produced an advertisement for my company and saw a word or phrase that would improve the ad, I stopped the presses or held up a publication while I made the correction. I'm certainly not perfect, and many mistakes have slipped through my careful eye, but I still strive for excellence.

I'm not a perfectionist. A perfectionist is a portrait in frustration. Rarely, if ever, is perfection achieved. But excellence is something else. I strive for excellence in advertising. Not perfection. And in order to make my ads excellent, I really have to work at it.

No matter what you do, strive for excellence. Don't accept sloppy work. Remember that everything you do is a direct reflection of you.

You are often going to be confronted with a choice while striving for excellence. If you remember that every time you opt for excellence over average, you're tipping the scale toward greater success.

11) The 80/20/30 Rule

You've all heard of the 80/20 rule in its many forms. It is said, for example, that 20% of a company's employees usually produce 80% of the work. Or that 20% of your time is productive and you waste the other 80%.

My philosophy goes beyond the standard concept of the 80/20 rule in that it suggests an action that will result in 30% more profit—hence the 80/20/30 rule.

My philosophy is that in business 20% of your profits create 80% of your headaches. For example, you might have ten clients, eight of whom are just great but two of whom create 80% of your problems. They pay late, fail to live up to their promises, and cause you a great deal of unproductive work.

My rule says that if you sacrifice the 20% of your profits—those profits that create 80% of your headaches—you'll end up making 30% more profit.

Think about it. Eliminate those two headache accounts, or 20% of your profits, and what happens? First, you'll have more time to devote to your really good accounts. Your time will be more productive and you'll be able to make room for another good account. You'll soon find that by getting rid of your headaches, even though they represent 20% of your profits, you'll end up with 30% higher profits and greater peace of mind.

This rule can be applied to many situations. For example, at one point in JS&A's history, we accepted purchase orders from major corporations for the purchase of calculators. This activity represented 20% of our volume.

However, the program required three people to follow up on the late payments and a great deal more paperwork. We found that many people who bought on credit tended to use our products, never pay for them, and return them months later.

One day I decided to eliminate open account billings and request checks from anyone purchasing our products. It represented 20% of our business and theoretically 20% of our profits, but it also represented 80% of our headaches.

It didn't take me more than a few months to realize that it was the best move I ever made. The three people I needed to collect on delinquent accounts were soon reassigned to other areas of the company, and that gave us the opportunity to expand. There was less trouble with returned products, and we were saving a great deal of time and effort. Most of our credit customers started paying by check. Our business actually grew as a result of this move.

Take a look at the areas in your life that create 80% of your headaches. The best way to do that is first to select those areas that you really enjoy and those areas you do best in. Then make a list of those areas you do poorly in or don't enjoy.

You'll be amazed to discover that the unpleasant areas that cause you 80% of your aggravation and discomfort represent only 20% of your financial return. Simply by eliminating those areas (often at what appears to be a sacrifice) your life will improve, you'll be happier and you'll profit overall from the move.

12) Success Pressures

If you become successful, you'll find that the hardest thing you have to learn is not how to make money but rather how to hold on to it.

You suddenly become everybody's best friend. You get calls from people you don't know but who know somebody you do know and they end up asking for loans.

You get very worthwhile charities calling you and asking for donations. You get entrepreneurs calling you with business deals that "can't lose." And you may feel compassionate towards the entrepreneur because you were once in his or her position when you started out. People pitch you their hard luck stories to win your favor.

People don't change that much when they achieve success but what they are is more amplified. For example, if I was a collector of small miniature model cars and became rich, I may start collecting the real cars. Everything is magnified.

Let's take, for example, lottery winners. An unusually high proportion of lottery winners lose everything within a very short period of time. Certainly these people don't have the experience and knowledge necessary to protect themselves, manage their money and live a normal life.

According to University of Connecticut sociologist Dr. Mark Abrahamson, winning big can be a bummer. Dr. Abrahamson studied 164 men and women who had won the Connecticut State Lottery. He found that far from making life easier, their easy winnings often created great stress.

Another good example of the pressures wealth brings is the child actress or successful rock star who eventually goes broke or out of control famous boxers who lose everything, and you wonder, "How could they lose so much? They made millions. How did it all disappear? Michael Jackson and Mike Tyson—they all made millions and they lost it.

Take for example, Tony Hsieh of Zappos, a very successful marketer of shoes and other products on the Internet. Tony sold his first company, Link Exchange, to Microsoft for 250 million dollars. He then started Zappos and sold it to Amazon.com for over a billion. At first blush, you might think he's a pretty lucky guy. But he too had to struggle to get to a point to sell to Microsoft and then when he did, he took the money and invested in other ventures, none of which worked out until he was almost broke. Then the concept of Zappos was presented to him.

He had lost almost all he had made from Microsoft to the temptations of investing in other start up ventures. And his venture with Zappos would have failed if it wasn't for outside capital that came to his rescue.

And if you're raising children, be careful to instill in them the importance of hard work and persistence. You don't want them growing up as the children of rich parents but more as individuals who worked for what they wanted and earned it. The one thing we did with our children is travel a great deal. This gave them an education and they got a pretty good idea how other people lived. They saw children in poverty, in terrible living conditions and realized how fortunate they were. They also learned the importance of giving to the less fortunate.

If you remember one thing from this chapter, it is simply that with all your success, expect pressures from people and opportunities you never experienced before and realize that it is much easier to make your fortune than it is to keep it.

I don't invest in any company unless I really know and understand their business. And even then, I consider the risks involved and have a limit I will invest even if more capital is required.

A true entrepreneur is somebody who makes a fortune, loses it all, and then makes it all back again. So don't despair even if you failed once. Just get back up and try again.

Yes, making money is really the easier part. Keeping it and not going broke is the hard part. But with all of the above, I'd rather have those success pressures and be wealthy than the alternative.

And Finally...

When I wrote the original Success Forces over 30 years ago, I covered my life experiences and then used that as a background to introduce my *Success Forces*.

Obviously there has been a lot more to learn since then. About 10 years ago, I decided to conduct my last seminar and then sit down and write a book on what I had learned and taught in the 20 years since I wrote *Success Forces*. The book looked like it was going to be over 1,000 pages and I realized that maybe I really had three books, not one.

So I came up with three books that covered copywriting, print marketing and TV marketing. Then the publisher, Wiley and Sons, came to me and asked me to write a book on copywriting which I did. The book was written as part of the Adweek Magazine book series. The Adweek book is called *The Adweek Copywriting Handbook*.

The Adweek Copywriting Handbook

This is an updated version of the copywriting book I wrote which I called, "*Advertising Secrets of the Written Word*." But the book is really much more than just about copywriting. This book guides and teaches you not only how to write copy but also how to make what you write even more effective. We cover selling on the Internet with valuable suggestions on building your business. There are plenty of illustrations to help guide you into becoming a first-rate copywriter. The second book is called *Marketing Secrets of a Mail Order Maverick*.

Marketing Secrets of a Mail Order Maverick

This 400-page book is packed with stories and lessons on how to find a product and then market it through various forms of print advertising. I show you how to use catalogs, direct mail and print ads. The use of magazines and newspapers is discussed and there are a lot of tips on how to make media work for you. If you're a salesperson, many of the stories will give you valuable strategies that you can implement immediately. The final volume in my three-book trilogy is a 300-page book entitled *Television Secrets for Marketing Success*.

Television Secrets for Marketing Success

Here is a book that contains insights for getting your product on national television and promoting it to the mass market via one of the most powerful mediums ever created for the sale of products. But wait, there's more. If you have a product that you'd like to put on a home shopping show or use in an infomercial or even tailor for the Internet, this is the book to invest in. There are plenty of stories and experiences to enjoy and learn from. And finally, there's my very popular book *Triggers.*

Triggers: 30 Sales Tools You Can Use to Control the Mind of Your Prospect to Motivate, Influence and Persuade

This book evolved from a chapter I wrote in my copywriting book that I called *Psychological Triggers*. So popular was this single chapter that I realized I could easily expand it into a book by itself. And instead of teaching just the techniques to use in copywriting, I could expand it to cover personal selling and thus increase the market for the book. Triggers will entertain you, capture your imaginations and teach you some of the secrets of effective copywriting. Some triggers will double your response. Some will build trust and still others will set the atmosphere for the perfect selling environment. I urge all my customers to get a copy of this book.

Social Media

Social Media has become such a major part of our communications that I would like to continue to share my life lessons with you on the various social media platforms. I feel so honored to have so many friends and followers who continue to benefit from what I have to share. Here are a few links where I share my experiences and insights.

Visit: **www.JoeSugarman.com**

Connect with me on LinkedIn:
www.linkedin.com/pub/joseph-sugarman/1/4/b47

Follow me on Twitter: **@joesugarman**

Visit my Facebook Fan Page: **www.facebook.com/sugarmanjoe**

And be sure to visit and continue to support and enjoy
BluBlocker sunglasses: **www.blublocker.com**

APPENDIX

Joe's Photo Album

"The aspiring entrepreneur at the tender age of two."

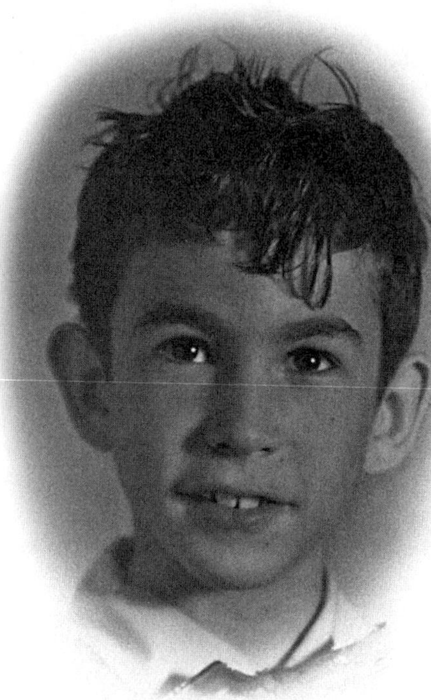

Joe living in Chicago at 8 years old in 1946.

Joe at 3 years old in 1941. Joe was quite a Romeo. He had a sister to play with and also captured the attention of all the girls in the neighborhood.

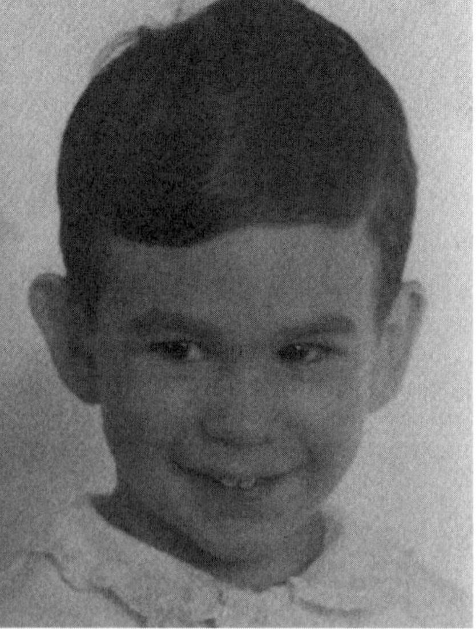

Joe at 4 years old in 1942. When he reached this age he already had two younger sisters with a third one to come later.

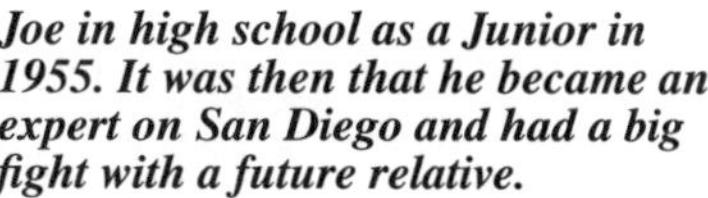

Joe in high school as a Junior in 1955. It was then that he became an expert on San Diego and had a big fight with a future relative.

Entering college presented many challenges, but Joe was cool and handled his new surroundings quite nicely.

Joe in New York in 1958 running the Spectra 59 exposition. He had to hire an actor to represent him as he wasn't even old enough to sign a binding contract at 20 years of age.

Joe in the woods near Oberammergau in Southern Germany 1964. This isolated location was where Joe attended classes to learn the German language at the request of his Army Intelligence unit.

Joe with Maui friend and neighbor Steven Tyler—both wearing BluBlocker sunglasses in 2012. Tyler bought a home across a remote bay where Joe had his Maui home.

Joe had a beard for 27 years starting in 1968 at 30 years old and shaved it off in 1995. He felt that the beard made him look older so prospective clients would not judge him by how young he looked. It was also the fashion at the time.

Joe and friend Nick Nanton at the Kentucky Derby. Joe was invited to give a speech at a hotel near the Derby in 2013. The Batman shirt was used to tell the Batman credit card story. The card is now over 48 years old.

Joe giving a speech on Maui in 2011. Joe has spoken all over the world on a variety of subjects involving direct marketing and motivational talks to entertaining presentations always winning accolades for his speaking ability.

JS&A Advertisements

Many of our ads became classics and taught me many lessons. The following are some of the more memorable ads I ran while building JS&A.

Digital Watch Breakthrough

There are several big changes taking place in digital watches. Here are all of them in one product.

Your digital watch is either too thick, uses up batteries quickly, has just a few functions or is hard to read under certain lighting conditions. You still have to press a button, flick your wrist, or hold your watch at just the right angle to read the time.

The digital watch industry has gone through four years of rapid change, but the disadvantages cited above have finally been resolved in one totally new product—the Sensor Laser 440 Digital. The Laser 440 is so different that it represents a dramatic departure from conventional digital watches.

NO BUTTON TO PRESS

There is no button to press since the display glows in the dark. A glass ampoule, charged with tritium and phosphor and sealed by a laser beam, is placed behind the new CDR (crystal diffusion reflection) display. When room lights dim, the self-contained tritium light source will compensate for the absence of light by glowing brightly and illuminating the display.

No matter when you wear your watch—day or night—just a glance will give you the correct time. There's no button to press, no special viewing angle required, and most important, you don't need two hands to read the time.

CHANGE YOUR OWN BATTERIES

The Laser 440 is only 8 millimeters thick—thinner than many of the so called thin digitals being advertised today. The new CDR display draws 100,000 times less current than an LED watch when displaying the time so your single commercially-available Union Carbide battery lasts years longer. In fact, part of our warranty includes all the batteries you'll ever need, free of charge, for five full years. To replace a battery, simply open up the battery hatch on the back of your watch, tap out the old battery and drop in the new one.

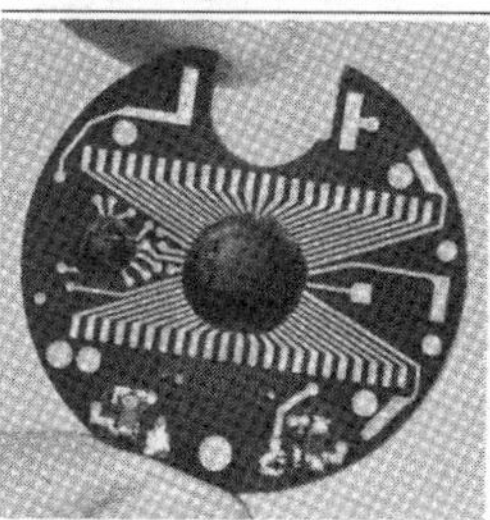

Most digital watches have dozens of electronic components. The Laser 440 has only six—two integrated circuits, a crystal and three micro-capacitors. All components are bonded directly on the printed circuit board. By hermetically sealing the integrated circuits and using fewer components, the Laser 440 is considerably more reliable than other watches that do not yet have this complete integration.

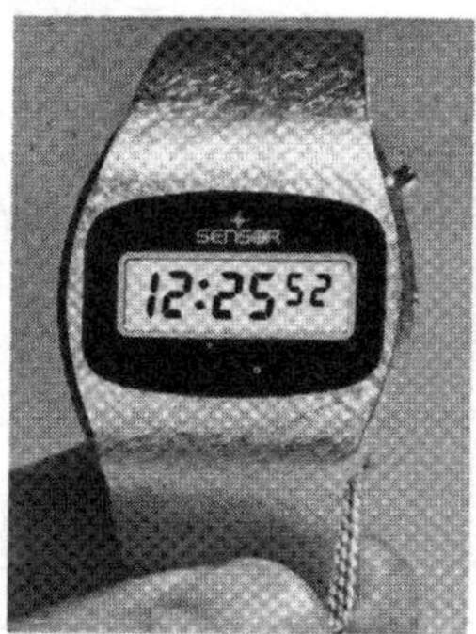

The new Sensor Laser 440 digital watch glows in the dark so there's never a button to press to read the time in darkness or in sunlight.

THE ULTIMATE ACHIEVEMENT

Other manufacturers have devised unique ways to produce a watch you can read at a glance. The $300 LED Pulsar requires a snap of the wrist to turn on the display, but the Pulsar cannot be read in sunlight and its display uses 100,000 times the current of the Sensor display. The $400 Longine's Gemini combines both an LED and liquid crystal display. (Press a button at night for the LED display, and view it easily in sunlight with the liquid crystal display.) But you must still press a button to read the time. All these applications of existing technology still fail to produce the ultimate digital watch: one you can read under all light conditions without using two hands. Until the new Laser 440.

And if you've owned a digital watch for a year, chances are you've had it in for repair more than once—a very common consumer complaint. The Laser 440 is so service-free and has such high quality that it should rarely, if ever, require service. It is backed by a solid five-year warranty—your assurance of our commitment to this outstanding new product.

The Laser 440 has both time and stop watch functions. Six digits are on display—four large digits and two small ones. You choose between hours, minutes and seconds or hours, minutes and date by pressing a button. The Laser memory remembers the number of days in a month and resets automatically on the first day of the new month.

The 440 is also available in an 11 function chronograph (stop watch) and is truly the ultimate Laser timepiece. You can time two separate laps of a multilap race keeping one lap in memory. You can accumulate time; you can view the time of one lap while continuing to time a lap stored in memory. As a business executive, you can time long distance phone calls and interviews. Lawyers can keep track of their services, and doctors can time the vital signs of their patients. Even while the chronograph is functioning, you can still view the time—something even many of the expensive digital chronographs cannot do.

BUILT DIFFERENTLY

All wires have been replaced with circuitry printed on one single thin surface. On this same surface are two integrated circuits which use gold contacts and are hermetically sealed to protect their several thousand micro components. The American-made Laser is shock resistant and uses a tough mineral glass crystal to protect the rugged electronics from the everyday water and humidity tortures normally given any watch.

NEW QUARTZ BREAKTHROUGH

Digital watch accuracy depends on the quartz crystal. Even the best crystals change frequency with shock or age (especially when first produced). The Laser 440 uses the new and very expensive, tuning fork crystal. It is first aged to not shift frequency more than five parts per million per year (more accurate than most radio or TV time signals) so the extreme accuracy you expect is built into your watch from the first day you wear it. The crystal is cushioned and solidly bonded to the crystal carrier eliminating all fine wires that may break from shock. In short, the advanced design of the crystal will assure guaranteed accuracy greater than 5 seconds per month—year after year after year.

The Laser 440 is ideal for pilots because of its cockpit visibility and chronograph functions, perfect for the businessman who depends on his watch for split-second accuracy and the ultimate watch for anybody who wants unquestionably the finest digital watch ever offered at any price.

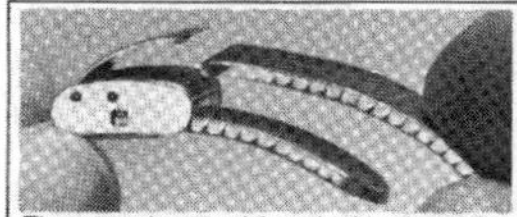

The expensive metal bracelet has the equivalent of 92 finely-hinged links and is completely adjustable. Simply slide the adjustment mechanism to the most comfortable position on the band for your wrist size and lock it into place. Then, whenever you have to put on your watch, simply hook the strap into the already pre-set adjustment mechanism and snap it shut. It's fast and simple and gives you the most comfortable fit of any watch by conforming exactly to the contour of your wrist.

HOW WE PROVIDE THE FINEST SERVICE

Can our company provide better service than even your local jeweler? We think so. If your Laser malfunctions during its unprecedented five-year warranty, just call us on our toll-free line. We have made arrangements with United Parcel Service to pick up your Laser at your door, at our expense, and we give you a loaner watch to use while your Laser is repaired. You pay nothing to have your watch serviced during its five-year warranty (that is if service is ever required) and we are as close as your phone or door.

WHO WILL BACK YOUR 5 YEAR WARRANTY?

Two solid companies are behind your new Laser. JS&A is America's largest single source of space-age products—a substantial company and a leader in electronics for over a decade. Our commitment to the consumer and to service is a matter of record. Check with the Better Business Bureau in your very own community, the Northbrook, Illinois Chamber of Commerce (312) 498-5555, or any of the 100 national magazines and newspapers in which we advertise. We realize that a quality watch warranteed for five years is a serious investment and our reputation for service and customer satisfaction must be unsurpassed. Most important, check with our customers. For almost two years we have sold and serviced the Sensor watch. We are proud of our record and will gladly share it with anyone who inquires.

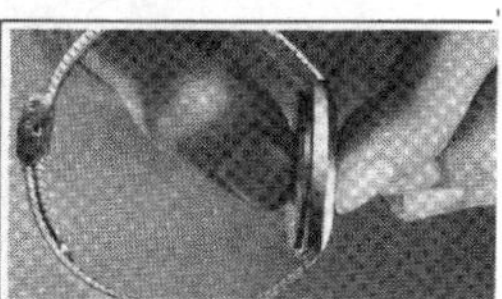

The Laser 440 is not only thin but is designed to conform to the contour of your wrist. A bulky digital watch can become annoying to wear—especially if you have a thin wrist.

The Sensor Laser 440 is manufactured exclusively for JS&A by Micro Display Systems, a leader in the new emerging watch technology and a well-financed company backed by one of the world's major manufacturers.

STANDING BEHIND A PRODUCT

The Laser 440 is everything you would want in a digital watch: a major advance in digital watch technology, all the really important functions you'll need, a service contract so solid that you'll never have to leave your home if service is ever required, and a product of unsurpassed quality and accuracy. But it is only after you receive it that you will convince yourself of its beauty, its design, its fit and the accuracy of our claims. For that reason we give you a one month trial period. Wear the Laser 440 for one full month. Check its accuracy, its feel and show it to others. Compare it to all other digitals. If you are not totally convinced that the new Laser is the finest digital watch at any price, then return it for a prompt and courteous refund.

To order your Laser 440 for a personal trial, simply call our toll-free number below and give us your credit card number or send us your business or personal check. There are no postage or handling charges (Illinois residents add 5% sales tax) and it will be sent to you promptly by United Parcel Service unless you specify otherwise.

A REVOLUTION IN TECHNOLOGY

There is a revolution taking place in the watch industry. Some digitals are getting thinner, some have dozens of new functions and some claim exceptional visibility. None have all the features in one quality timepiece. The new Laser 440 does. Order yours at no obligation today.

Stainless Steel With Time and Date.... $139
Gold Plated With Time and Date....... 159
Stainless Steel With Chronograph 199
Gold Plated With Chronograph 219

JS&A ranked first among all watch manufacturers in total unit sales of quality digital watches during 1976.

Dept. OO One JS&A Plaza
Northbrook, Ill. 60062 (312) 564-9000

CALL TOLL-FREE.... 800 323-6400
In Illinois call .... (312) 498-6900

January, 1977

We had focused primarily in the Wall Street Journal but this ad gave us the courage to advertise in every magazine we could get our hands on.

An unretouched photo of the world's first ambient light liquid crystal memory pocket calculator—the DataKing 800 manufactured by Rockwell International. The 800 can operate for one year on the same set of disposable batteries.

the End

A new memory calculator breakthrough means the end of the AC adapter, rechargeable battery and small display and the introduction of a new memory system.

$59.95 NATIONAL INTRODUCTORY PRICE
SUG. RETAIL: $79.95

If you've been waiting for the world's most advanced memory calculator—your timing is perfect.

Powered by two inexpensive 9 volt batteries, the 800 will last almost one year on the same set of batteries or ten times longer than even the lowest drain pocket calculators. But there are several other very exciting new feature breakthroughs.

RECHARGEABLE VS THROWAWAY BATTERIES

It all boils down to convenience vs savings. Rechargeable batteries cost roughly $3.00 per year to power the average pocket calculator. That isn't very expensive. But the calculator owner who wishes to recharge his batteries is always at the mercy of his AC adapter/charger. And the adapter 1) is always subject to malfunction, 2) is often heavier than the calculator and 3) requires AC power to drive it.

If you've ever been on an airplane when your calculator pooped out or if you have been unable to use your calculator because your AC adapter didn't work, you can appreciate the convenience of the throwaway battery. But throwaway batteries are more expensive—an average of about $4 to $7 to operate the average calculator per year.

The DataKing 800 costs roughly $1.00 per year to operate using readily available 9 volt batteries. Therefore no AC adapter is required nor is one provided.

BIG DISPLAYS VS SMALL DISPLAYS

The display is the biggest consumer of battery power in a calculator. The bigger the display, the more power required to light it. Sunlight can easily overpower the display's light-emitting elements making legibility impossible.

The DataKing 800 has a large easy-to-read liquid crystal display. When small electrodes, arranged to form digits, are charged by micro-currents of electricity, the liquid crystal turns opaque. The resulting numbers must then be illuminated by a light source to provide the contrast needed to read the display. The 800 employs a light-gathering prism that eliminates any need for an internal lighting system and consequently uses a mere fraction of the power required by other conventional calculators. And the brighter the room light, the easier it is to read—even in sunlight.

CLICK-ACTION VS FULL-THRUST KEYS

Most calculators have either 1) click-action keys that move a fraction of an inch and then click to indicate entry or 2) full-thrust keys that are spring-loaded and create contact after moving a distance. Both have advantages and disadvantages. Click-action keys can easily enter the wrong data should your finger overlap or accidentally touch another key, and full-thrust keys do not have the snap of click-action keys to confirm data entry.

The DataKing 800, using the advantages of both keyboard systems, has taken the full-thrust feel and added a click to provide the world's first "click-thrust" keyboard. Not only do you get a very positive data entry feel, but your chance of false entry is greatly minimized by the unique widely-spaced keys.

CHAIN MEMORY VS ACCESS MEMORY

Memory on a calculator is such an important feature that units without it are practically outdated. Chain memory (one of the most advanced systems) permits you to store individual numbers or answers to calculations in a memory bank and then recall the total of those numbers directly onto your display without erasing the total in your memory.

The DataKing 800 has access memory—the latest memory logic breakthrough. You can now take any number on your display and divide or multiply your memory total by that number—all without affecting what is shown on your display.

MANY OTHER FEATURES

Now that we've told you all about those revolutionary features, here are some additional qualities that make the DataKing the nation's unquestioned memory leader.

1) Easy to use Even if the 800 is your first pocket calculator, you'll find it a snap to learn. The algebraic logic (you perform the functions as you think) makes it easy to perform chain calculations. The automatic constants on all six functions require no separate switch to turn on, and there's a separate memory-plus and memory-minus entry system.

2) The best percentage system To add 5% to a $50 purchase, simply enter $50, then press the times key, the 5 key and then the percent key. The percentage amount of $2.50 is displayed. Then press the equal key—$52.50 is displayed. In short, you perform percentage problems exactly as you think for both addition, subtraction, multiplication and division.

3) The finest display The large 8-digit liquid crystal display with floating decimal has negative balance and overflow indicators. You can also clear any overflow condition and continue your calculations.

4) Access memory To achieve access into the memory with a number on the display, simply press the "M" key and then the corresponding function. For example, to add a number to memory, press "M" and the plus key. To divide a number into memory, press "M" and the divide key.

COMPARED TO TEXAS INSTRUMENTS

America's leading brand-name calculator is Texas Instruments. TI recently announced their new TI 2550 memory unit for $99.95. That same calculator is now outdated by the introduction of the 800. The TI 2550 uses rechargeable batteries and has a small display and the older chain memory system. Compare price, features, performance and dependability, and you can easily see why the DataKing is America's greatest memory calculator value.

5) Handsome styling Rarely do you find so many outstanding features in a highly-styled calculator. The DataKing 800 measures only 1½" x 3½" x 6" and weighs only 10½ ounces. Other features include a clear entry system for memory or mistaken entries, zero suppression, and fixed decimal point for addition or subtraction.

You are no doubt familiar with Rockwell International and their approach to quality. The DataKing 800 is no exception. Although the 800 was designed to be service-free, your unit is backed by a one year warranty and DataKing's national service-by-mail facility. DataKing, Inc. is a well financed and established company and a leading consumer electronics firm—further assurance that your modest investment is fully protected.

JS&A is so convinced that the 800 is the best memory unit you can buy that we are making the following offer: try the DataKing 800 for a full month. Compare it with every other calculator on the market for features, value, keyboard—whatever. If you are not absolutely convinced that it is the finest calculator value ever offered, return it anytime within that month for a prompt and courteous refund.

EXCHANGE YOUR PRESENT UNIT

Want to exchange your old, outdated calculator for the DataKing 800 without losing too much money? We've got a way. After you are absolutely satisfied with your DataKing 800, send us your outdated unit. JS&A will then send it to a deserving school, non-profit organization, or charitable institution who in turn will send you a letter of appreciation and a certificate acknowledging your contribution. Then use that contribution as a legitimate deduction on your income tax return. You'll be helping somebody in need, while justifying the purchase of the latest calculator technology.

TO ORDER BY MAIL

Simply send your check for **$62.45** ($59.95 plus $2.50 postage and handling) with your name, address, city, state, and zip code to the address shown below. If you wish to charge the 800 to your Master Charge, BankAmericard, Diners Club, or American Express credit card account, call our toll-free number or send us a brief note with your account number, signature and telephone number. Illinois residents add 5% sales tax. Order your DataKing 800 at no obligation today.

CREDIT CARD BUYERS CALL:
(800) 323-5886
IN ILLINOIS CALL (312) 498-6900

JS&A NATIONAL SALES GROUP
4200 Dundee Road, Northbrook, Illinois 60062
(312) 498-6900

March, 1974

The Halloween Sale was one of our biggest sales ever. The prices were spectacular but the availability was limited.

Halloween Sale

All treats and no tricks in America's most spectacular calculator sale.

TEXAS INSTRUMENTS $9.95 BOWMAR $19.95 APF $29.95 KEYSTONE $39.95 DATAKING KINGSPOINT $99.95

Unbelievable but true! JS&A has 5,000 calculators in various quantities set aside for this spectacular sale. The more sensational the price, the smaller the quantity, the more realistic the price, the larger the quantity—but each calculator represents a tremendous value and, in our opinion, an outstanding product in its price class.

JS&A is America's largest single source of electronic calculators. Our company introduced the nation's first pocket calculator three years ago and has since been the first company to break every price barrier, often months ahead of any other company. But prices have practically bottomed out, and with inflation and shortages, there may be no more major price drops. Even those $19.95 calculators are turning out to be more like toys than computers.

So in one unprecedented crowning sale spectacular, JS&A will reduce its inventory by breaking every conceivable price barrier and offering the greatest selection of the finest calculator products ever manufactured.

HERE'S HOW WE'VE ARRANGED THE SALE

We have commissioned a nationally recognized public accounting firm to objectively administer every aspect of this sale. Although their professional ethics prohibit us from mentioning their name, they are one of the nation's largest accounting firms and their name will be sent to those who request it.

All orders will be sent to a post office lock box and retrieved by the accounting firm on November 12, 1974. This firm will then supervise the opening of the mail to objectively insure that the rules of this sale will be strictly adhered to.

All envelopes will be placed on a table and selected and opened one by one until all calculators are sold. If your envelope is chosen and your first selection is sold out, you can have your second choice if it is still available. Envelopes will be chosen at random so everyone has an equal opportunity to get their first selection.

HOW TO ORDER

1. On a sheet of paper, write down the calculator of your choice. Make sure you indicate your first, second, and third choice if you wish to select alternates. You may order no more than 12 of each calculator model.

2. Include your check for the amount of your highest-priced selection. If your first choice was the $9.95 Texas Instruments unit and you listed a DataKing 800 @ $39.95 as your alternate selection, include enough money to cover the DataKing unit. In this manner you will have a greater chance of getting something from this sale.

3. Add a total of $3.50 to your check per entry (not per unit) to cover postage, handling and profit. The $3.50 will actually go towards paying the cost of this ad and the mailing of your selection if we fill your order. Illinois residents pay 5% sales tax on your purchase only.

If your envelope is chosen after we run out of all your selections, we will immediately mail back your check. If you obtain the lowest priced item of your selections, we will refund the difference to you.

SOME HELPFUL HINTS

1. Don't assume that because a price is so low, you'll have no chance of getting your selection. We have enough stock of even the lowest-priced merchandise to surprise quite a few people and remember, every entrant has an equal opportunity to receive the desired purchase.

2. Follow the rules carefully and choose alternate selections. You'll have a greater opportunity to obtain a bargain-priced calculator. There will not be a second chance, and this may possibly be the last sale of its type.

3. Christmas shopping? Order the maximum of twelve units. If you're lucky, you'll get all twelve.

4. Make sure you address the envelope properly. The correct address is:

JS&A Halloween Sale
Lock Box 777
Northbrook, Illinois 60062

5. Make all checks payable to the "**JS&A National Sales Group, Inc.**" and endorse the check properly.

Remember: JS&A will not make any sale decision. All sales will be determined by an independent public accounting firm in a fair and objective manner.

This is not a contest, sweepstakes, or gimmick, but a truly unique consumer buying opportunity. Dealers may also order. Many of the products offered are well below factory costs and a great profit opportunity for any wholesale calculator dealer. All orders must be accompanied by a check for the full amount. No credit card charges, C.O.D.'s or purchase orders can be accepted.

If you feel that the calculator you receive is not the spectacular value we say it is, return it within a week for a prompt refund. There is no way you can lose.

JS&A has introduced practically every major new calculator price and feature breakthrough. It is with great pride, therefore, that we present the most spectacular calculator sale in our nation's history. Join us in this tremendous buying opportunity.

TEXAS INSTRUMENTS 2550 memory and percentage calculator. The TI 2550 is really our most spectacular value and our first $9.95 calculator. Each unit comes complete with carrying case, one year warranty, rechargeable batteries and AC charger. A $69.95 retail value, only $9.95

BOWMAR MX75 memory calculator. This automatic accumulating memory and percentage calculator currently retails for $69.95. This unit comes complete with AC charger, rechargeable batteries, carrying case and one year warranty. Only $19.95

APF Mark 14 This four-button memory and percentage calculator has a bright LED display, five function constant, and sign change feature. Truly one of the easiest and best memory calculators to operate. Priced to sell retail at $59.95, only $29.95

DATAKING 800 pocket memory calculator has an exclusive, large liquid crystal display, true access memory and an easy-to-operate percentage system. The DataKing 800 has the longest battery life of any calculator sold today and comes complete with batteries and a one year warranty. Considered a superior calculator at $59.95, only $39.95

KEYSTONE Exponent 1 Scientific memory and square root calculator is rechargeable. It comes complete with charger, carrying case and one year warranty. A great bargain for school or science. Only $39.95

APF Mark VII 4-function 8 digit desk calculator comes with built-in digital clock, floating decimal, constant, and a large display. A great gift idea only $39.95

KINGSPOINT SC40 10 digit scientific calculator has scientific notation, bracket memory system, square root, pi, exponential functions, trigonometric functions, rechargeable batteries and a one year warranty. Comes complete with charger and carrying case only .. $99.95

SCIENTIFIC 8-digit calculator features fully addressable memory, trigonometric functions, pi, square root and exponents. The unit comes with a one year warranty, rechargeable batteries, carrying case only $69.95

SPECIAL BONUS We've obtained thousands of a brand name electric shaver rated highest in a leading consumer testing publication along with a handsome travel case. The shaver is a heavy duty 110/220 volt unit with several unique features. Your cost for either the man's or lady's version is only $19.95

4200 DUNDEE ROAD
NORTHBROOK, ILLINOIS 60062
(312) 498-6900

October, 1974

We received so many orders that we had to hire armed guards to guard the mail as there were hundreds of thousands of dollars in checks in our offices.

The Results

Here's the story behind America's most spectacular calculator sale and an exciting new digital watch offer.

This quarter page ad in the Wall Street Journal offered spectacular value and drew a tremendous response.

JS&A's Lorri Russin selects another lucky customer from a portion of the 57 feet of mail totalling over 12,000 envelopes in which over one half million dollars in checks were enclosed.

It was the most spectacular sale in our history.

HOW WE DID IT

In the ad shown above, JS&A offered a variety of high-priced calculators at exceptionally low prices. The more sensational the price, the smaller the quantity; the more realistic the price, the larger the quantity. But each calculator represented a tremendous value.

We offered a total of 5,000 calculators. We knew that there would be a great demand for the limited number of lower-priced units, so we engaged a nationally-recognized public accounting firm to assure our customers a fair and impartial selection of orders. Everyone had an equal opportunity to obtain the calculators of his or her choice since the orders were accumulated in a post office lock box and removed on the day the sale ended (Tuesday, November 12, 1974).

Participants could order up to 12 of the same item and choose alternate selections. JS&A had no access to the lock box nor any knowledge of the total response.

THE BIG DAY ARRIVES

On November 12th, the final day of the sale, the public accounting firm drove to the post office and picked up the mail which was later protected by two armed guards. When the 12,000 responses were stacked, they extended 57 feet, turning our office into a sea of mail.

THE BIG JOB BEGINS

We sequentially numbered each of the 12,000 envelopes and then produced a computer printout of all 12,000 numbers randomly listed. The public accounting firm then supervised the random selection to insure that each lucky customer was fairly chosen. With over 12,000 letters, it wasn't until late Thursday that the lucky participants eligible for the 5000 calculators were selected and the remaining steps of order-processing and typing began.

In the process we discovered that one customer had submitted over fifty letters. Many submitted two or three but, for the most part, there were single entries. Incidentally, despite the totally objective random selection, the gentleman submitting 50 letters did not have one of his letters chosen.

OVER ONE HALF MILLION DOLLARS

A total of over one half million dollars was enclosed in the envelopes. Consequently, a contingent of armed guards kept constant watch until all checks were either processed or returned. Checks ranged from $13.45 for the Texas Instruments calculator to over $1,200 for 12 of the KingsPoint units. Several people were disqualified because they either forgot to sign their checks or they sent the wrong amount. But, for the most part, thousands of calculators were sold to many delighted customers.

With eleven others in his office, a man bought 12 Texas Instruments calculators at $9.95 each and regretted not ordering all twelve for himself. Entire engineering departments were pleasantly surprised when they were notified that their scientific calculators were going to cost them up to 40% less than what they'd have to pay at any retail outlet.

OUR BIG SURPRISE

But we did have one surprise. DataKing made a quantity of their units available to sell at $39.95 as part of the Halloween Sale. Worried that JS&A would be unable to liquidate DataKing's entire inventory, DataKing overreacted by offering the unit for $34.95 directly to readers of the Wall Street Journal. They later apologized and credited our account so that we could offer the same unit with carrying case at $34.95. All those who ordered the DataKing 800 will be receiving a refund and a carrying case.

A NEW MARKETING TOOL

JS&A's Halloween Sale was the first promotion of its type and may be the year's greatest new consumer-oriented idea. The concept is simple. Many manufacturers who have heavy inventories and wish to liquidate them by dropping prices are often afraid to do so. They don't want to upset their present channels of retail distribution.

JS&A has found a way to create an exciting sale, make it appear like a contest, all without upsetting the normal channels of retail distribution. And the consumer benefits through spectacular values. Already a car dealer in Texas is planning to use portions of our concept to sell cars, and several companies have asked us for our consulting services.

QUANTITIES KEPT CONFIDENTIAL

The one thing we can't reveal are the quantities. Again, the reason is simple. We did not want to discourage participants by listing the smaller quantities of lower-priced units nor did we want to embarrass any suppliers by listing the larger quantities of higher-priced units.

JS&A will repeat a similar offer in a private calculator sale to all those whose orders were returned unfilled. And because the offer will not be published in a newspaper, all quantities will be specified.

JS&A also saved on the processing of orders. With all orders accumulated, processed, and shipped in one batch, the processing costs were reduced. By insisting on checks with orders, we also saved on credit card charges. We were literally able to sell calculators with a one dollar mark-up and make a profit.

So it all added up to tremendous savings, lots of fun, and another example of the creative marketing approach that has made JS&A America's largest single source of electronic calculators and other space-age products.

OUR NEXT SPECTACULAR OFFER

JS&A has 5,000 of the new space-age liquid crystal quartz digital watches. This nationally-advertised, solid-state, stainless steel field-effect watch is the same one shown in many Christmas catalogs for $150. Its lowest price to date has been $119.95. JS&A's price: only $69.95.

There are two types of solid-state digital watches. With the L.E.D. watch, you press a button and the readout is displayed in red digits. With the liquid crystal or LCD, small power requirements permit the constant display of time. Our LCD displays the hours and minutes constantly in black numbers while a colon pulses out the seconds. JS&A's new LCD watch has an accuracy of plus or minus one minute per year and comes with an unconditional one year parts and labor warranty.

Rather than go through the random selection process, JS&A has decided to sell it on a first-come, first-served basis. We feel there are enough watches to last about ten days, however, we promise to return your check promptly if we are unable to fill your order. Simply send us your check for $69.95 plus $3.50 postage, handling and profit (Illinois residents add an additional $3.50 sales tax) to the JS&A Digital Watch Sale, 4200 Dundee Road, Northbrook, Illinois 60062.

If you are not totally satisfied after you receive your watch, you may return it within two weeks for a prompt and courteous refund. There is no obligation! If you're doing your Christmas shopping early or if you're looking for an excellent buy, we urge you to act promptly and take advantage of this spectacular value.

We can't mention the name of the watch nor the manufacturer for if we did, his current channels of retail distribution would be adversely affected. By our insisting on checks with your order and with your trust and confidence in our selection and integrity, we have made possible the most exciting, spage-age digital quartz watch sale in history. Please join us by acting today.

November, 1974

Our Mickey Math calculator was originally designed for children, but we pitched it to business people without success.

©WALT DISNEY PRODUCTIONS

Impress your friends, figure little deals, close sales and feel smarter with the world's most powerful calculator.

Alco, one of America's largest manufacturers of paper clips and rubber bands, has developed a space-age computer miracle.

HERE'S WHAT IT CAN DO

You're a salesman. You're at lunch with a prospective customer. While discussing prices, your customer pulls out his $400 Hewlett Packard HP-80. You pull out your $19.95 Mickey Math. Two minutes later you walk out with the sale.

You're the financial vice president of a major U.S. corporation. You're at the board of directors meeting. The chairman of the board poses an important financial question and points to you for the answer. You open your briefcase and pull out your Mickey Math. The next day you're promoted to president.

Success stories like the above are real possibilities when you own a Mickey Math calculator. In fact our guarantee of satisfaction clearly states, "If the Mickey Math calculator does not make you rich, famous, more interesting and smarter, return it any time within two weeks for a prompt and courteous refund." And no other calculator company could dare make that guarantee.

FOR LITTLE DEALS ONLY

Mickey Math has six large, yet powerful digits. That's why we recommend it for little deals only. Its full-floating decimal, four-function constant and algebraic logic (you perform the functions as you think) make working complex problems a breeze.

You can do chain calculations, derive negative balances and figure all kinds of answers automatically, all by pressing little round buttons. It's truly the ultimate calculator.

Mickey Math is only 1" x 7½" x 7½" and fits conveniently in your briefcase, suitcase or the trunk of your car. It weighs only 14 ounces and its built-in, space-age handle makes it fun to lug around.

THEY'LL NEVER FORGET YOU

Give Mickey Math to somebody you want to impress: your boss, banker, State Farm insurance salesman or favorite General Motors executive. They'll not only be getting the latest in space-age technology, but they'll never forget you.

It is true that the Mickey Math calculator was designed for children. The instruction booklet with its colorful pictures and clear examples is designed to stimulate math interest and create little geniuses.

But as America's largest single source of electronic calculators and other space-age products, we feel Mickey Math's place is with the executive—as a business tool and as a major element in his day-to-day, decision-making process.

If you're looking for the perfect gift or a great business tool, we urge you to act quickly and order your Mickey Math electronic calculator at no obligation today!

EXECUTIVE ORDER FORM

○ Yes, please rush me___ Mickey Math electronic calculator(s) @ $22.45 each ($19.95 plus $2.50 postage and handling) complete with one year warranty and explicit Mickey Mouse instructions. I understand that if I do not become rich, famous, more interesting or smarter, I may return Mickey Math within two weeks for a prompt and courteous refund.

○ Please add the $4.95 AC adapter which will allow me to conserve battery power while using the calculator at my desk or during lengthy executive conferences.

○ Please add the $3.00 padded carrying case.

Clip out Executive Order Form and mail with your check to the address shown below:

JS&A NATIONAL SALES GROUP

DEPT WMM 4200 DUNDEE RD.
NORTHBROOK, ILL, 60062 (312) 564-9000

©JS&A GROUP, INC., 1975

January, 1975

We had an exclusive to sell this new innovation in checkbook design, but it was offered during a major recession and sales really suffered. We lost on this one.

Checkbook with a brain

Never make another checkbook error with America's first computerized banking center in a case.

The new Corvus CheckMaster is a checkbook holder with a built-in computer—a time-saving device that will keep you in perfect balance for every check you write, every day of the year.

YOUR BANK WILL LOVE YOU

If you're like most Americans, your checkbook is a disaster area. And your electronic calculator isn't helping much.

Now, there's a great new space-age product called the Corvus CheckMaster designed specifically to keep you in perfect balance, for every check you write, every day of the year. And it's actually easier to use than a calculator.

HERE'S HOW IT WORKS

Open your checkbook holder and turn on the built-in computer. Press the "Balance" key, and your bank balance is recalled on the display. The CheckMaster memory is so powerful that it never forgets your balance—even months after you last recall it.

Enter the amount of your check, and press the "Check" key. The check amount is automatically deducted from your balance, and your new balance is displayed—and all with just one key stroke.

Or enter the amount of a deposit, and press the "Deposit" key. Your deposit is automatically added to your balance, and again, your new balance is displayed.

MANY EXTRA FEATURES

The Corvus CheckMaster does so much, so easily, and it's great fun to use. Here are seven reasons why:

1. Easily corrects mistakes If you enter the wrong digits, press the "Clear" key. Only your mistake will be cleared—never the balance.

2. Worry-free decimal Just enter the digits. The unit's dollar-position decimal always keeps the decimal point where it belongs.

3. Low battery signal The unit's penlight batteries will last one year with average use. A low battery signal on the display will indicate when it's time to replace them.

4. Overdraft alert CheckMaster will signal an overdrawn account plus show the overdraft amount and help you avoid the embarrassment of having a check accidentally bounce.

5. Safety switch If you forget to turn off your computer, don't worry. Whenever you close your case, your unit shuts off automatically.

6. Private viewing angle Don't worry about anyone seeing your balance. The red display can only be viewed by the user and registers up to $9,999.99 or any six digits.

7. Perfect size The CheckMaster's handsome tan and cream-colored case measures 7/8" x 3 5/8" x 6 3/4" and weighs only 8 ounces.

To find out your exact balance, even months after you've last recalled it, simply open your case and press the balance key. CheckMaster's memory never forgets. Designed for both men and women, CheckMaster holds any standard-sized personal checks, check register, credit cards and important papers.

RUGGED AND SHOCKPROOF

Drop it, sit on it, drop it again—CheckMaster's shock-proof case will withstand plenty of abuse. The integrated circuit is hermetically sealed for a lifetime of trouble-free service. A spot of gold is even used in the circuit's final sealing process to insure CheckMaster's very high level of reliability.

CONTROL YOUR PURCHASES

Take CheckMaster with you to the supermarket. Set a dollar limit on what you intend to buy. Then enter each item you purchase as if you were writing a check. When your balance reaches your limit, stop buying and head for the check-out counter. It's a great way to control your budget and prevent overcharging by the check-out clerk.

THE PERFECT GIFT

CheckMaster makes the ideal gift for your wife, husband, friend or anybody who has a personal checking account. Even a person who already owns a calculator will appreciate CheckMaster's value and convenience.

$39.95 NATIONAL INTRODUCTORY PRICE

The CheckMaster is perfect insurance against bounced checks, overdrafts, arithmetic errors and bank errors. Its powerful memory, simple operation, and many extra features make it another example of how space-age technology has made fun out of one of the most time-consuming household tasks.

MORE THAN GUARANTEED

The Corvus CheckMaster will make such an improvement in helping you balance your checkbook that we make the following unusual money-back guarantee: use the CheckMaster until your next bank statement arrives or for one full month. If the CheckMaster does not balance your checkbook perfectly and actually pay for itself in either convenience or actual savings, return it for a prompt and courteous refund. You can't lose.

A NATIONAL INTRODUCTORY PRICE

The American-made CheckMaster is manufactured by Corvus, a wholly—owned subsidiary of Mostek Corporation and a leading consumer electronics manufacturer. Mostek was the first company to manufacture the integrated circuit—the heart of today's pocket calculator. JS&A is the world's largest single source of electronic calculators, digital watches and other space-age products. We have purchased the entire initial CheckMaster production to sell exclusively through the mail for only $39.95 during its national introduction.

HOW TO ORDER

Credit card buyers may order by calling our national toll-free number or any of the local numbers listed below. Or you may send your check or money order for $42.45 per unit ($39.95 plus $2.50 postage, insurance and handling—Illinois residents add 5% sales tax) to the address shown below. But act quickly! See for yourself how easy it is to keep your checkbook in perfect balance every day of the year. Order your CheckMaster at no obligation today.

ONE YEAR WARRANTY

CALL TOLL-FREE.................. (800) 323-6400
In the State of Illinois call.......... (312) 498-6900
In the Los Angeles area call........ (213) 629-1190
In the San Francisco area call..... (415) 391-1700
In the New York City area call... (212) 964-0690
In Montreal Canada call.............. (514) 332-9523
In Toronto Canada call............... (416) 445-8136
In Australia call.................... Melbourne 53 5286

DEPT. BAN 4200 DUNDEE ROAD
NORTHBROOK, ILLINOIS 60062
(312) 564-9000 © JS&A Group, Inc., 1975

March, 1975

Pocket CB: We sold over a quarter of a million of these units during the hot CB craze in the mid 70's.

Pocket CB

New integrated circuit technology and a major electronic breakthrough brings you the world's smallest citizens band transceiver.

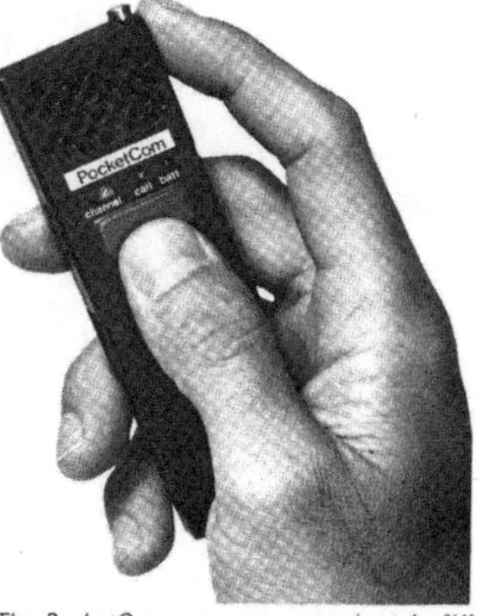

The PocketCom measures approximately ¾" x 1½" x 5½" and easily fits into your shirt pocket. The unit can be used as a personal communications link for business or pleasure.

SMALL ENOUGH FOR YOUR POCKET

Scientists have produced a personal communications system so small that it can easily fit in your pocket. It's called the PocketCom and it replaces larger units that cost considerably more.

MANY PERSONAL USES

An executive can now talk anywhere with anybody in his office, his factory or job site. The housewife can find her children at a busy shopping center. The motorist can signal for help in an emergency. The salesman, the construction foreman, the traveler, the sportsman, the hobbyist—everybody can use the PocketCom—as a pager, an intercom, a telephone or even a security device.

LONG RANGE COMMUNICATIONS

The PocketCom's range is limited only by its 100 milliwatt power and the number of metal objects between units or from a few blocks in the city to several miles on a lake. Its receiver is so sensitive, that signals several miles away can be picked up from stronger citizens band base or mobile stations.

VERY SIMPLE OPERATION

To use the PocketCom simply turn it on, extend the antenna, press a button to transmit, and release it to listen. And no FCC license is required to operate it. The PocketCom has two Channels—channel 14 and an optional second channel. To use the second channel, plug in one of the 22 other citizens band crystals and slide the channel selector to the second position. Crystals for the second channel cost $7.95 and can only be ordered after receipt of your unit.

The PocketCom components are equivalent to 112 transistors whereas most comparable units contain only twelve.

A MAJOR BREAKTHROUGH

The PocketCom's small size results from a breakthrough in the solid state device that made the pocket calculator a reality. Mega scientists took 112 transistors, integrated them on a micro silicon wafer and produced the world's first transceiver lineai integrated circuit. This major breakthrough not only reduced the size of radio components but improved their dependability and performance. A large and expensive walkie talkie costing several hundred dollars might have only 12 transistors compared to 112 in the Mega PocketCom.

BEEP-TONE PAGING SYSTEM

You can page another PocketCom user, within close range, by simply pressing the PocketCom's call button which produces a beep tone on the other unit if it has been left in the standby mode. In the standby mode the unit is silent and can be kept on for weeks without draining the batteries.

SUPERIOR FEATURES

Just check the advanced PocketCom features now possible through this new circuit breakthrough: 1) Incoming signals are amplified several million times compared to only 100,000 times on comparable conventional systems. 2) Even with a 60 decibel difference in signal strength, the unit's automatic gain control will bring up each incoming signal to a maximum uniform level. 3) A high squelch sensitivity (0.7 microvolts) permits noiseless operation without squelching weak signals. 4) Harmonic distortion is so low that it far exceeds EIA (Electronic Industries Association) standards whereas most comparable systems don't even meet EIA specification. 5) The receiver has better than one microvolt sensitivity.

EXTRA LONG BATTERY LIFE

The PocketCom has a light-emitting diode low-battery indicator that tells you when your 'N' cell batteries require replacement. The integrated circuit requires such low power that the two batteries, with average use, will last weeks without running down.

The PocketCom can be used as a pager, an intercom, a telephone or even a security device.

MULTIPLEX INTERCOM

Many businesses can use the PocketCom as a multiplex intercom. Each employee carries a unit tuned to a different channel. A stronger citizens band base station with 23 channels is used to page each PocketCom. The results: an inexpensive and flexible multiplex intercom system for large construction sites, factories, offices, or farms.

NATIONAL SERVICE

The PocketCom is manufactured exclusively for JS&A by Mega Corporation. JS&A is America's largest supplier of space-age products and Mega Corporation is a leading manufacturer of innovative personal communication systems—further assurance that your modest investment is well protected. The PocketCom should give you years of trouble-free service, however, should service ever be required, simply slip your 5 ounce PocketCom into its handy mailer and send it to Mega's prompt national service-by-mail center. It is just that easy.

GIVE IT A REAL WORKOUT

Remember the first time you saw a pocket calculator? It probably seemed unbelieveable. The PocketCom may also seem unbelieveable so we give you the opportunity to personally examine one without obligation. Order only two units on a trial basis. Then really test them. Test the range, the sensitivity, the convenience. Test them under your everyday conditions and compare the PocketCom with larger units that sell for several hundred dollars.

After you are absolutely convinced that the PocketCom is indeed that advanced product breakthrough, order your additional units, crystals or accessories on a priority basis as one of our established customers. If, however, the PocketCom does not suit your particular requirements perfectly, then return your units within ten days after receipt for a prompt and courteous refund. You cannot lose. Here is your opportunity to test an advanced space-age product at absolutely no risk.

A COMPLETE PACKAGE

Each PocketCom comes complete with mercury batteries, high performance Channel 14 crystals for one channel, complete instructions, and a 90 day parts and labor warranty. To order by mail, simply mail your check for $39.95 per unit (or $79.90 for two) plus $2.50 per order for postage, insurance and handling to the address shown below. (Illinois residents add 5% sales tax). But don't delay.

Personal communications is the future of communications. Join the revolution. Order your PocketComs at no obligation today.

$39⁹⁵ NATIONAL INTRODUCTORY PRICE

DEPT. PS JS&A Plaza
Northbrook, Illinois 60062
CALL TOLL-FREE . . 800 325-6400
In Missouri call. . . . 800 323-6400

©JS&A Group, Inc., 1976

September, 1975

We got the rights to offer a Picasso product and did very well, rapidly acquiring 12,000 new customers with our profitable promotion.

Only 1250 sets of four special Picasso *les Artistes* tiles will be offered to a select group of collectors.

This advertisement in the Wall Street Journal will be the only one you will ever see on this special release.

This advertisement is being run for what may well be the most unusual limited edition offer ever made. And for good reason. First, your chances of purchasing it, even if you have the funds, are very remote. Secondly, the concept behind its issuance gives even art collectors, with meager means, the same opportunity to purchase the series, at its initial offering, as wealthy collectors. Finally, it is a ceramic tile series—an innovative new art form with reproductions by one of the world's most admired names in art—Pablo Picasso.

There have been no licensed coins or collectors plates issued with reproductions by Picasso since his death. In an historic decision, approval was granted for a special release of tiles, but under the strict supervision of the official Picasso licensing group. The price of seven dollars per tile was established or twenty eight dollars for the complete series.

Each ceramic tile in the four-part series was processed initially in England using the highest quality clay. The exact Picasso drawing is then silk-screened on the tile and then baked at 1862 degrees Farenheit until the image is firmly in the ceramic.

Several authentification steps are then taken. Each tile 1) is sandblasted on the reverse side; 2) has a 14 karat gold spot glazed in the tile itself; 3) is numbered and the thumb print of an agent of the official licensing group is imprinted and ceramitized on the reverse side. All tiles are registered, a certificate is issued, and the owner's name is kept on file in a registry. Any sale or transfer of the tile can also be registered.

UNLIKE ANY OTHER LIMITED EDITION

A limited edition is simply the production of a specific quantity of an item. Usually the molds or dies are destroyed after production to preserve the value and uniqueness of the specific art form. Franklin Mint, for example, normally limits the quantity by the number of participants who apply for the series before the registration date closes. The Picasso *les Artistes* series, however, is the world's first *Random Selection Collectors Series*—a series whose quantities will not meet the demand created for them necessitating a form of objective random selection to select participants.

To acquire the series you must fill out the coupon below and mail it to Battram Galleries. All applications will be entered into a computer and numbered consecutively. A public accounting firm will then generate a random number list equal to the number of participants. The first 1250 participants whose numbers correspond to the first 1250 numbers on the random list will be eligible to purchase the series. All applicants will be notified of the results. No money is required with your application and duplicate applications will be disqualified.

The first tile will be issued in April, 1976 and the remaining three tiles at three month intervals. If you are selected to receive the series, you will receive a reservation form insuring your participation in this exclusive offering.

When the licensing group licensed the Picasso *les Artistes* tile series, it did so with two provisos: that the offering company be prohibited from purchasing the series itself and not greatly profit from the initial offering.

To insure that little or no profit was made on the initial offering, the licensing group accepted the proposal of Battram Galleries to market the collectors tiles through a *Wall Street Journal* advertisement.

OFFERING DISCLOSURE

Gross Sales
Offering price of \$7.00 per
tile x 4 tiles per set x 1250 sets \$35,000
Costs
5 col. x 16" advertisement
(1120 lines x \$15.75 per line) .. \$17,640
1250 sets x 4 tiles per set
x cost of tiles (\$2.88 each) \$14,400
Minus Costs \$32,040
Gross Profit **\$2,960**

NOTE: The gold embedded in each tile was contributed, at no charge, by the licensing group and is not included in the cost of the tiles.

The profit to Battram Galleries will probably be absorbed by the handling costs but the prestige of being associated with this new Picasso art form and the ancillary benefits are well worth our association.

THIS LIMITED EDITION IS DIFFERENT HERE ARE FOUR REASONS WHY:

- **Your chances of acquiring the series from this advertisement are very remote.**
- **We'll guarantee to buy back your entire collection anytime within five years.**
- **Little profit, if any, will be realized from the sale of these tiles.**
- **No money is required to participate.**

For its participation in the initial offering, Battram Galleries will also be designated the official registry and transfer agent for the tile series. When title to the series transfers from one collector to another, if the collection is registered, a \$5 registration fee is paid. Battram Galleries will also act as broker for the re-sale of the series and will receive a 20% brokerage fee for this service.

ABOUT THE SERIES

Picasso went through at least a half dozen identifiable periods in his prolific artistic career. In one of the phases, called the Classical period, he specialized in figures and narratives reminiscent of the art of ancient Greece and Rome. The four scenes portrayed on the *les Artistes* tiles are from that period. Each set of four tiles comes with a complete background explanation of the sketches written by nationally renown art critic and art authority Franz Schulze. In his contribution, Mr. Schulze describes the exceptional ease with which Picasso's line traces a common theme: The relationship of artist, model and art work.

The Picasso *les Artistes* tile series consists of four 6" x 6" square ceramic tiles with a green felt easel backing. The series can either be displayed in its own handsome presentation case on a counter with attached easel or hung on a wall. The square format, the fine craftsmanship, the exclusive nature and the limited distribution all add to its value but the name Picasso adds a dimension not available on any other similar art form.

FIVE YEAR BUY-BACK GUARANTEE

Battram Galleries will also buy back the collection from the original collector anytime within the first five years after issuance at the full original purchase price including the postage and insurance expenses incurred by the collector for the return of the collection.

HOW TO OBTAIN THE SERIES

All applicants may either send a post card or fill out the application form below and mail it to the address indicated. Remember, any applicant sending in duplicate applications will be disqualified. **Please do not send any money.** All applicants, including those selected, will be notified by March 10, 1976 and applications will not qualify if postmarked after February 29, 1976. No offer of any kind, whether it be for substantially more than the offering price or for special favors will be accepted. The Board of Governors of Battram Galleries, and suppliers and employees of the other JS&A Group companies will not be allowed to participate and will be disqualified if selected. If any buy-back request is made to Battram Galleries anytime within five years, we agree to advise the collector of the then current value of the *les Artistes* tile series and any other orders pending, as brokers for that series, before arrangements are completed for the return of the collection.

Battram Galleries further states that it will not substantially profit from the initial sale or offering of the tile series in accordance with the requirements of the Picasso licensing group and that any subsequent sale by Battram Galleries will be within the licensing provisions.

AN INVITATION TO PARTICIPATE

Battram Galleries extends an invitation to all of America's serious collectors to participate in this offering. If you have the honor of being selected, you will join an extremely small group of collectors who have distinguished themselves by both the process with which they were selected and the artistic value and achievement of owning a very limited Picasso reproduction. Your participation is invited.

INVITATION TO PARTICIPATE

I wish to be entered, at no cost or obligation, in the random selection process to determine those eligible for the Picasso *les Artistes* tile series.

Name ______
Address ______
City ______ State ______ Zip ______
Country ______ Phone ______
Signature ______

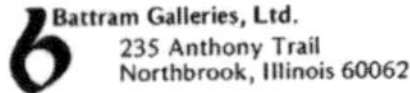

Battram Galleries is a JS&A company.

©JS&A Group, Inc., 1976

February, 1976

I ran his ad offering my services to work for any company selected in a random drawing if they would also send a check made payable to the American Cancer Society as a tribute to my mom who died of cancer around that time.

(The entire cost of this advertisement was paid for by Mr. Sugarman)

I'm the world's highest paid copywriter.

Nobody can buy my services, but for a few dollars I'll write your next ad.

By Joseph Sugarman

My gross income last year was $3,737,452. I worked a total of 64 hours writing copy to earn that salary and, if you've got one of our company's calculators, that figures out to be $58,397.69 per hour. Not bad for a guy who flunked English.

I write the mail order ads for the JS&A National Sales Group—ads that appear in The Wall Street Journal and every major U. S. publication. I also own the company.

It takes me about two days to write an ad around a product my staff selects for me. Then they test my copy in an advertisement, and roll out in every major national publication. We're a well organized company with a unique creative approach to marketing that depends on the ability of my copy to move millions of dollars in merchandise.

So here I am. 37 years old and financially secure beyond my wildest expectations. And think of it—all through the power of my pen.

About three months ago my mom died of cancer. Two years prior she was a beautiful woman of 59 years who looked 10 years younger.

Cancer crept throughout her entire body and literally ravaged her during two incredibly agonizing years. Her doctors and family stood by helpless as we saw her painfully disintegrate into a human vegetable. You've never known the feeling of helplessness until you've experienced cancer slowly eating away the life fibers of your loved ones.

And like many people whose families were touched by this disease, there were questions. Why hasn't a cure been found? Why are we spending billions for defense and foreign aid when one billion dollars for research could do so much to find a cure?

In this election year, why can't just one of the presidential candidates get up there and say, "As you can see, I'm not that much different than anybody else running for president, but if elected I want to be known for just one thing—the president who started the first major all-out war against cancer."

I contribute to the American Cancer Society as do millions of other Americans. But with the creative power of my pen, I felt I could do more to combat this disease than the sheer force of my dollars.

I've devised a way to provide someone with over 3 million dollars of my time ($58,397.69 per hour x 12 hrs/day x 5 days per week = $3,503,861.40) for an "investment" of just a few dollars.

Send me your name and address and a contribution made payable to the American Cancer Society for any amount—from $5 to $500 to $5,000. I will personally open each envelope, assign a sequence number to it, and then drop you a handwritten thank you note. I will then, through the use of my company's computer, randomly select my lucky client.

If you are selected, I will fly to your city, spend one week at your offices and work 12 hours per day—all at my expense including air fare, hotel and meals. I will work with your creative department or write copy for your next brochure, mailing piece or advertisement.

All checks received will be given directly to the American Cancer Society and all expenses, including the full cost of this advertisement, will be paid by me. The winner will be announced to the participants through a news release and I will call and congratulate the winner.

Send your special American Cancer Society contribution to me: Joseph Sugarman, JS&A, Northbrook, Illinois 60062. This offer is open to the business and advertising community or anyone who could use my services. April is National Cancer Month so entries must be postmarked by April 30, 1976. The American Cancer Society will also send you a receipt acknowledging your contribution for tax purposes.

Then what is my next step? Convince the American Cancer Society that my small idea could raise millions of dollars for them. I'd get every manufacturer of a consumer product to contribute one of their items to a random selection drawing similar to the one in this advertisement. There would be 20 automobiles, 100 TV sets, 50 dishwashers, 60 refrigerators—a huge collection of consumer products that could be used in a national cancer awareness promotion that could generate a substantial return for the American Cancer Society.

A dream? Not if you make it happen. Please send your contribution and let me select you as my next client. Thank you.

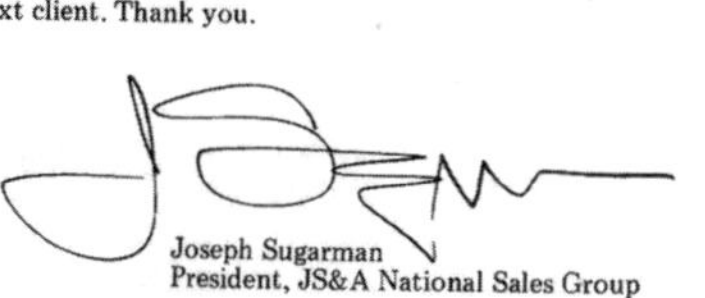

Joseph Sugarman
President, JS&A National Sales Group

These are a few of the ads I've written during the past year. I've also written successful copy for almost every conceivable type campaign from humor to specific trade applications.

March, 1976

Consumers Hero was another company I started from scratch selling refurbished electronics supplied by a friend of mine who repaired these products.

HOT

A new consumer concept lets you buy stolen merchandise if you're willing to take a risk.

We developed an exciting new consumer marketing concept. It's called "stealing." That's right, stealing!

Now if that sounds bad, look at the facts. Consumers are being robbed. Inflation is stealing our purchasing power. Our dollars are shrinking in value. The poor average consumer is plundered, robbed and stepped on.

So the poor consumer tries to strike back. First, he forms consumer groups. He lobbies in Washington. He fights price increases. He looks for value.

So we developed our new concept around value. Our idea was to steal from the rich companies and give to the poor consumer, save our environment and maybe, if we're lucky, make a buck.

A MODERN DAY ROBIN HOOD

To explain our concept, let's take a typical clock radio retailing for $39.95 at a major retailer whose name we better not mention or we'll be sued. It costs the manufacturer $9.72 to make. The manufacturer sells the unit to the retailer for $16.

THE UNCLE HENRY PROBLEM

Let's say that retailer sells the clock radio to your Uncle Henry. Uncle Henry brings it home, turns it on and it doesn't work. So Uncle Henry trudges back to the store to exchange his "lousy rotten" clock radio for a new one that works ("lousy" and "rotten" are Uncle Henry's words).

Now, the defective one goes right back to the manufacturer along with all the other clock radios that didn't work. And if this major retail chain sells 40,000 clock radios with a 5% defective rate, that's 2,000 "lousy rotten" clock radios.

CONSUMERS PROTECTED ALREADY

Consumers are protected against ever seeing these products again because even if the manufacturer repairs them, he can't recycle them as new units. He's got to put a label on the product clearly stating that it is repaired, not new, and if Uncle Henry had his way the label would also say that the product was "lousy" and "rotten."

It's hard enough selling a new clock radio, let alone one that is used. So the manufacturer looks for somebody willing to buy his bad product for a super fantastic price. Like $10. But who wants a clock radio that doesn't work at any price!

ENTER CONSUMERS HERO

We approach the manufacturer and offer to steal that $39.95 radio for $3 per unit. Now think of it. The manufacturer has already spent $9.72 to make it, would have to spend another $5 in labor to fix and repackage it, and still would have to mark the unit as having been previously used. So he would be better off selling it to us for $3, taking a small loss and getting rid of his defective merchandise.

Consumers Hero is now sitting with 2,000 "lousy rotten" clock radios in its warehouse.

Here comes the good part. We take that clock radio, test it, check it and repair it. Then we life test it, clean it up, replace anything that makes the unit look used, put a new label on it and presto—a $39.95 clock radio and it only cost us $3 plus maybe $7 to repair it.

Impossible-to-trace ★ ★ Guarantee ★ ★

We guarantee that our stolen products will look like brand new merchandise without any trace of previous brand identification or ownership.

We take more care in bringing that clock radio to life than the original manufacturer took to make it. We put it through more tests, more fine tuning than any repair service could afford. We get more out of that $10 heap of parts and labor than even the most quality-conscious manufacturer. And we did our bit for ecology by not wasting good raw materials.

NOW THE BEST PART

We offer that product to the consumer for $20—the same product that costs us $3 to steal and $7 to make work. And we make $10 clear profit. But the poor consumer is glad we made our profit because:

1) We provide a better product than the original version.
2) The better product costs one half the retail price.
3) We are nice people.

BUT THERE'S MORE

Because we are so proud of the merchandise we refurbish, we offer a longer warranty. Instead of 90 days (the original warranty), we offer a five year warranty.

So that's our concept. We recycle "lousy rotten" garbage into super new products with five year warranties. We steal from the rich manufacturers and give to the poor consumer. We work hard and make a glorious profit.

To make our concept work, we've organized a private membership of quality and price-conscious consumers and we send bulletins to this membership about the products available in our program.

Items range from micro-wave ovens and TV sets to clock radios, digital watches, and stereo sets. There are home appliances from toasters to electric can openers. Discounts generally range between 40 and 70 percent off the retail price. Each product has a considerably longer warranty than the original one and a two week money-back trial period. If you are not absolutely satisfied, for any reason, return your purchase within two weeks after receipt for a prompt refund.

Many items are in great abundance but when we only have a few of something, we select, at random, a very small number of members for the mailing. A good example was our $39.95 TV set (we had 62 of them) or a $1 AM radio (we had 1257). In short, we try to make it fair for everybody without disappointing a member and returning a check.

EASY TO JOIN

To join our small membership group, simply write your name, address and phone number on a slip of paper and enclose a check or money order for five dollars. Mail it to Consumers Hero, Three JS&A Plaza, Northbrook, Illinois 60062, %Dept. AI.

You'll receive a two year membership, regular bulletins on the products we offer and some surprises we would rather not mention in this advertisement. But what if you never buy from us and your two year membership expires. Fine. Send us just your membership card and we'll fully refund your five dollars plus send you interest on your money.

If the consumer ever had a chance to strike back, it's now. But act quickly. With all this hot merchandise there's sure to be something for you. Join our group and start saving today.

CONSUMERS HERO®

JS&A NATIONAL SALES GROUP Consumers Hero has been made possible by grants from the JS&A National Sales Group.

© Consumers Hero, Inc., 1977

January, 1977

Nixon was exposed for recording his phone conversations so why not sell products that could record them as well? This ad ran and the FBI stopped by. The Wall Street Journal said they would not run my ads anymore. We stopped running it.

SYSTEM 3

The legal recording of phone conversations grows in popularity. Here's how you can save time, money, and improve your efficiency with America's newest business concept.

Tap Your Phone.

A 1971 United States Supreme Court decision clearly made the recording of telephone calls between two parties legal if one of the two parties arranged the recordings. The legal recording of phone conversations thus opened a new concept of business record keeping.

A NEW BUSINESS PRACTICE

You can now record important phone conversations or complicated business discussions and have both a permanent record of the call and an important reference. Very often the inflection and tone in a recording tell more about the conversation than the written facts.

AN ERA OF RESPECTABILITY

Phone tapping has always been associated with espionage, Watergate-type scandals, and controversy. The fact that President Nixon was using this form of record keeping did two things for telephone communication recording. First, it emphasized its legality. Secondly, it paved the way for business use of phone tapping as a new form of business record keeping.

SEVERAL BUSINESS USES

If you have an order taking department think of how much money you'll save in phone bills if you first record the orders and transcribe the results later. In addition you'll always be able to confirm a discrepancy if an error is made. Letters can be dictated and facts can be relayed over the phone quickly and later reviewed or put in written form. Combining your telephone with a good recording device makes sense and saves money.

THREE RECORDING SYSTEMS

The JS&A National Sales Group has developed three recording systems to be used with an induction-type phone pick-up. The pick-up is attached to the telephone head set by means of its suction cup and plugged into any one of three different Craig recording systems with a special cable. There's no installation necessary. The suction cup can be removed in seconds and because nothing is hard-wired to your telephone, there is no way to detect its use during a conversation. Each system has automatic level control to maximize clarity and volume and uses commonly available cassette tapes that range in length from 15 minutes to one hour.

RESPONSIBILITY IS IMPORTANT

With the right to record phone conversations comes an important degree of responsibility. For example, you should always advise your caller that you wish to record the call. Extending this courtesy will be both appreciated by the other party and pave the way to play back the recording if required in the future.

PHONE COMPANY TARIFFS

The telephone company tariffs suggest that a beep tone be placed on the recording at 15 second intervals. Non-compliance with this regulation however violates no law. The telephone company tariffs are simply the regulations under which the telephone company operates as approved by the Federal Communications Commission. To conform to these regulations, you must go "beep" every 15 seconds during your conversation or obtain an electronic beeping device.

THE FINEST RECORDING EQUIPMENT

JS&A offers the famous Craig line of recording equipment for several reasons. Craig Corporation maintains hundreds of affiliated service locations throughout the country with one probably located in your city. It's always good to know that service is available locally whenever needed or at one of three Craig service-by-mail locations. The line of Craig cassette recorders have always led the industry in value, performance and features—further assurance that the system you purchase is the best recording system for the money. All Craig portable units accept long lasting rechargeable nickel cadmium batteries and the AC adapters act as battery recharging units.

System 1: The Craig portable cassette recorder complete with induction phone pick-up and AC power supply. The unit comes complete with an external remote-control microphone and two cassette tapes. **$59.95**

System 2: The Craig portable cassette recorder with AM/FM radio, built-in condenser microphone and built-in AC adapter. This very attractive portable system can record directly off the AM or FM radio or the induction phone pick-up supplied with each unit. Four free cassettes are supplied. System 2 can also be used as an unobtrusive conference recorder. If you do not have a good AM/FM radio on your desk, the System 2 is a wise investment. **$99.95**

System 3: This is the ultimate in the Craig line of recorders. The System 3 has a built in telephone recording circuit and is a complete dictation and transcribing machine with back spacing and automatic tape counter. Your secretary can transcribe directly from the System 3 just as she does with her current dictation equipment. The System 3 operates on AC current only and comes complete with the telephone pick-up and six cassettes. **$219.95**

The use of phone tapping equipment in legitimate business and record keeping applications makes a great deal of sense. Its constructive and responsible use can save time, money and improve the efficiency of any business.

We hope this ad has opened your eyes to the good aspects of phone tapping. We also hope you consider purchasing your phone tap from us. We promise prompt delivery, good value and the right to return your purchase within two weeks for a prompt refund if you are not absolutely satisfied. We're in business to improve your business. Order a phone tap today.

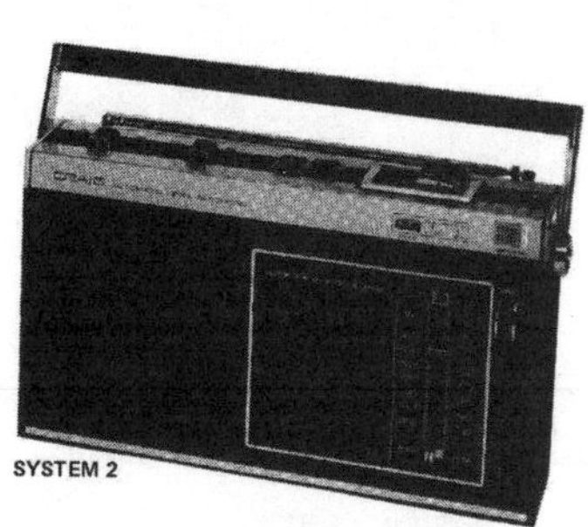

SYSTEM 2

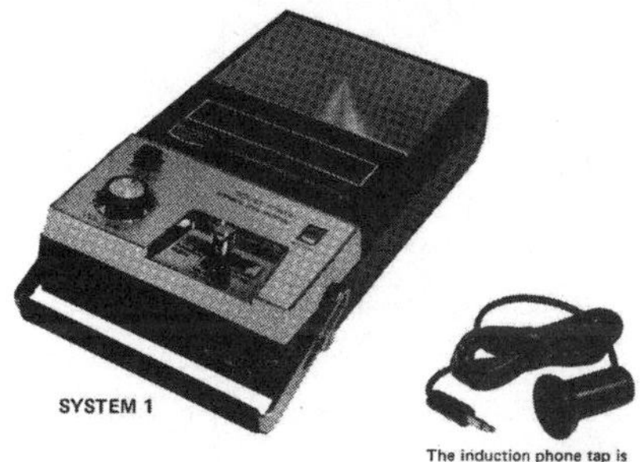

SYSTEM 1

The induction phone tap is supplied with each system.

ORDER FORM

Please rush me the following phone tap system. I understand that if I am not absolutely satisfied I may return my purchase within two weeks for a prompt refund.

System 1: ____ @ $59.95
System 2: ____ @ $99.95
System 3: ____ @ $219.95

Enclosed please find my check for $________
Which includes $2.50 for postage and handling.

Mail all orders to: JS&A National Sales Group 628 Michelline, Northbrook, Illinois 60062

☐ Please charge my Master Charge, (also include four numbers above name) Bank Americard, Diners Club, or American Express (be sure there are 13 digits) credit card account:

NO. ________ EXP. ____
SIGNATURE ________
NAME ________
COMPANY ________
ADDRESS ________
CITY ________ STATE ____
ZIP ________ PHONE ____

The JS&A National Sales Group is one of the leading national distributors of electronic calculators and other consumer and business related electronic products. Despite our size we insist upon complete customer service and satisfaction. Our descriptions must be accurate, our products must represent good value and you must be completely satisfied. You deal with people (not computers) and you receive answers to your letters and prompt refunds if you so request. The names of our customers are kept confidential and not sold for mailing lists. Our insistence on the highest standards of customer service is your assurance of complete satisfaction.

JS&A

NATIONAL SALES GROUP
628 Michelline, Northbrook, Ill. 60062 (312) 498-6900

April, 1973

The Bone Fone was a very popular product until Sony came out with the Walkman. Sales plummeted and we were left with a big loss.

STEREO BREAKTHROUGH

Bone Fone

T.M.

A new concept in sound technology may revolutionize the way we listen to stereo music.

The Bone Fone surrounds your entire body with a sound almost impossible to imagine.

You're standing in an open field. Suddenly there's music from all directions. Your bones resonate as if you're listening to beautiful stereo music in front of a powerful home stereo system.

But there's no radio in sight and nobody else hears what you do. It's an unbelievable experience that will send chills through your body when you first hear it.

AROUND YOU

And nobody will know you're listening to a stereo. The entire sound system is actually draped around you like a scarf and can be hidden under a jacket or worn over clothes.

The Bone Fone is actually an AM/FM stereo multiplex radio with its speakers located near your ears. When you tune in a stereo station, you get the same stereo separation you'd expect from earphones but without the bulk and inconvenience. And you also get something you won't expect.

INNER EAR BONES

The sound will also resonate through your bones—all the way to the sensitive bones of your inner ear. It's like feeling the vibrations of a powerful stereo system or sitting in the first row listening to a symphony orchestra—it's breathtaking.

Now you can listen to beautiful stereo music everywhere—not just in your living room. Imagine walking your dog to beautiful stereo music or roller skating to a strong disco beat.

You can ride a bicycle or motorcycle, jog and even do headstands—the Bone Fone stays on no matter what the activity. The Bone Fone stereo brings beautiful music and convenience to every indoor and outdoor activity without disturbing those around you and without anything covering your ear.

SKI INVENTION

The Bone Fone was invented by an engineer who liked to ski. Every time he took a long lift ride, he noticed other skiers carrying transistor radios and cassette players and wondered if there was a better way to keep your hands free and listen to stereo music.

So he invented the Bone Fone stereo. When he put it around his neck, he couldn't believe his ears. He was not only hearing the music and stereo separation, but the sound was resonating through his bones giving him the sensation of standing in front of a powerful stereo system.

AWARDED PATENT

The inventor took his invention to a friend who also tried it on. His friend couldn't believe what he heard and at first thought someone was playing a trick on him.

The inventor was awarded a patent for his idea and brought it to JS&A. We took the idea and our engineers produced a very sensitive yet powerful AM/FM multiplex radio called the Bone Fone.

The entire battery-powered system is self-contained and uses four integrated circuits and two ceramic filters for high station selectivity. The Bone Fone weighs only 15 ounces, so when worn over your shoulders, the weight is not even a factor.

BUILT TO TAKE IT

The Bone Fone was built to take abuse. The large 70 millimeter speakers are protected in flexible water and crush resistant cases. The case that houses the radio itself is made of rugged ABS plastic with a special reinforcement system. We knew that the Bone Fone stereo may take a great deal of abuse so we designed it with the quality needed to withstand the worst treatment.

The Bone Fone stereo is covered with a sleeve made of Lycra Spandex—the same material used to make expensive swim suits, so it's easily washable. You simply remove the sleeve, dip it in soapy water, rinse and let the sleeve dry. It's just that easy. The entire system is also protected against damage from moisture and sweat making it ideal for jogging or bicycling.

The sleeve comes in brilliant Bone Fone blue—a color designed especially for the system. An optional set of four sleeves in orange, red, green and black is also available for $10. You can design your own sleeve using the pattern supplied free with the optional kit.

YOUR OWN SPACE

Several people could be in a car, each tuned to his own program or bring the Bone Fone to a ball game for the play by play. Cyclists, joggers, roller skaters, sports fans, golfers, housewives, executives—everybody can find a use for the Bone Fone. It's the perfect gift.

Why not order one on our free trial program and let your entire family try it out? Use it outdoors, while you drive, at ball games or while you golf, jog or walk the dog. But most important—compare the Bone Fone with your expensive home stereo system. Only then will you fully appreciate the major breakthrough this product represents.

GET ONE SOON

To order your Bone Fone, simply send your check or money order for **$69.95** plus $2.50 postage and handling to the address shown below. (Illinois residents add 5% sales tax.) Credit card buyers may call our toll-free number below. Add $10 if you wish to also receive the accessory pack of four additional sleeves.

We'll send you the entire Bone Fone stereo complete with four AA cell batteries, instructions, and 90-day limited warranty including our prompt service-by-mail address.

When you receive your unit, use it for two weeks. Take it with you to work, or wear it in your car. Take walks with it, ride your bicycle or roller skate with it. Let your friends try it out. If after our two-week free trial, you do not feel that the Bone Fone is the incredible stereo experience we've described, return it for a prompt and courteous refund, including your $2.50 postage and handling. You can't lose and you'll be the first to discover the greatest new space-age audio product of the year.

Discover the freedom, enjoyment, and quality of the first major breakthrough in portable entertainment since the transistor radio. Order a Bone Fone stereo at no obligation, today.

*Pending FCC approval.

Dept.WJ One JS&A Plaza
Northbrook, Ill. 60062 (312) 564-7000
Call TOLL-FREE 800 323-6400
In Illinois Call .... (312) 564-7000
©JS&A Group, Inc.,1979

November, 1979

Designed by Josh Reynolds, this was the first ion generator ever offered and was successful for three straight years.

NEW INVENTION

The new Energaire ionized oxygen generator will make a handsome addition to any desk.

Miracle Fuzz

A new space-age invention and the same effect as lightning combine to create the world's first home oxygen regeneration system.

You need oxygen to live. You can live without food for 60 days, without water for seven days, but without oxygen, you won't make it past two minutes.

That small piece of fuzz located on top of the cylinder shown above emits negatively-charged electrons which attach themselves to molecules of oxygen thus creating ionized oxygen.

You are already familiar with ionized oxygen if you've smelled the air after a thunderstorm. You feel great, revitalized, and alert. The lightning from the storm adds a small negatively-charged electron to each oxygen molecule in a process called ionization.

POSITIVE ADVANTAGES

Ionized oxygen performs several positive functions. First, it cleanses the air by attaching itself to anything floating in the air, causing it to fall to the ground.

Secondly, when inhaled, it has an effect very similar to pure oxygen. It is more readily absorbed by your system. It energizes your brain. You feel more alert and alive.

The new space-age product shown above is an oxygen ion generator called Energaire. The copper mesh fuzz on top of the unit is one of the secrets of the system.

Although it has no moving parts, you can actually feel a wind of ionized oxygen produced from the fuzz which spreads to fill an average-sized room in one minute.

EFFECTS FELT QUICKLY

A trip into the mountains exposes you to nature's freshly ionized oxygen. The Energaire produces this same effect. It will clean your room of odor-causing bacteria and stale, musty, or smoky air. Energaire will keep you alert. With a fresh supply of ionized oxygen, you will have more energy, be less fatigued, and you will sleep better.

Our polluted cities often deprive us of enough oxygen to make us feel healthy and alert. The Energaire solves this problem by providing a personal environment–an area that surrounds your body and work location with fresh ionized oxygen.

NEW SCIENCE

The oxygen ion generator is a relatively new product, yet its use in the home may make it more important than any filter system.

The Energaire is a new breakthrough. Ionized oxygen generators have been under development since the early 60's. The Energaire, using the latest in solid-state electronics, is the first cost-efficient system that produces several times the ion production of other commercial units that cost considerably more than the Energaire.

USED IN HOSPITALS

Ionized oxygen creates a germ-free environment–proven through research at several universities. Many hospitals are now converting their operating rooms and burn centers to ionized oxygen systems. Ionized oxygen also eliminates allergy-causing irritants making it ideal for homes as well as hospitals.

The heart of the Energaire is this small yet powerful component that replaces the much larger and heavier power supplies previously required by more expensive systems.

TRY THIS DRAMATIC TEST

To show the dramatic effect of ionized oxygen, take the ion generator, blow cigarette smoke into a clear bowl, and hold the bowl inverted over the system. The smoke will vanish. The charged oxygen particles appear to dissolve the smoke particles, precipitating them from the air.

In a room, Energaire surrounds you with these oxygen ions and cleans and purifies the air so even in a smoke-filled room, you will be breathing clean, country-fresh air all day long.

Ionized oxygen should not be confused with ozone. Ozone has a molecular formula of O_3, whereas the molecular formula for ionized oxygen is O_2 with a negatively charged ion.

DRAMATIC LIFE CHANGES

Working in an ionized oxygen environment, you think clearer, are more alert, and your brain functions better. In actual brain wave tests, there was an increase in alpha waves when ionized oxygen was used, indicating greater alertness, deeper relaxation, less stress, and more creative brain functioning.

The Energaire is actually a miniature lightning machine. The minute you plug it in, energy is converted into ionized oxygen. This efficient system uses one watt of power or less than a penny per week to operate, so you leave it on continuously.

We are so impressed with the pleasant effect of Energaire that we urge you to personally test it yourself in your home or office.

Order one at no obligation. Put it by your desk, or in any room where you spend a great deal of time. See if it doesn't make you feel better or make you more productive. See how it rids your room of allergy-causing particles and freshens the air.

SLEEP EASIER

At home, use the Energaire to reduce odor-causing bacteria. Use it by your bed and see how fresh, country-like air makes you sleep easier, deeper, and more relaxed.

You should notice the difference within one day–especially in a work environment. But use it for a full month. Then, if you do not feel better and totally convinced of the positive effects of ionized oxygen, return your unit for a prompt and courteous refund.

The Energaire is manufactured by the Ion Foundation, one of America's leading ion research laboratories.

Service should never be required, but if it is, there's a prompt service-by-mail center as close as your mailbox–further assurance that your modest investment is well protected. The Energaire measures 9" high by 3" in diameter and weighs 24 ounces.

To order your Energaire ionized oxygen generator, send **$69.95** plus $3.00 for postage and handling (Illinois residents, please add 5% sales tax) to the address shown below or credit card buyers may call our toll-free number below. We will send you your Energaire ion generator complete with 90-day limited warranty on the electronics, a five-year limited warranty on the fuzz, and full instructions.

Let space-age technology revitalize your life with the world's first home ionized oxygen generator. Order one at no obligation, today.

JS&A NATIONAL SALES GROUP ®

Dept.WJ One JS&A Plaza
Northbrook, Ill. 60062 (312) 564-7000
Call TOLL-FREE 800 323-6400
In Illinois Call .... (312) 564-7000

©JS&A Group, Inc.,1978

August, 1978

We challenged the Soviet chess champion to play our new Chess Computer. The Soviet Union didn't like the idea but we finally worked out a deal.

CHESS DIPLOMACY

Soviet Challenge

This is the computer that may change the course of chess playing history.

Can an American chess computer beat the Soviet Chess Champion? A Confrontation between American space-age technology and a Soviet psychological weapon.

The Soviet Union regards chess as a psychological weapon, not just a game. It is a symbol of communism's cultural struggle with the West.

So when Russian Anatoli Karpov competed against the Russian Defector, Victor Korchnoi, he had the entire Soviet Union's resources at his disposal, including a hypnotist and neuro-psychologist.

Karpov won. And with it the world's undisputed chess championship. Karpov however, has never confronted American space-age technology and in particular JS&A's new Chess Computer.

So representatives of JS&A met with Karpov's representatives in Hong Kong in an effort to arrange a match between the Soviet Champion and the JS&A Chess Computer.

It wasn't easy negotiating with the Soviets. We offered them a $50,000 guarantee against royalties from the sales of our chess computers. But negotiations broke down.

Was the Soviet delegation afraid that American space-age technology would win? Were the Soviets fearful of negative publicity if Karpov lost to a $100 computer? Or were they fearful of a circus-type atmosphere that would degrade their prestige, even if he won?

Honestly, we don't know. We do know that our offer is still open, but we suspect Karpov will not accept.

Why did we challenge Karpov? Simple. We thought that having Karpov play against our computer would focus world-wide attention on our product. This attention would increase its sales and win or lose, we would sell more computers.

We had to sell more computers. We wanted to sell our unit for $100 even though it compares with units that sell for more than $300. But we had to do two things in order to sell our unit for $100. First, we had to manufacture it in Hong Kong where labor costs are very low. Secondly, we had to sell large quantities.

SOPHISTICATED DESIGN

The JS&A Chess Computer is designed to look several moves ahead to determine its next move. When we first designed it, it played five levels of chess. Level one was for beginners and as you played against the computer, you could increase its level of difficulty until the computer became more of a challenge. Level five was quite a challenge.

We thought we had the ultimate unit with five levels, until we developed our most sophisticated unit which has six levels. With six levels and all its previous features, the system is now a challenge for any Soviet Chess Champion.

The JS&A Chess Computer is a small unit that comes without a board or chess pieces. We felt that most players prefer their own board and pieces anyway.

LIKE PLAYING KARPOV

The system is the perfect way to sharpen your chess skills. It not only has six different skill levels, but if you are playing against the computer at level two and you are beating it, you can switch the unit to level six. It's like having Karpov as your new opponent—right during mid game.

To play against the computer, you enter your move on the unit's keyboard. You then wait until the computer examines all its options and selects its move. You then move the computer's chess piece to correspond with its request as shown on the display. A board layout is provided to show you where each chess piece should be moved.

SHARPEN SKILLS

If you already play chess, the JS&A unit provides a new chess dimension. If you haven't played chess, the system is a good way to learn and sharpen your skills.

The JS&A Chess Computer measures only 2⅛" x 4⅞" x 8⅞" and weighs just a few ounces, so if service is ever required you can slip it in its handy mailer and send it back to our prompt service-by-mail center. Service should never be required, but it is reassuring to know that service is an important consideration in this program.

JS&A is America's largest single source of space-age products—further assurance that your modest investment is well protected.

We suggest you order a JS&A Chess Computer on our 30 day trial period. Play against it. Raise or lower the level as you play and watch how the computer's personality can change right in mid-game—from a tough competitor to a push over.

TEST LEVEL SIX

Test our level six and see if you'd have much of a chance against the Soviet Champion Karpov. Then, after you've really given it a workout, decide if you want to keep it. If not, you may return your unit for a prompt and courteous refund, including your $2.50 postage and handling charge. There is no risk. Each JS&A Chess Computer comes complete with instructions and an AC adapter (no batteries are required).

To order your JS&A Chess Computer, send your check for **$99.95** plus $2.50 for postage and handling (Illinois residents please add 5% sales tax) to the address below or credit card buyers may call our toll-free number below.

The Soviet Union may have the World's Chess Champion, but JS&A has a very powerful Chess Computer and something the Soviets don't have—a pretty good advertising department.

Why not order a JS&A Chess Computer at no obligation, today.

JS&A PRODUCTS THAT THINK®

Dept.WJ One JS&A Plaza
Northbrook, Ill. 60062 (312) 564-7000
Call TOLL-FREE 800 323-6400
In Illinois Call .... (312) 564-7000
©JS&A Group, Inc.,1978

November, 1978

After the FTC attacked me, I countered with a national campaign featuring my request for an oversight hearing which I eventually received.

FIRST OF A SERIES

FTC Revolt

You've heard of the tax revolt. It's about time for an FTC revolt. Here's my story and why we've got to stop federal bureaucratic regulation.

My story is only one example of how the FTC is harassing small businesses but I'm not going to sit back and take it.

By Joseph Sugarman,
President, JS&A Group, Inc.

I'm pretty lucky. When I started my business in my basement eight years ago, I had little more than an idea and a product.

The product was the pocket calculator. The idea was to sell it through advertisements in national magazines and newspapers.

Those first years in the basement weren't easy. But, we worked hard and through imaginative advertising and a dedicated staff, JS&A grew rapidly to become well recognized as an innovator in electronics and marketing.

THREE BLIZZARDS

In January of 1979, three major blizzards struck the Chicago area. The heaviest snowfall hit Northbrook, our village—just 20 miles north of Chicago.

Many of our employees were stranded—unable to get to our office where huge drifts made travel impossible. Not only were we unable to reach our office, but our computer totally broke down leaving us in even deeper trouble.

But we fought back. Our staff worked around the clock and on weekends. First, we processed orders manually. We also hired a group of computer specialists, rented outside computer time, employed a computer service bureau, and hired temporary help to feed this new computer network. We never gave up. Our totally dedicated staff and the patience of many of our customers helped us through the worst few months in our history. Although there were many customers who had to wait over 30 days for their parcels, every package was eventually shipped.

WE OPENED OUR DOORS

During this period, some of our customers called the FTC (Federal Trade Commission) to complain. We couldn't blame them. Despite our efforts to manually notify our customers of our delays, our computer was not functioning making the task extremely difficult.

The FTC advised JS&A of these complaints. To assure the FTC that we were a responsible company, we invited them to visit us. During their visit we showed them our computerized microfilm system which we use to back up every transaction. We showed them our new dual computer system (our main system and a backup system in case our main system ever failed again). And, we demonstrated how we were able to locate and trace every order. We were very cooperative, allowing them to look at every document they requested.

The FTC left. About one week later, they called and told us that they wanted us to pay a $100,000 penalty for not shipping our products within their 30-day rule. (The FTC rule states that anyone paying by check is entitled to have their purchase shipped within 30 days or they must be notified and given the option to cancel.)

NOT BY CONGRESS

The FTC rule is not a law nor a statute passed by Congress, but rather a rule created by the FTC to strengthen their enforcement powers. I always felt that the rule was intended to be used against companies that purposely took advantage of the consumer. Instead, it appears that the real violators, who often are too difficult to prosecute, get away while JS&A, a visible and highly respected company that pays taxes and has contributed to our free enterprise system, is singled out. I don't think that was the intent of the rule.

And when the FTC goes to court, they have the full resources of the US Government. Small, legitimate businesses haven't got a chance.

We're not perfect. We do make mistakes. But if we do make a mistake, we admit it, accept the responsibility, and then take whatever measures necessary to correct it. That's how we've built our reputation.

BLOW YOUR KNEE CAPS OFF

Our attorneys advised us to settle. As one attorney said, "It's like a bully pulling out a gun and saying, 'If you don't give me a nickel, I'll blow your knee caps off.'" They advised us that the government will subpoena thousands of documents to harass us and cause us great inconvenience. They warned us that even if we went to court and won, we would end up spending more in legal fees than if we settled.

To settle would mean to negotiate a fine and sign a consent decree. The FTC would then issue a press release publicizing their victory.

At first we tried to settle. We met with two young FTC attorneys and agreed in principle to pay consumers for any damages caused them. But there were practically no damages, just a temporary computer problem, some late shipments, and some bad weather. The FTC then issued a massive subpoena requesting documents that will take us months to gather and which we feel was designed to harass or force us to accept their original $100,000 settlement request.

Remember, the FTC publicizes their actions. And the higher the fine, the more the publicity and the more stature these two attorneys will have at the FTC.

If this all sounds like blackmail—that's just what it appeared to be to us.

We did ship our products late—something we've admitted to them and which we publicly admit here, but we refuse to be blackmailed into paying a huge fine at the expense of our company's reputation—something we've worked hard eight years to build.

We're not a big company and we realize it would be easier to settle now at any cost. But we're not. If this advertisement can attract the attention of Congressmen and Senators who have the power to stop the harassment of Americans by the FTC, then our efforts will be well spent.

ALL AMERICANS AFFECTED

Federal regulation and the whims of a few career-building bureaucrats is costing taxpayers millions, destroying our free enterprise system, affecting our productivity as a nation and as a result is lowering everybody's standard of living.

I urge Congressmen, Senators, businessmen and above all, the consumer to support legislation to take the powers of the FTC from the hands of a few unelected officials and bring them back to Congress and the people.

I will be running this advertisement in hundreds of magazines and newspapers during the coming months. I'm not asking for contributions to support my effort as this is my battle, but I do urge you to send this advertisement to your Congressmen and Senators. That's how you can help.

America was built on the free enterprise system. Today, the FTC is undermining this system. Freedom is not something that can be taken for granted and you often must fight for what you believe. I'm prepared to lead that fight. Please help me.

Note: To find out the complete story and for a guide on what action you can take, write me personally for my free booklet, "Blow your knee caps off."

One JS&A Plaza, Northbrook, Ill. 60062

In this ad we actually make fun of a thermostat that we were selling. We ran this ad for three years and created a strong response.

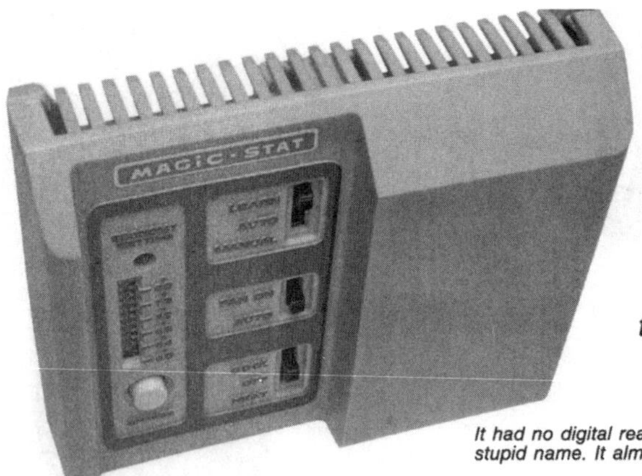

Magic Baloney

You'll love the way we hated the Magic Stat thermostat until an amazing thing happened.

It had no digital readout, an ugly case and a stupid name. It almost made us sick.

You're probably expecting our typical sales pitch, but get ready for a shock. For instead of trying to tell you what a great product the Magic Stat thermostat is, we're going to tear it apart. Unmercifully.

When we first saw the Magic Stat, we took one look at the name and went "Yuck." We took one look at the plastic case and said "How cheap looking." And when we looked for the digital readout, it had none. So before the salesman even showed us how it worked, we were totally turned off.

REAL LOSER

So there it was—at first blush a real loser. But wait, we did find one good feature—a feature that led us to a discovery. The Magic Stat installs in a few minutes and no serviceman is required. Thermostat wires in your wall follow standard color codes. So when you install Magic Stat, you attach the red wire to the red location and the white to the white. That's playschool stuff. And it's safe. Conventional thermostats installed over the past 20 years are generally only 24 volts, so you can either turn off the power or work with the "live" wires without fear.

OK, LET'S TEST IT

The Magic Stat installation was so easy that the least we could do was test it. And that's when we made an incredible discovery. We discovered that the Magic Stat was probably the most consumer-oriented, technologically-advanced and most sophisticated thermostat ever developed on the face of this earth and in our galaxy for all times ever. What made us switch from hating the thing to loving it? Read the following.

The Magic Stat has six setback settings per day and a seven day program. That means that you could set it for 70° when you get up in the morning, drop the temperature to 54° when you go to work, raise it to 68° when you return for dinner, raise it up to 72° after dinner as you watch TV and then drop it down to 62° when you go to sleep. Count them—five settings with one to spare.

In one day the Magic Stat is programmed for the whole week and for the weeks to come. If you want a different schedule for weekends, you can individually program the thermostat for those days, too. "Big deal," you might think. "What's so great about that?" Read on.

You set most electronic setback thermostats to the time you want the furnace to go on in the morning, so when you wake up, your room is once again warm. But what if one morning it's bitter cold outside and the next morning it's much warmer? This means that setting your furnace to go on at the same time may, on one morning, leave you cold and on the next morning cause you to waste energy by warming up your house too soon.

By golly, the Magic Stat has everybody beat on this one too. Throughout the night it senses and computes the drop in temperature and the time it will take to get your room to your exact wake up temperature. So if you want to wake up at 7 AM to 70 degrees—that's the temperature you'll wake up to every time. Because it's a patented concept, no other thermostat has this feature. But wait. There is also a patent on the setting feature.

SIMPLE TO SET

To set the thermostat, you press just one button. A small LED light scans the temperature scale until you reach your desired temperature and then you release the button. You change the temperature naturally, throughout the day, up to six times. The unit responds and remembers that exact living pattern. The present temperature is displayed by a glowing red LED on the scale.

The system also computes the ideal length the furnace should stay on to keep the temperature within a range of plus or minus one and one-half degrees. A battery backup lets you keep your stored program in its memory so power outages as long as eight hours won't let your unit forget. And if something happens and your power is out for a few days, the unit will automatically maintain 68 degrees when the power is restored.

Quite frankly, we were so impressed with the unit, its ease of installation and setting plus its many energy-saving features, we seriously considered advertising it until we realized that our customers would probably not want to trust their future comfort to a product called Magic Stat. What if something went wrong with the unit? How substantial was this Magic Stat outfit? Remember, a thermostat is something you live with as long as you live in your home, and they're supposed to last ages. After all, your comfort depends on it.

Well, we did our homework, We found the company to be a sound, well-financed organization. They have been in business for several years, and they back their products with a three-year limited warranty. In addition, the company has a policy of buying back your unit in one year if you haven't saved its full cost in energy savings. We were satisfied with the company, the people, the product, its incredible features, the company's commitment to the product and above all, the energy savings.

We are so impressed now with the Magic Stat that we're going to make buying one irresistible. Buy one from us for only $79. Install it yourself in a few minutes or hire a handyman to install it.

Or order the new deluxe unit for $99 with the exact same features as the regular model, but with a beautiful new case.

Then enjoy the savings this next winter, Not only will you save up to 30% on your heating bills, but you're eligible for the 15% energy tax credit. Then if you're not absolutely in love with this product one year later, return it to JS&A. You'll get all your money back and you can reinstall your old thermostat.

REALIZE SAVINGS

But we're counting on a few things. First, you will realize an energy savings and a comfort that will far surpass what you are currently experiencing. Secondly, you probably will sleep better breathing cooler air yet wake up to just the right temperature.

Beauty is only skin deep and a name doesn't really mean that much. But we sure wish those guys at Magic Stat would have named their unit something more impressive. Maybe something like Twinkle Temp.

To order, credit card holders call toll free and ask for product by number below or send check plus $4 delivery for each unit ordered.

Magic Stat (0040G) **$79**
Deluxe Magic Stat (0041G) **99**

One JS&A Plaza
Northbrook, Illinois 60062
CALL TOLL FREE 800 323-6400
IL residents add 6% sales tax. ©JS&A Group, Inc.,1983

Teen Club Flyers

The following are some of the flyers used to promote the dances at the teen clubs.

the
APOCRYPHALS
ARE ALIVE AND
WILL PLAY AT
FRANK BOND'S
THIS SUNDAY
FEBRUARY 18th

come
blow
your
mind!

SEE THE
METALICS
and the
BEL ESPIRITS
Play at BONDS
come to Bond's
BIG COMPUTER DANCE
January 14th
7pm to 10:30 Admission only $2.00

BATTLE

of the BANDS

APOCRYPHALS

v.s.

APOCRYPHALS

Frank Bond's, March 3rd at 7pm in Berwyn

BOND DANCE BIG

the APOCRYPHALS

along with the Green Gook will play in a Big St. Patrick's Day Dance at Frank Bond's Teen Club, 3243 South Harlem, Berwyn, Sunday, March 17th... 7pm to 10:30

Frank Bonds was sold to new owners who agreed to continue the club. So in this flyer we announced the final dance.

... then in this flyer we announced the start of Richard's Teen Club with a big grand opening event.

WCFL's Jim Stagg presents:

the fantastic sound of the

APOCRYPHALS

with the FAMILY

☆at the GREAT GRAND OPENING of ☆☆

RICHARDS

TEEN CLUB

3243 S. Harlem, Berwyn, Sunday,☆April 7th

the Family

the APOCRYPHALS!

GO-GO DANCERS

DANCE CONTEST

7pm to 10:30 Admission only $2.00; All invited to attend!!

FRANK BOND'S

SUN.

Blow your mind!

DECEMBER 10th

Picture Gallery

A picture of my mom and me at age 2 years posing for a picture. Mom was a beautiful woman and had four wonderful kids.

Breakfast of Dog Champions. From time to time I would use our boxer dog as a model. She was well trained.

Here I am spending time at the beach with two friends. Note how conservative the women's bathing suits were compared to how they are today.

Since I was a ham radio operator, I had the opportunity to broadcast from the Army's powerful radio facility in Frankfurt Germany. Note the postcards on the wall in the background. When you contacted somebody in the world, you would typically acknowledge that contact by sending what was called a QSL card. I spoke to people all over the world. My call letters were K4TDL while in school and W9IQO at home in Illinois.

In 1958 I entered the Fisher Body Contest and submitted a car design. I carved the car out of a solid block of wood during a craft course at the University of Miami. I won an honorable mention and some cash for my submission.

While a Junior in high school, I designed and built a car that won the Illinois Institute of Technology award for the best car in its class.

WINS AUTO EXHIBIT TROPHY—Joseph Sugarman, 1201 Woodbine, shows the trophy, and the car that won it, he brought home from the Illinois Institute of Technology's "Technorama" open house program recently. The restyled car, called a "custom" in auto jargon, won in its division of the show. Sugarman is a junior at Oak Park-River Forest high school.

Mary Stanke and I look over the layout of an advertisement for a new product.

The Army sent me to their intense language school in southern Germany in a quaint town called Oberammergau. I often had to clear the snow from my Volkswagen.

I took almost all the pictures to illustrate the products featured in the ads I wrote. Here is a dramatic shot and a good example of my photography.

As pledges we were on a scavenger hunt and one of the goals was to meet Jimmy Durante who is holding my arm in this candid shot.

The Jaguar XKE I drove while in Frankfurt. It was part of my cover for a mission I had undertaken.

Visits Joe Sugarman

Lovely Sandra Dee, on a recent trip to Chicago, visited with Joe Sugarman, manager of Frank Bond's Teen Club, 3243 S. Harlem ave., Berwyn. Sandra Dee is co-star of the recently released "Rosie." This Sunday evening the Apocryphals will appear at Frank Bond's, Chicagoland's most respected Teen Club.

Many celebrities would stop by our teen clubs and surprise even me. This picture shows me greeting the late Sandra Dee.

Wendy and I pose for a publicity shot at the New York Toy Show where we exhibited the Teeny Bopper. OK, you probably guessed that wasn't me in the picture.

In basic training at Ft. Carson, Colorado. I won a marksman medal and enjoyed the Army experience as I prepared to leave for the Ft. Holibird spy school in Maryland.

Pizza Hut had us supply them with four futuristic sunglass styles to be used in the movie Back to the Future II as part of a major world-wide promotion. We supplied them with 10 million pairs. Although the promotion was very successful, the sunglasses never appeared in the movie.

Since Spectra '59 was an international show, why not have an international beauty pageant to tie into the event? We did and it drew a lot of publicity and it was a lot of fun.

Candidates for "Miss Spectra '59," beauty contest being held by International Graphic Arts Exposition in the New York Trade Show Building, September 6-12. From left to right: Isabella Rye, representing Germany; Dorothy Dollivar, Czechoslovakia; Linda Powers, United States; Olga Darina, Japan; Lily Lind, Sweden; Vicky Ardiss, France and Kim Kane, Switzerland.

OFFICE OF THE MAYOR

CITY OF CHICAGO

RICHARD J. DALEY
MAYOR

February 9, 1956

Mr. Joe Sugarman, Editor,
The Atom
1201 North Woodbine Avenue,
Oak Park, Illinois

Dear Mr. Sugarman:

Thank you for your letter and kindness in sending me a copy of your publication "The Atom."

I firmly believe in the essential goodness of our young people in general and in their desire to become good and useful citizens. I am sure that your publication is extremely interesting and worthwhile and speaks well for them all. I shall be glad to read it at my first opportunity.

With my best wishes,

Sincerely yours,

Richard J. Daley

Mayor

Even Mayor Daly acknowledged the Atom publication we created while we were in high school.